FAMILY AND FARM IN PRE-FAMINE IRELAND

Kevin O'Neill

FAMILY AND FARM IN PRE-FAMINE IRELAND

The
Parish
of
Killashandra

THE UNIVERSITY OF WISCONSIN PRESS

Published 1984

The University of Wisconsin Press
114 North Murray Street
Madison, Wisconsin 53715

The University of Wisconsin Press, Ltd.
1 Gower Street
London WC1E 6HA, England

Publication of this book has been aided by a grant
from the Trustees of Boston College
First printing
Printed in the United States of America

For LC CIP information see the colophon

ISBN 0–299–09840–0

To my family, in its most extended form

The whole landscape a manuscript
We had lost the skill to read,
A part of our past disinherited;
But fumbled, like a blind man,
Along the fingertips of instinct.

John Montague, "The Rough Field"

Contents

Maps
and
Figures

Tables

Acknowledgments

It is a wonder that such a slim volume could have involved so many. On the long road that led to its publication I have received the help and encouragement of many. The longest standing debt is to Lawrence J. McCaffrey, who first provoked my interest in Irish history and who provided the critical and early encouragement and assistance without which the journey would never have begun.

L. P. Curtis of Brown University directed the dissertation from which this book evolved; his suggestions, questions, and encouragement helped make this work take its initial form. Perhaps more important, by his example he taught me the high regard for precision in research and argument which sustained me through the heavy revisions which followed.

The quantitative work contained in this volume could not have been completed without the enormous help and guidance which R. B. Litchfield provided. Barbara Anderson also gave important advice on the measurement of marriage age, and thanks are due to Hunter Dupree, who encouraged me to move beyond my empirical orientation.

My research in Ireland was carried out with the assistance of a Hayes-Fulbright fellowship. During that time I benefited from the direction of Kevin B. Nowlan of U.C.D. (who also had a great influence on my undergraduate education.) Alf MacLochlainn, then director of the National Library of Ireland, offered valuable assistance, as did William Crawford of the Public Records Office, Belfast; E. R. R. Green of Queens University, Belfast; William Vaughn of Trinity College, Dublin; and Cormac O'Grada and Tom Garvin of U.C.D.

While revising the dissertation, I was very fortunate to have the stimulation of the "Boston group"—Eric Almquist, Frank Carney, and Ruth Ann Harris—who met regularly to discuss Irish social and economic history. I also owe a great debt to Joseph Lee, whose enthusiasm provided an important "push" at a critical moment. James Donnelly and Paul Spangoli read parts of the manuscript and offered numerous comments and suggestions.

A special thank you is due to David Doyle of U.C.D., whose friendship, encouragement, and assistance on both sides of the Atlantic have made every step a little easier.

Gretchen Dietz O'Neill assisted with the formidable task of coding the 1841 Census forms and, more important, helped me to maintain my perspective on work, theory, and reality.

All of the above contributed to the strength of this work. Its weaknesses are solely my responsibility.

FAMILY AND FARM IN PRE-FAMINE IRELAND

Introduction

From the very beginning, the historiography of nineteenth-century Ireland has been predominantly concerned with political issues. Despite the importance of early works, such as George O'Brien's *Economic History*,[1] Irish historians until very recently have been largely preoccupied with the nature and the course of Ireland's struggle for independence from Britain. This political bias is perhaps understandable in light of the unhappy nature of the Anglo-Irish problem and its prolonged, bitter, and violent history, but it is still unfortunate. Ireland's economic and social experiences during the nineteenth and early twentieth centuries could be of particular importance to studies of both the general economic history of Europe and agricultural and demographic changes in peasant societies.

Ireland's position during the nineteenth century was extreme for Europe, but typical of many non-European nations attempting to modernize their agricultural production as a first step toward general economic development. In many ways, Ireland was isolated and "backward." Her traditional communal economy had avoided both Roman and feudal conversion until the seventeenth-century conquests firmly entrenched the English system of private property

3

relations. Her economic infrastructure was primitive; outside of the coastal areas where Viking settlement had taken place, towns did not become common until the sixteenth and seventeenth centuries. Roads were rare in most parts of the country before the seventeenth century, and only the eastern seacoast, Galway, and Limerick had what could be considered a rudimentary commercial economy. Most Irish people lived on a purely subsistence level well into the eighteenth century. Isolated from their rulers by language, customs, and religion, the peasantry were able to preserve much of their traditional Gaelic culture.

Yet, despite Ireland's apparent isolation on the western fringe of Atlantic Europe, she was too close geographically and politically to the momentous economic changes taking place in Britain to avoid direct involvement in the first Industrial Revolution. The eastern parts of Ireland actually were closer to the early stages of industrialization than large parts of England. The effects of the rapid urbanization of the western regions of Great Britain upon a culturally and economically isolated island make Ireland an excellent area in which to study the nature and effects of the expansion of capitalism into isolated rural areas. Unfortunately, very little work has been done in this field.

A number of specialized works dealing with textile production in Ulster (most notably those of Green, Gill, Crawford, and Gibbon) provide valuable information on the early industrialization of Ireland.[2] However, until very recently little attention has been paid to the commercialization of agriculture. Kenneth Connell's *The Population of Ireland* and Raymond Crotty's *Irish Agricultural Production* provided the impetus for the increased interest of economic historians in pre-famine topics.[3] Connell stressed the essential importance of economic structure and the potato in determining pre-famine population trends, arguing that the population increases of the pre-famine period were due to economic deprivation coupled with an increased food supply; but he was unable to offer any substantial proof of this connection between economic and demographic trends. Crotty provided a controversial reinterpretation of Irish agricultural history based on limited aggregate data which stressed the economic rationality of Irish agriculture.[4] Both of these works provoked considerable interest, criticism, and defense, but as there was little published material either to confirm or deny the agricultural or demographic theories presented, the argument remained primarily theoretical, prompting Joseph Lee to comment that "a line of evidence is worth a page of hypothesis."[5]

Since the publication of Connell's and Crotty's work, the drift of Irish historical studies has been toward a more empirical study of economic and social structure before and after the famine.[6] The present study is a part of this response. It will attempt to fulfill two separate and occasionally competing goals: (1) to provide an empirical view of critical demographic and family structure variables for an Irish parish during the pre-famine era; and (2) to place this demographic information within its economic environment and attempt to provide an analytical model of agricultural and demographic development. This model may prove useful in interpreting other Irish and European data from the past, and it may suggest some different perspectives for viewing contemporary problems of rural poverty and economic development.

Models, by their nature, are speculative; and as one of the more useful discussions of the theory of peasant economy has indicated, the attempt to provide a single model for peasant society is a particularly risky business.[7] Much of the difficulty inherent in the exposition of the dynamics of rural, social, and economic life lies in the preoccupation with the identification of *the* independent or control variable. Such monistic patterns of argument may prove useful in the basic formulation of research questions, but it is doubtful that they will provide an adequate understanding of such a complex relationship. Yet, since the time of Malthus's assumption that "land supply" and "agricultural production" could be interchanged as the independent variables of the agriculture/population function, monism has dominated the debate.

Malthus's original assumption led him to his famous conclusion that population confronted fixed barriers which demanded periodic and painful readjustment of human population. Since Engels's harsh criticism of this assumption, its weakness has been much discussed, but in general those who challenge Malthus have been satisfied to offer revisions which either modify Malthus's independent variable to accommodate a flexible carrying capacity, or provide an alternative independent force. The neo-Malthusian argument exercises powerful influence; Kenneth Connell used it impressively in *The Population of Ireland*, where he argued that the potato, by increasing the carrying capacity of available land, provoked an inevitable increase in population. But much of the best work in agriculture and population has tended to reverse the direction of control in Malthus's model. From Chayanov to Boserup, the emphasis has shifted steadily toward population itself as the controlling variable. Chayanov's identification of the mechanism controlling traditional agricultural productivity has been extended to Boserup's challenging and controversial anti-Malthusian thesis that population growth can cause agricultural development.[8]

Chayanov's model is particularly important, both because of its highly empirical origin and its wide influence. Chayanov identified the consumer/worker ratio as the critical factor in determining Russian peasant economic activity. As the number of consumers per family unit increased, the level of economic activity rose accordingly.[9] In Chayanov's Russia, this normally meant that as family size increased, so too did farm size. However, he indicated that even in areas with no additional land, the process could be maintained through more intensive agricultural labor on a given area of land, offering the adoption of the potato as the classic example of an agricultural change intended to increase labor intensity. Chayanov's thesis can be extended and used to argue that an increase in population should lead to labor intensification across a population, and hence to a rising level of agricultural productivity.

As brilliant and convincing as Chayanov's model is, there are a number of problems with its indiscriminate application to other areas and time periods. Richard Smith and others have observed that the operation of the market "tended to produce social differentiation of a level such that only a minority of the rural populace were able to maintain what we can term a Chayanovian equilibrium."[10] Smith's comment is based on the English evidence, yet there is great difficulty in transplanting Chayanov's model of family agriculture to other areas of traditional European peasant production. The evidence presented in this study strongly supports Smith's argument. Even in neighboring Poland, Jacek Kochanowicz has concluded that "family size and structure were mainly determined by the produc-

tive capacity and the amount of land under cultivation,"[11] thus
standing Chayanov on his head.

Could Kochanowicz's and Chayanov's descriptions of the dynamic connecting family and economic structures in peasant communities be reconciled within one model? Is it possible that the
consumption ratio (Chayanov) and the productive capacity (Kochanowicz) represent successive independent (or control) variables
within a single evolving peasant economy? Could a sense of time
reconcile the work of these authors?

It was Marx who first pointed toward some of these questions and
provided an outline of their answers. Marx, like most historians,
conceptualized his linear and cumulative model in terms of periods
or stages. The application of this general idea of historical development to population theory is obvious enough. As Marx put it, "an
abstract law of population exists for plants and animals only" (he
went on to note that man's presence on the planet had placed even
this abstraction in question).[12] As part of his general discussion of
social organization, Marx argued that, in place of an abstract law,
each form of social and economic structure produced its own laws of
population. Marx did not concern himself with the nature of these
laws in a "traditional" (or, in his terms, "feudal") economy, but
he did comment specifically upon the nature of the population dynamic in emerging capitalistic agriculture: "As soon as capitalist
production takes possession of agriculture, and in proportion to the
extent to which it does so, the demand for an agricultural laboring
population falls absolutely, while the accumulation of the capital
employed in agriculture advances . . ."[13]

The qualifications "as soon as" and "in proportion to" are worth
consideration. Clearly Marx had some sort of transition period in
mind where the forces of both the old and new relationships would
operate. Marx did not elaborate on either the demographic or economic nature of such a period of transition, most likely because he
believed it was already under way and that it would be a very brief
experience. In any case, from his perspective the end point was
clear enough and identical to that of society as a whole; hence,
separate examination of the rural economy was unnecessary. Unfortunately, the evidence presented below and the general outline of

peasant experience in the nineteenth and twentieth centuries suggest that this transition period can be (and perhaps normally is) prolonged over several generations. It may even be "short-circuited" and evolve into something quite different from Marx's capitalist "factory" agriculture.[14] Thus, from the perspective of the national historian, the historical demographer, or the agricultural economist, Marx's model is inadequate because it tells us too little about the rural economy before close contact with capitalism; and more important, because it assumes so much about the nature of that contact.

This study presents a three-stage model which I believe provides a conceptual device for the study of peasant economy before, during, and after involvement with capitalistic production. The model is eclectic; rather than offering much new theory, it attempts to fit existing theory into a system that removes some of the problems and limitations already noted. Because of the critical importance of exogenous market forces within the model's operation, I call it a "market impulsion model." This appelation was chosen to underscore the dynamic power which the market must exercise in order to overcome the low-level equilibrium found in traditional agricultural economy. In the absence of such intense market pressure, other variables are able to control the agricultural and demographic operation of the system. Thus the model is multicausal rather than monistic, and although it is time-specific and cumulative, it does not assume a particular rate of development nor does it *require* the achievement of some end point. The market may impel the system in the direction of greater commercialization, but unless certain conditions are met and unless market pressure is maintained at a critical level the system may stagnate or even regress. The model is clearly "Marxist" in many of its elements, especially its emphasis on the control of the means of production, the production of surplus, and social differentiation; yet because it permits rising market development and capitalism to *increase* labor demands in agriculture, and because it rejects one-directional motion, it is perhaps best classified as "neo-Marxist" (if one needs to classify it).

A fitting introduction to the model developed in this book is Black's paradox: "Only by being unfaithful in some respects can a model represent its original.''[15] The market impulsion model is most "unfaithful" in its exclusion of cultural factors which influence some of the more important decisions involved in both agricultural and demographic events. This is not because I consider their influence unimportant, but because of the methodological necessity to provide logical pathways. Moreover, because these cultural influences normally change very slowly, they can feasibly be treated as constants, not variables. In a sense, these cultural factors provide an atmosphere within which economic forces operate. They influence the way in which a population perceives change; they affect ideological and political responses to change; and, in the most extreme case, they may condition the nature (but not the direction) of change. If the model is successful at representing the abstraction of economic and demographic relationships devoid of cultural influences, it should be possible for the cultural historian/anthropologist to provide the appropriate modifications for specific societies.

The model consists of three stages of agricultural and social organization (see figures I.1–I.3). The first stage, schematically depicted in figure I.1, represents the "traditional" or "feudal" stage of agricultural organization and reflects the Irish land-poor and rent situations, which are the subject of this study. The terms *feudal* and *traditional* are too vague and abused to recommend themselves. So, despite the danger of trivializing Chayanov's theory, I shall characterize this stage of organization as his and refer to it as "Chayanovian." In this stage, the Malthusian trap is avoided via two possible pathways. As population and consumption needs grow, the required increase in labor intensity has two independent results. First, it increases overall agricultural productivity through a variety of means, such as more careful cultivation of traditional crops or the adoption of a more intensive crop mix. This increased productivity permits a greater population to be supported on a static land supply. But intensification and crop substitutions have limits (although they are amazingly elastic, as rice agriculture demonstrates); and eventually, without some check on growth, a crisis is likely. The second result of increased labor intensity provides such a mechanism. Increased labor inputs, rising productivity, and rising population all tend to increase competition for available land and thus make new

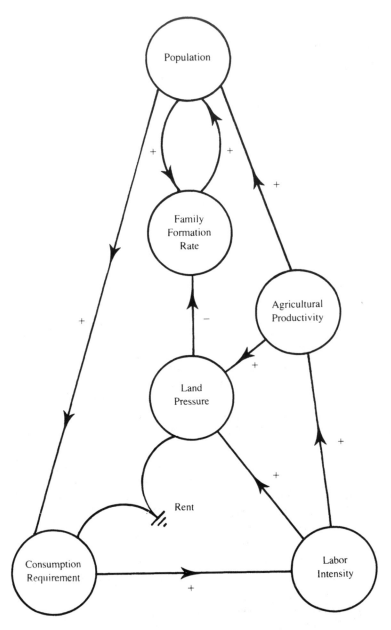

Figure I.1 Chayanovian Stage of Economic Development

family formation more difficult. This provides a brake to population growth through rising ages at marriage and/or a falling proportion marrying.

The model does not assume that this system is necessarily in equilibrium. Indeed, it is quite possible for it to operate cumulatively, with population and productivity tending to increase fairly steadily over time. However, the critical factor remains the *possibility* of the negative feedback from land pressure counteracting the general tendency toward growth. Obviously, this would be most likely to occur at the point when land competition reaches a crisis stage, when no new land is available, when intensification of labor reaches extremes, and when a history of population growth produces increasingly large cohorts of potential farmers seeking settlements.

Two further observations should be offered here. It may surprise some that in this stage of the model "rent" plays a rather insignificant role in the operation of the system. This does not imply that peasants in the Chayanovian system did not feel pain when paying rents (or taxes). They did, but such payments were generally of a fixed nature, varying little over time and generally serving as a fixed base of the consumption need of the individual farm household. In some rare cases, rents may have been adjusted to the actual productivity of the land (or the intervening variable of land pressure), but there is little evidence of such careful management in Ireland before the eighteenth century.

Secondly, a key assumption implicit in this stage of the model, an assumption which Chayanov and Connell share, is that the social structure of peasant society is basically homogeneous. The hypothesized check upon population growth assumes that the majority of those people who wish to marry need access to land as a precondition of marriage—i.e., that the society is predominantly composed of farming families. Where large numbers of landless laboring families exist, it is quite possible for increased labor demands to encourage marriage among laborers at the same moment that increased competition for land discourages marriage for the farming class. This is one of the central elements of the market impulsion model's second stage. Indeed, this social differentiation is the most visible aspect of pre-famine Cavan society, and it serves as a useful quick test for categorizing communities.

The process of change between the Chayanovian and the second
or "surplus-producing" stage is important in this construction. Inherent in the Chayanovian stage is the ability to attain high levels of
productivity and population. However, as the intensity of labor
nears the saturation point at which marginal returns of increased
labor input fall very low, we can begin to talk about a surplus of
population, and we can expect the negative feedback mechanism to
grow in strength.

There is, however, another possibility. Suppose a moment is
chosen before this crisis when a system carries a fairly high level of
population, but does not fully exploit its labor resources.[16] In this
situation, the Western economist might talk of surplus or "underutilized" labor.[17]

If a community in such a state of economic and social organization encounters certain key extra-local forces, it may realign its
productive variables to conform to the "surplus-producing" stage
of organization. The extra-local factors include a strong demand for
agricultural products and a market mechanism for transmitting this
demand to the community. In a process described by economists as
"vent for surplus," such underutilized resources as virgin land or
"a large supply of underemployed labor" can serve as the base of
economic development.[18] In this scenario, a peripheral area with
underutilized resources may take advantage of external market opportunities to exploit those resources. The income from this initial
exploitation provides the capital for the further development of the
region. However, the response is not automatic; as F. Tipton notes,
it depends upon "the willingness and ability to reorganize the region's economic and social structure in favor of production."[19]
Irish data as well as other peasant experiences suggest that the
"willingness" which Tipton speaks of can be replaced by coercion.
Peasants involved in a Chayanovian system serve their self-interest
best by protecting that system. From their individual and "communal" perspective, further development carries no guarantee that
it will provide for the consumption needs of the rural population,
and it most benefits an urban population distant in culture and economic interests. Thus, this type of development requires some sort
of coercion to overcome the inevitable resistance of an economically rational peasantry. In Ireland and in many other examples, this

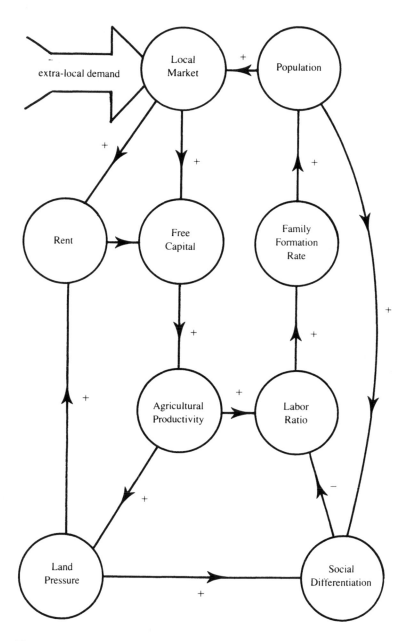

Figure I.2 Surplus-Producing Stage

coercive element was the landlord system backed by a harsh and violent legal apparatus. In the market impulsion model, this coercion is represented by "rent," but taxation or the more inventive means of peasant coercion employed in this century by some national governments can operate just as effectively.

In Killashandra, landlords responded to the steadily rising corn prices of the late eighteenth century by raising rents *and* rationalizing their estates (i.e., bringing the actual tillers of the fields under their more direct control). It is worthwhile to consider here the relationships involved in this process to show how the model can be used to provide an additional perspective to traditional questions. Doing so will also illustrate the relationship of political and cultural attitudes to the market impulsion model.

In Ireland the rent system was almost classical. The rationalization of land ownership carried out during the seventeenth century by English conquerors left the Irish peasantry economically the most "modern" in Europe (assuming English farmers no longer qualified as peasants). All claims to land ownership *and* use were reduced to the cash nexus; and as all ownership was in the hands of the alien aristocracy and most production in the hands of "native" tenant farmers, the rent system functioned in an unusually visible and exploitative way.

Yet the bitterness of landlord-tenant relations in nineteenth-century Ireland was not due primarily to the structural competition inherent in any tenancy arrangement. It represented a much more profound and explosive clash of social and economic systems, a confrontation which affected every aspect of the contact between the two communities: "native" and "planter." The landlords viewed rent as a capitalistic process of resource utilization. Their modern idea of rent explains why the "objective" modern observer has tended to reject the polemical characterization of this system as a "rack rent" operation.[20] Given the productive capacity of the land, the market forces operating in the British Isles, and the general productivity of capital in the economic system of which Ireland was a part, landlord rent charges in the early nineteenth century were capitalistically rational. Furthermore, as I shall argue below, the rising rents of that era were probably more the result of landlords catching up with the markets than some new form of cannibalism.

Nonetheless, the "people's" bitterness was very real, and for good reason. Tenants did not object to the payment of rent per se, as long as it was a fixed component of their overall consumption needs and was determined by the carrying capacity of land utilized in the traditional system of mixed agriculture. What they understandably resisted was the movement to a system of variable rent based on extra-local factors over which they had no control and about which they could predict little. As landlords subjected their land investments to the tests of capital productivity available in the British economic system, their tenants were forced to replace their consumption-ordered family economy with a more modern production-oriented system. The agricultural community protested vehemently and often violently, because this new system threatened their always precarious economic system and the social and moral values which supported it. In the nightmare of the Great Famine, the proof of *their* reading of the nature of this system would emerge with horrific clarity.

In addition to rent, there are three other key factors—market, capital, and agricultural productivity—which are either radically transformed or newly introduced during the transition from stage 1 to stage 2. By definition, the transition begins when landlords recognize that radically increased market contact is both possible and profitable enough to outweigh the economic and political difficulties which it may bring. Thus the market becomes a key variable which must be introduced into the model. Certainly there was some limited market contact in nearly every peasant society. What distinguishes the transitional phase is not the arrival of the market, but its inclusion in the central economic activity of the region.

Capital is another "new" key variable. Like the market, it was certainly not unknown before the transition; indeed, in its literal sense, agriculture is impossible without the capital represented by the seeds or stock which begin a farm's production. But again, what is noteworthy is the "new" function of capital. It no longer represents just the fixed elements of land, seed, and tools. It now assumes a dynamic role as well, facilitating greater productivity through the use of additional fertilizers, lime, and other "improvements" (the most obvious in County Cavan being drainage). Before entering into a full discussion of capital, I would like to note here the curious and uncertain nature of the relationship between rent and capital. In the vent for surplus models, the continued development of a region is supported by the reinvestment of the profits provided by resource exploitation. Hence the nature of the relationship between rent and capital should be positive. I have represented it as negative. The reason for this anomaly lies in the nature of Irish landlordism. A great deal of the profit from the increasing agricultural productivity of Ireland went into the landlords' hands, but very little of it was ever reinvested in either Irish agriculture or Irish industry.[21] In fact, as the proportion of profit which went to rent increased, the remaining profit which the farmers themselves could possibly reinvest decreased, creating the negative relationship. Very little is known about the investment patterns of either landlord or tenant, but I believe that tenant investment clearly played the major role in agricultural development in Ireland.

This rent/capital connection is part of the key set of relationships which controls development in this stage of agricultural organization. Since the rent/capital pathway can "short-circuit" the positive impact of the market/capital/agricultural production relationship, the relative strength of market and rent will determine whether any increase in market activity will translate into sustained productivity growth or cause merely a short-term ripple in the production/rent ratio. In other words: in order for agricultural productivity to increase, the market intervention must be on a scale large enough and of a duration long enough to overwhelm the negative effect of rent increases—hence a market "impulsion." In any other set of conditions, the braking effect of this rent relationship will be the major factor preventing sustained economic development.

The very nature of "agricultural productivity" also changes as we move into the surplus production system. In Chayanov's system the key function of economic activity was to provide the most food for the least labor. But as rent requirements rose and the object of agricultural activity began to shift, farmers had to be increasingly concerned about maximizing their "profit." Only in this way could they acquire the cash needed for rent. *Profit* can be simply expressed as:

$$P = \text{Market Value of Produce} - (\text{Capital Input} + \text{Labor Costs})$$

Thus market value replaces home consumption as the major influence on the nature of agricultural activity. In Europe, during the period 1750–1815, this meant the production of corn for market was likely to become an increasingly common characteristic of those fringe areas that were just entering into market production. The particular nature of this eighteenth-century European demand was to have enormous consequences for some parts of Ireland.

The surplus producing stage of the market impulsion model represented not only fundamental structural economic changes, but dramatic social transformations as well. The latter changes were caused by two parallel relationships. As demands for corn products increased and farmers were coerced through the rent system to fulfill that demand, productivity was increased by placing more land into labor-intensive tillage operations. This led to an increasing demand for labor (and hence the labor ratio, which equals labor demand/labor supply), which quite often exceeded family means. The increase in economic activity and in agricultural productivity also made agriculture more "competitive." In the Chayanovian system, deficiencies in a farm's efficiency could be counteracted by taking more land under control or devoting more land to the most intensive uses available. With the rising costs of land access and the increasing labor costs of the surplus system, these solutions became less viable. Together, the increased demand for labor and the increasingly competitive nature of farming helped spur the differentiation of rural society. Two large groups emerged with separate economic interests: the farmers and the landless agricultural laborers. This "proletarianization" of much of rural society completely transformed its demographic dynamic.

Landless laborers were not bound by the same logic of family formation that characterized the Chayanovian system and which continued to operate among the farming groups in this new organization. A male did not have to await access to land, designation as an heir, or inheritance in order to seek a bride. Likewise, the need of a dowry did not impede the marriage of laboring women. For both men and women, peak earning power came early and was easily lost; there was no rational economic reason to postpone marriage as long as labor demand remained strong. Because of its encouragement to early and widespread marriage, this system could simultaneously and dramatically increase population and the competition for land, something which was difficult or impossible in the previous system.

As one might expect, the system had a self-regulating mechanism of sorts. As population increased, primarily among the landless, social differentiation became more pronounced. The more rapidly the population grew, the more proletarian society became. This in turn lowered the labor ratio by increasing the available supply of wage labor. As the opportunity for labor declined, it might be expected that family formation became increasingly difficult. Eventually this would happen, but the system of control was weak and very slow to operate. Because the landless youth found it difficult to foresee their employment opportunity, and because their peak laboring and wage-earning years were still their twenties, they could see little reason to postpone marriage until a severe crisis situation arose. During this stage of peasant economic organization, the new "rural proletariat" would be subject to many of the same problems that their urban counterparts experienced; as individuals they faced increased vulnerability to misfortune, sickness, and age, and as a group they were dramatically vulnerable to shifts in an increasingly complicated economy.

At this point it is sufficient to note that the same mechanism which provided for population growth would, under altered conditions, operate to curb the rate of growth. As population growth became an increasingly important part of the system and the labor ratio began to fall, the momentum of the system decreased; family formation became more difficult, marriage age rose, fertility began to decline, and emigration began to rise.

In the market impulsion model and, I believe, in the real world, this system might have survived indefinitely, meeting new problems caused by market fluctuations through readjustments of its social and economic organization. These readjustments could be every bit as painful as Malthus's periodic crisis, but they had a very different origin, and as the history of Irish agriculture demonstrates, this system could transform itself into a modern form of fully commercialized agriculture.

The subject population of this study did not complete transition to the "developed" stage of the model during the study's time frame. Yet it is important to note the major features of the new relationships, because some of the producers were clearly moving into this form of economic organization, and the crisis of agricultural labor signals the beginning of this transition in Ireland.

The most obvious characteristic of the developed stage is its relative simplicity (see figure I.3). Capital assumes a central and controlling influence in the local economy. The major change between the surplus and developed stages which permits this is the reordering of capital's impact upon labor. In the surplus stage, an increase in market activity leads to an increase in agricultural production, which in turn has a positive effect upon the labor ratio. In the developed system, the relationship is more direct and its impact reversed. Increased market activity provides and encourages more capital investment, which now increases productivity through "man-saving" developments (this does not require mechanization; it came about in Ireland by a shift to dairy production). Thus, as the economy continues to grow, there is a general loss of population, primarily through out-migration to the growing urban areas which provide market demand.

The importance of emigration accounts for the absence of two variables important in the other stages. Family formation becomes increasingly irrelevant to the operation of the economic system. In fact, family formation is in many ways replaced in stage 3 by emigration. Young people of both sexes and across all social groups have little incentive to remain in the community unless they are designated heirs of substantial farms. For the children of agricultural laborers and small farmers, the increasingly important role of capital in agriculture makes for a continuingly declining horizon of opportunity, and even the competitive edge of the larger farmers can be transferred to only one or two children. A seemingly endless rural depopulation of Ireland replaced the unusually wide opportunity for marriage and family which the previous system had supported. Indeed, on the personal level, the limited opportunity for marriage may often have been the most visible aspect of declining labor ratios and hence a major cause of emigration.[22] The other "missing" variable, social differentiation, is also largely "replaced" by emigration. Clearly this system tends toward increasing homogeneity, not differentiation. Both small farmers and laborers are encouraged out of agriculture, leaving the remaining larger farmers as the heart of the community and its future.[23]

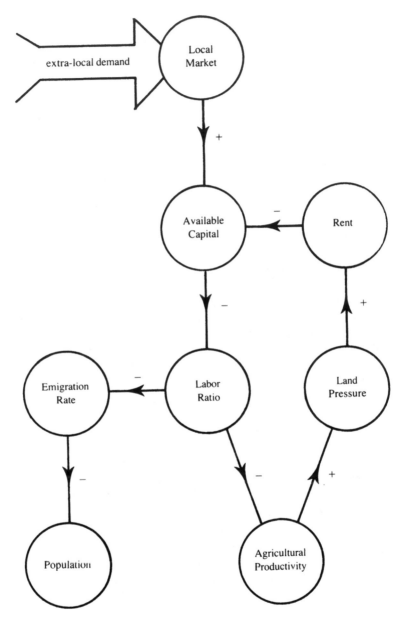

extra-local demand

Local Market

+

Available Capital

−

Rent

−

+

Labor Ratio

Land Pressure

Emigration Rate

−

−

+

Population

Agricultural Productivity

Figure I.3 Developed Stage

This brief explanation of the model which emerges from the Cavan and Killashandra data must conclude with a caveat. Although the model was built to explain the direction of development in a rural community, it does not assume that such development is linear or inevitable. The timing of outside forces, the ecology of an area, and the type of landholding system can all affect its operation. It has been developed to provide a framework for understanding the demographic and economic changes in a specific community; and if it is to be of any comparative usefulness, it must be applied in a similar way. Modifications will most likely be necessary, even for many other Irish communities; but if the basic formulation is correct, the relationships and pathways outlined here will provide the framework for exploring the forces which either create or, just as important, retard economic development.

The model presents a schematic representation of social and economic organization, and this reduction of complexity gives it whatever usefulness it possesses; but we should not be deceived into conceptualizing its stages as mutually exclusive "moments" of development. It is possible, even likely, that a given rural area would contain aspects of two (perhaps even all three) stages at one time. The rural economic "system" is in reality composed of the relationships and decision-making processes of many production/consumption units (over 800 in Killashandra, a parish of 12,529 people). These units of varying size and quality certainly varied in their response to the forces which the model contains. Pure subsistence activity can accompany the most sophisticated commercial operations. Like all models and abstractions, this one is directed at describing the norm or the dominant pattern of activity at any given moment. The persistence of "obsolete," or the apearance of precocious, relationships should not deter us from recognizing and categorizing communities according to their prevailing form of organization.

KILLASHANDRA: AGRICULTURAL DEVELOPMENT

This study of County Cavan and its parish of Killashandra covers the period 1780–1845. In many parts of Ireland, the transition from the Chayanovian to the surplus stage of economic organization occurred during the early years of this period. As has been suggested, the rent system was of primary importance in this transition. The landlord system and its increasingly hungry demands necessitated a more intensive utilization of the land than the traditional, or Chayanovian, system of mixed tillage and pasture could provide. The resultant intensive tillage system permitted the movement of large amounts of capital out of the agricultural system (in the form of rents) through the exploitation of the only productive factor over which the farming population had control: labor.

With the severe capital shortage endemic in Ireland, grain tillage required even greater labor inputs than in other parts of Europe. On the small farms predominant in most of Ireland, draft animals were uneconomical and much of the tillage labor was carried out by the spade. The potato was the perfect mate for corn under these conditions because it sustained the high population densities needed for corn tillage to survive in an undercapitalized system.

Thus, contact between intensive agricultural production for a capitalist market (i.e., grain production) and a predominantly subsistence crop (the potato) substantially altered all sectors of the agricultural economy. But the relationship between subsistence and commercial sectors of the rural economy was not really competitive. By virtue of its dual role as a restorative crop in the grain rotation and the food source of the laboring population, the potato served as a link between the high and rising population density and the increasing agricultural production. In this way, the expansion of the corn market helped to create and to confirm an ecological niche for the potato in commercial agriculture in pre-famine Ireland, even though only the corn crop had a direct link with commercialization.[24]

From this perspective, the potato, the large numbers of agricultural laborers, and the resultant rising population of the pre-famine era appear not as the legacy of an old subsistence form of agriculture, but as the foundations of surplus production. In a very real sense the agricultural laborers of pre-famine Ireland provided the ''primitive accumulation'' necessary for the commercialization of Irish agriculture. Of course many small farmers also contributed to the intensification of agricultural productivity through greater ''self-exploitation," and in some parts of the country they may have played a more important role than the laborers. But the small farmers in this case could, with fair justification, be described as "hidden" wage earners.

This form of agricultural development had social dangers which are apparent to us from the post-famine perspective; but it also had several economic and ecological shortcomings which would have required major changes even if potato production had remained stable. By requiring large labor inputs, the system encouraged the laboring population to increase rapidly; yet there was a biological limit beyond which the land could no longer benefit from additional labor. When this point was reached (and, as will be seen shortly, it had been reached in Cavan before the famine), the laboring population was left to bear the burden of the community's survival. There was an even greater potential problem ahead. In some parts of the country the entire process of commercialization rested upon the high corn prices of the late eighteenth century and the inflated prices of the Napoleonic wars. When those prices fell, the survival of commercial agriculture in Ireland would depend on the ability of the agricultural community to reorganize itself along the more capital-intensive lines of dairy and beef production. This could not be done without the removal of large numbers of the rural population and the redirection of agricultural capital.

If market forces were of primary importance in spurring agricultural change, geographic location obviously played an important role in determining the experiences of any given community. In this study of County Cavan I am suggesting a model of economic development in which a shift from the Chayanovian to the surplus-producing stage began sometime around 1789. The transition was a response to landlord demands for higher rents facilitated not only by the growing demands for food in industrial Britain, but by transportation improvements which enabled Cavan producers to participate in the British market. Landlords themselves probably were motivated by the need to make their Irish investments as profitable as contemporary British investment. This stage of economic development was directly responsible for the growth of population in Cavan through its demands for agricultural labor. By the third decade of the nineteenth century, the demand for labor had been exceeded by the rapidly growing laboring population, and living conditions of the laboring population began to decline. My research shows that the response to this altered situation was the reassertion of pre-famine social controls over population growth.

The transition to the developed stage of economic development is difficult to date precisely. Sometime in the immediate pre- or post-famine period, emigration, the introduction of rail transport, and social controls on fertility, permitted Cavan farmers to begin a slow shift toward dairy production which was necessitated by falling grain prices. This final reorganization of Cavan agriculture along capital-intensive lines was made possible only by the changing tastes and demands of the British urban population, and it necessitated the continuous rural depopulation which became a hallmark of Irish population dynamics until the very recent past.[25]

This study does not follow the transformation of Cavan agriculture to its modern capitalized state. It is concerned with the initial period of market development in which the critical social and demographic developments took place—with the manner in which rural society accommodated itself to the changing economic circumstances of early industrial Europe, and the nature of the social controls over production and population. My major concern will be to document the changes in agricultural organization during the pre-famine period and to relate these changes to family structure and population trends.

Such a study of the interaction of social and economic factors can be carried out only at a local level. The choice of County Cavan as the subject area was largely determined by the unusual richness (by Irish standards) of that county's demographic sources for the pre-famine period. The vast majority of the individual census forms from the pre-famine census of Ireland were destroyed during the Irish Civil War. For the 1841 census, only the forms of Killashandra parish in Cavan have survived as a group. The 1841 census marks the first reliable (and perhaps the most accurate) census of Ireland. It is also the first to inquire into marriage age, a critical variable in the Irish demographic debate. Information contained in the individual forms, supplemented by other data on landholding and religion, was transformed into a computerized file which has served as the base for much of the information presented below. The existence of this important and, in some ways, unique data base determined the selection of the geographical study area. There are other areas better served with secondary sources, newspapers, and estate papers still awaiting the historian. I cannot hope to reproduce the economic landscape of Cavan with the same clarity that James Donnelly did for Cork, but my task is different and in some ways more limited. This is not an attempt at a study of economic organization over a century; rather, it is an attempt to describe the environment in which a number of critical demographic changes occurred. By definition, this entails considerable economic footwork, and at times the lack of some desirable data (such as a detailed time series of agricultural wages) has been as exasperating to me as it will be to the critical reader.

Still, the traditional sources do deal with Cavan. The Poor Law Commission, the Devon Commission, and the Railroad Commission all produced important local data bases for Cavan, and there are a number of complete estate surveys and rentals which I believe are important to the examination of agricultural and demographic interaction. I cannot provide precise dating of the economic change suggested here, nor can I produce indices of change. However, it is possible to test earlier models of Irish demographic behavior and advance an additional one which better fits both the economic and demographic data.

One of the basic questions for any Irish local study seems to be the "typicality" of the area under scrutiny. This is true in Irish historiography because of a tendency among some historians and anthropologists to concentrate attention upon certain regions of the country which they consider to be most representative of Irish "peasant" society. From this perspective, the most Gaelic, the most subsistence-oriented, and the most remote areas seem particularly important. This approach is obviously of limited use to those trying to understand economic development, but it is just as limited for any attempt to understand the country as a whole. The poorest counties are no more typical than the wealthiest, the most remote no more than the most accessible, and the most underdeveloped no more than the most commercially oriented.

In a sense, typicality is a chimera; no one county can be a micro-

cosm of the country. Nineteenth-century Ireland contained places as
diverse as the Lagan Valley and West Mayo, Belfast and Belderg.
Indeed, no national description can be written until a series of local
studies is completed and the true extent of the variations is known.
The most to be hoped for in a quest for national significance is that
the county selected not deviate too far from the experiences of the
other counties, and that it resemble several other counties fairly
closely. If these requirements are met, it is reasonably certain that
the county is not "atypical" and that the conclusions have some
national significance. Cavan meets these criteria; but only the completion of thirty-two county studies will permit a decision as to
whether Cavan was indeed "typical."

There is even a sense in which the quest for typicality can be
counterproductive. The boundaries of "communities" or "regions" are not congruent with the geographic and political boundaries within which the historian must normally operate. The records
used here and elsewhere were collected without regard to any particular definition of *community* other than the historical accident of
administrative boundaries. Hence the researcher must try to treat
these administrative communities cautiously, using them as a basis
for collecting data but withholding the use of the term *community* as
an heuristic concept until it is clear that some internal logic or
system functions within the area under study. Of course this is a
difficult, if not impossible, task because of the need, even in the
earliest stages of data collection, to make some assumptions regarding the nature of a community. The two uses of "community"
become even more confused once data analysis begins. These con-
cerns might be immobilizing were it not for the fundamental importance of small-scale studies in the understanding of large-scale
phenomena.[26] The best to be hoped for is not that the study area
have a precise fit with some already identified pattern or region, but
that it provide a useful image for comparative study, both within
and beyond Ireland.

This problem of community "identity" is made even more difficult in this case by defects in the economic data. While the demographic data is highly specific, from the single parish of
Killashandra (population 12,552),[27] the economic data is drawn
from the entire county (population 243,158). There was (and is)

Ireland and England

considerable local variation within Irish counties. For Cavan the major regional division was between the western "panhandle," which was wild and mountainous, and the larger area of the county (including Killashandra), which was hilly but much more hospitable (see map of Ireland). The bulk of the evidence comes from this part of the county, but only some of it is actually from Killashandra parish itself. There are some estate data on about one-fifth of the land of the parish, but they are insufficient for much analysis on their own. Therefore, the study must assume a certain amount of continuity in the social and economic organization of the eastern part of the county. A survey of the physical and social geography of this region will establish the grounds for that assumption.

Topographically, Cavan is part of the Upper Erne Valley and the Northwest Midlands. The underlying bedrock is covered by glacial deposits (except for parts of the western panhandle). The main feature of these glacial deposits are several thousand drumlins, which with their interspersed lakes, marshes, and bogs form a landscape of numerous hills with highly varied soil and drainage conditions. Although most of these drumlin hills are in the 400- to 900-foot range, their irregular arrangement and the numerous lakes which separate them make communication in this region difficult. The northwest region has higher elevations and is dominated by the bleak Cuilcagh Mountains and Slieve Russell.

The soils of Cavan vary a good deal depending on altitude and drainage conditions, but in general they are primarily drumlin gleys with some acid brown earths and grey-brown podzolics developed on dense clays and glacial till. The predominance of the gleys demonstrates the poor drainage and aeration in the drumlin regions, where the underlying clay is often so impermeable that internal drainage is almost impossible.[28] Because of this, and the wet climate of the region, the most valuable farmland in Cavan was (and is) generally hillside land of moderate slope rather than the level areas between hills. This helps to explain the resistance of Cavan tillage to the plow, since the land most suitable for the plow was the least productive.

These soil conditions were very unfavorable to tillage, but they also made the land susceptible to overgrazing. Furthermore, throughout the pre-famine period the high rent structure which worked against fodder crops forced cattle owners to put their stock out to pasture early in the spring, preventing the natural rejuvenation of the grassland. With careful drainage, management, and reseeding and proper fertilizer, the soil is capable of very high grass yields, but all of this requires capital, which, as we shall see, the Cavan farmers did not possess during the pre-famine period.

This natural geography, which dominated all but the western uplands, closely resembled the drumlin country of Monaghan, Louth, and the Carlingford peninsula. The higher elevations of the panhandle resembled the neighboring counties of Leitrim, Roscommon, Longford, and Sligo. An indication of the general similarity of these counties can be found in the contemporary use of the land; by 1965 over 95 percent of the farmland in each of these counties was under hay or pasture.[29]

The human geography of Cavan was closely tied to the major characteristics of the environment. Towns were small but fairly close together due to the difficulties of transportation. The largest town, Cavan, had a population of only 3,749 in 1841. Other principal towns included Cootehill (2,425), Bailieborough (1,203; a major town because of its large market), Kingscourt (1,614), and Belturbet (1,620). A large group of smaller market towns and villages situated about eight to fifteen miles apart accounted for the county's remaining town population (see map of Cavan).

The manuscript census forms of the 1841 census used in this study are from the parish of Killashandra and contain the returns for two towns, Killashandra (1,085) and Arvagh (615). These two towns were fairly typical of the small market towns of the country and region. Killashandra town was the more important market center in the pre-famine period. In 1840 it had thirteen public houses, twenty-seven shops, a brewery (which had been closed for three years), and a newly built market house where weekly markets and four yearly fairs were held.[30] Killashandra had been an important coarse linen market town at the turn of the century, but by 1840 her connection to the linen industry was largely reduced to that of supplier of flax and low-quality warps. The town also was the terminus of one of Gosson's coach lines from Dublin.[31] Arvagh's markets were smaller, and the town could boast only four pubs, but the monthly fairs were of considerable importance to local trade.

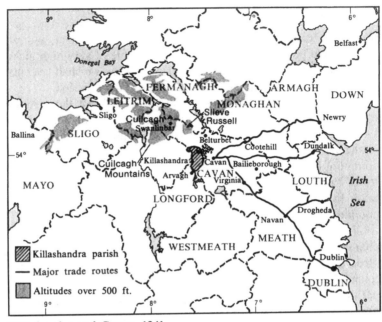

Killashandra and Cavan, 1841

   The hinterland around these two towns (approximately 22,000 acres) consisted largely of drumlin country. Killashandra itself was situated on the shores of Lough Oughter, one of the larger lakes of the drumlin region, which actually consisted of many twisting and confusing channels of the River Erne separated by drumlin islands. Arvagh, situated farther to the south, was on the shores of Garty Lough overlooked by Bruse Hill, the highest point of the parish. The land between the two towns ran along the Leitrim border and was divided mainly into small and medium-sized farms composed of many hillside fields separated by bog, marsh, and rough damp grazing. Flooding of the Erne was a perennial problem on the lower ground, of which the parish contained a good deal. In all this, Killashandra parish was typical of the Cavan/Fermanagh region of South Ulster.
   Regions such as this experienced the great population increases of

the pre-famine period; by 1841 Killashandra's population density reached the uncomfortable level of 361 people per square mile.[32] How areas of indifferent soils could support such levels of human population is the subject of this study. As already suggested, the answer lies in the increasing commercialization of agriculture based on labor-intensive tillage.

Agricultural
Structure:
Tenure,
Rents,
and
Farm
Size
1

It is difficult to categorize the agricultural system of Cavan within the framework traditionally used to describe Irish agriculture before 1848. Cavan's agriculture was not a fully capitalized system; the many holdings below five acres clearly were incapable of functioning in a competitive market system. Yet it certainly was not a subsistence-based system. The large farms produced primarily for the market, and even the smallest holder entered the market to procure his rent. In addition, laborers and even farm servants entered into cash transactions when hiring conacre.[1] One might say that Irish agriculture was in a transitional state between a peasant subsistence economy and a modern form of capitalized agriculture, but this presupposes that there was a definite direction of change and that Irish agriculture was following the same course as that of its English neighbor, assumptions which do not fit the traditional description of pre-famine agriculture. The purpose of this and the following chapter is to examine closely the pre-famine agricultural system of Cavan to see if evidence of economic development exists.

Agriculture in County Cavan was influenced by a number of economic and social factors, such as market integration, population density, land tenure, and capital supply, but these factors operated within a predetermined ecosystem which was largely beyond the control of the farming population. The cool, wet climate and the heavy, poorly drained soil made it all but impossible to produce a competitive wheat crop. Instead, it favored the production of potatoes, oats, and grass products. Cavan's grasslands were poorly drained and in most parts of the county needed more lime than was locally available. For these reasons there were few grazers in Cavan. Instead pasture was used either for dairying or the rearing of calves which were sold to the large grazers of Meath. Oats, the traditional tillage crop of Ulster, did not lose importance as a cash crop with the advent of the potato because of the extreme difficulty and expense involved in transporting the latter (the potato was not, however, entirely a subsistence crop; it was important to the small farmers and cotters as pig fodder).[2]

These natural restrictions on agriculture remained constant throughout the pre-famine period and formed the limits within which Cavan farmers accommodated themselves to external forces such as market prices. Within these limits, the opportunity to change agricultural organization was controlled by indigenous social and economic factors. Farm size, land tenure, rents, capital and labor supply, transportation facilities, and social organization all played important roles in determining the opportunity for change for individual farmers. Only through detailed study of these individual factors can we arrive at an understanding of the process of change within the agricultural system before the famine.

Among the factors affecting the agricultural system, those concerning the occupation of land were the most important to the farming classes. The type of tenure, rent per acre, and size of holding were the major determinants of the farm family's potential for survival and prosperity. Among these three, the question of land tenure must be examined first, because the labyrinth of tenure evidence often distorts the image of rent structure and farm size.

TENURE

In order to prevent confusion, it is important to distinguish between direct tenancies (perhaps *primary* would be a better term) and subtenancies. Direct tenure, conveyed by a formal agreement between a

principal landlord and a tenant, was the meaning which most
nineteenth-century commentators understood for the term *tenure*.
Such an agreement usually entailed a lease, and even when it did
not, both parties had obligations and rights which were recognized
by the courts. The landlord had the right to expect timely fulfillment
of the covenants of the lease or verbal agreement. The tenant had the
right to peaceful possession and use of the property as long as he
met the obligations which he had undertaken.

This tenure system by itself was not a destructive economic force.
However, it did place the Irish peasant in a situation unique among
the peasantry of Europe. This system of property rights, modeled on
the English system, did not recognize any form of limitation on land
usage as long as the terms in the lease were honored. There were no
recognized community rights, no commons, and no village decisions regarding land distribution, crop choice, or crop rotation.
There was no legally recognized preventive check on the use of the
land other than economic restraints. This made the Irish peasant,
however reluctant, the most market-oriented peasant in Europe and
helps to explain the extreme nature of Irish economic and social
developments as agriculture moved painfully into a fully capitalized
system.

The difference between this direct tenure and the actual way in
which many of the occupiers of the soil held their farms was due to
the prevalence of a middleman system[3] which had developed in the
seventeenth century. During this period landlords uninterested in
estate management and unaware of the pitfalls of inflation had let
their estates out in large parcels by long leases without covenants
against subdivision. Many of these tracts, such as the modest 288
acres held by the Groome family from the Bishop of Kilmore, were
intended for subletting, but with the growth of population, the increased profitability of tillage, and the advent of the potato, there
was strong economic and social pressure in favor of subletting[4] on
even smaller units, including those below 100 acres. As a result, the
number of actual occupiers of agricultural holdings grew far beyond
the number of direct tenancies.

The numerous subtenantry did not generally have the benefit of
leases, and their right to possession depended not on their payment

of their rent, but upon the ability of their overtenant to pay his rent to the head landlord. Also, in order to insure the genteel status which the larger middlemen often sought, the subtenants had to pay considerably higher rents than the landlord received. A more detailed account of this system follows the discussion of direct tenure. At this point it is sufficient to note that evidence from the landlords' vantage point (the majority of evidence before the famine) refers to legal or primary tenure and not the actual occupation of the land; consequently great care must be taken in drawing conclusions about rent, farm size, and security solely from these sources. Only by use of other evidence concerning the occupiers of the land themselves can we understand the real nature of tenure.

One of the reasons for the expansion of the middleman system during the eighteenth century had been the landlords' difficulty in finding individuals who had the necessary capital to undertake a large holding. Charles Coote, a native of Cavan, may have put it too strongly when he wrote that, "formerly, the landlord fought for a tenant to take his ground on a long lease,"[5] but by the time Coote wrote his *Statistical Survey of Cavan* (1800), it was quite clear that there was no longer a shortage of bidders. More important, by the turn of the century agriculture in Cavan began to profit from the general increase in farm prices after 1750. As this increase was accelerated by the war, Cavan landlords, wishing to insure that they, not their tenants, would be the major recipients of the boom, became increasingly reluctant to offer long leases. On the Garvagh estate in the Barony of Knockbride, leases granted in the 1780s and '90s were still long; granted for the life of the Prince of Wales, they averaged forty years. By 1806, however, leases on the same estate were being granted for only one life or twenty-one years.[6]

On the Groome property near Bailieborough the same trend was clear. Leases set in the '80s were for three lives or thirty-one years, while those set after 1809 were for one life or twenty-one years.[7] On the Greville estates a similar reduction in term was made.[8] The process, however, was slow, depending upon the irregular falling in of leases. On the Garvagh estate only twenty-five of ninety-four holdings were let between 1800 and 1829, and of course not all landlords participated in the movement. On the Royal School estates near Swanlinbar, leases set as late as 1813 were still of the older type and still in effect in 1841.[9] However, despite these restrictions, the trend to shorter leases was clear.

While landlords were responsible for this early shortening of leases, the Devon Commission found that by the 1830s (and probably sooner) some Cavan tenants were reluctant to accept long leases. With the bitter experience of the post-Napoleonic price collapse not long behind them, it is not surprising that the more solvent tenant might be wary of a long lease at a high rent in uncertain times.[10] The Commissioners also found not only that the term of leases was decreasing, but that the number of occupiers holding by lease was also dropping.[11] This may have been partially due to the reluctance of larger tenants to take long leases, but the landlords' actions were certainly more important. They too had learned a lesson from the postwar depression. Falling rent receipts, coupled with the default of many middlemen, gave the more efficiency-minded (and the more desperate) landlords both the opportunity and the incentive to take back direct control over their estates. A survey undertaken in 1832 on the Greville estate shows that 123 out of a total of 217 tenants held their land as yearly tenants without a lease.[12] These yearly tenancies (not to be confused with tenants at will)[13] were generally automatically renewed as long as rent was satisfactorily paid. Since a "hanging gale" was the normal practice on Cavan estates (i.e., tenants were always six months in arrears), there was really little difference between the legal security of the two groups of tenants. Removal for nonpayment of rent was relatively rare and generally limited to those cases where several years' rent was due. During the pre-famine era, evictions were generally carried out for other reasons, reasons which the peasantry as a whole found more offensive and, on some occasions, sinister.

No aspect of Irish rural history is so emotionally charged as this question of eviction, and no occurrence in the rural community was as certain to provoke a violent reaction. In a society so overwhelmingly dependent upon agriculture and in which even the industrial laborer had to have access to potato land to provide for his or her family's survival, it is easy to see why the community would claim a moral right to the land. In a historiography rife with political implications, it is equally easy to understand why the tremendously provocative image of the eviction came to symbolize all landlord/tenant relations. Unfortunately it is not so easy to uncover the actual state of affairs on the local level. Barbara Solow, among others, has already pointed out, when writing of the post-famine period, that the term *eviction* refers often simply to the issuance and serving of a process or writ of eviction, not necessarily to the forceful removal of a tenant.[14] On Cavan estates before the famine it was common practice to issue notices of eviction to force recalcitrant tenants to pay back rents or for other coercive purposes, such as forcing a tenant to accept a new lease before the term of his old one had expired. Once accommodation was reached, the tenant would be readmitted. Thus the statistics given for evictions do not necessarily tell us how many tenants were actually removed from their holdings; instead, they serve as a general indicator of economic conflict. Even where we know that tenants were removed, the balance between coercion and inducement is not clear. For example, on the Garvagh estate between 1831 and 1847, of over three hundred tenants, only eighteen were removed by eviction. Twelve of those received cash payments for peacefully giving up possession. It is not known how happy these twelve were, but even if they left angrily, this works out to a forcible ejection rate of about .4 percent per annum.[15]

Table 1.1 gives some idea of the eviction decree process in the middle years of the period. It is worth noting that the large majority

Table 1.1

Eviction Decrees from Killashandra Parish, 1827–33

	EVICTION DECREES SOUGHT		EVICTION DECREES GRANTED	
YEAR	For Overholding	For Arrears	For Overholding	For Arrears
1827	10	1	10	0
1828	4	5	1	3
1829	10	1	7	1
1830	8	2	6	2
1831	10	0	8	0
1832	1	0	1	0
1833	3	0	3	0
Total	46	9	36	6

SOURCE: Poor Inquiry, Supplement to Appendices D, E, F (H.C. 1836, xxxiv), pp. 214–43.

of decrees both sought and granted were for the expiration of a lease
and not for the more emotional question of nonpayment of rent. This
may indicate that many of these tenants were later readmitted; but
even granting the unlikely condition that all of these tenants were
actually removed, the yearly eviction rate in this parish of approximately 1,100 tenancies never reached 1 percent and over this seven-
year period averaged about .5 percent.

   In some parts of the country large-scale evictions were carried out
for the purposes of consolidation and economic rationalization of
archaic landholding patterns, but in Cavan the majority of removals
undertaken before the famine seem to have been for either political
or sectarian reasons. The Devon Commissioners could not find any
area of the county where improving evictions were taking place;
instead they found a tenantry greatly disturbed by sectarian attacks
upon their holdings.[16] During the 1770s some zealous Protestant
landlords carried out wholesale evictions of Catholic tenants in order to replace them with a more tractable Protestant tenantry. In
1794 such sectarian evictions on Henry Maxwell's (the future Lord
Farnham's) land led to serious conflict between the Catholic community and the Protestant militia. On 15 May of that year over thirty
Catholics were killed when the militia burned the small village of
Ballinagh.[17]

   It is more difficult to identify the actual motive of evictions in the
early nineteenth century, as landlords were reluctant to expose
themselves, their agents, and their Protestant tenantry to the hostile
actions of an aroused Catholic community. But there is no doubt
that sectarian motives continued to play an important role in Cavan
evictions, especially on large estates. At the turn of the century
there were major clearances of Catholics on the Farnham estates
southeast of Lough Ramor[18] and on the Headfort estates throughout
the county.[19] Large-scale evictions were also carried out in the
twenties on the property of Sir George Hodson, causing violence in
1829.[20] In the late thirties and early forties the Reverend Marcus
Beresford, a Church of Ireland clergyman and an active leader of the
Orange Order, was also engaged in removing Catholics, again causing violence.[21]

   Many of these evictions had political overtones; the struggles for
the abolition of tithes, Catholic Emancipation, and the repeal of the

Act of Union all polarized political relations along religious lines. Many Cavan landlords also had an indirect economic motivation for sectarian eviction. Protestant landlords often considered Catholic tenants greater risks than Protestants; this impression rested partially upon reality. Larger and therefore more substantial tenants were more likely to be Protestant, giving many less than objective observers the impression that Protestant tenants, as a group, were more industrious. In addition, the natural animosity inherent in the landlord/tenant relationship was somewhat offset by the common political interests among Protestants. Protestant tenants who looked upon their landlords as political champions in the fight against Catholic Emancipation were less likely to resist their landlords' economic actions, especially where these actions were aimed at the removal of a largely Catholic subtenantry.

FARM SIZE

Whatever the rationale behind evictions, the truly remarkable feature of the Irish tenure system was "not so much the extent to which evictions and clearances did take place, as the extent to which in a milieu which might reasonably have been described as tailored to give conditions of perfect competition, people were able to cling to the land in excess of the numbers which could possibly have been justified economically."[22] The true evil of this system of tenure was that by denying the right of the indigenous population to control access to the land, it removed an important barrier to population growth.

The overconcentration of people on the land had originated in the twin processes of subdivision and subletting made possible by favorable tillage prices and by the extremely high productivity of the potato. Its stability rested upon the continued success of these two independent variables. But even had corn prices remained high and the potato healthy, there were limits beyond which further subdivision and subletting would have become impossible. In Cavan, farm size was approaching these limits well before the famine. At the same time, corn prices (relative to other prices) were declining, creating a scissors effect which made subdivision difficult and subletting much less attractive to the tenant.

A detailed analysis of this process requires some specification of the actual size of farms and the change, if any, over time. This is an extremely problematic exercise. All observers agreed that Irish farms were small by English standards, but this tells us very little about the trends within Ireland during the nineteenth century. Estate papers must be used with extreme caution due to the effects of subletting and subdivision. Fortunately, there are other sources of information which when used with the estate papers allow an overall estimate of farm size and the nature and extent of fragmentation.

An example of the danger of relying on estate rent rolls in order to calculate average farm size can be found in the rental accounts of the Crofton estate. In 1796, four tenants held 189 acres by lease, but a note in the rent roll informs us that the land was actually "held by poor people, undertenants."[23] No number is mentioned, and it is probable that the agent did not really know how many people farmed the land which he managed. Unfortunately, it is equally unclear how many estate accounts are flawed in the same way without such a gloss. Coote in his *Statistical Survey* offered figures for the average size of farms in the various baronies of Cavan, but unfortunately his statistics were often highly imaginative generalizations rather than mathematical observations. In general his estimate for the whole county was an average of nine acres,[24] and in the vicinity of a town five acres. In Tullaghunco barony he stated that the "smaller farms" ran from three or five to ten acres, while those of twenty would be considered "very large."[25] Coote reported that in many parts of the county there was little room left for expansion. In Tullaghagavy there was "no waste ground. The population so great, every patch is brought in with the spade, which is inaccessible to the plough."[26]

Coote believed that the reason for fragmentation in his time was the spread of the linen industry. He found that the manufacture of linen cloth occupied large parts of the peasantry in all of the county except the northwest panhandle, where the older tradition of woolen cloth manufacture persisted. In the three baronies of Castleraghan, Clonmoghan, and Clonchee he claimed that "linen manufacture is at present more or less engaged in by every peasant in this district."[27] He went as far as to claim that in many parts of the county the cotter was not longer an agricultural laborer but a weaver working for a master employer: "This wretched member of society works at the loom for his rapacious employer and his tenure is called a dry-cot take; if he has the grass of a cow, he pays for it from one to two guineas additional . . . these cot-takes are not leased to the weaver."[28] Coote argued that by greatly increasing the rent which the landless could pay to farmers for a small garden, these weavers drove up the profitability of renting land and reduced the amount necessary to produce a "comfortable" living, thus permitting the subdivision of a farm family's holding without any diminution of the farmer's standard of living.

However, Coote was a bit of a zealot when it came to the linen industry, and his statements must be treated with care. Most weavers were not engaged full time at their looms. They, and their wives and daughters who supplied thread from their wheels, worked only during the slack summer and winter months. As often as not these weaving families were farmers, not cotters. An 1824 survey of the Sneyd property in Drumlane parish shows that out of sixty tenants, eight were weavers, of whom six held property individually, their average holding being fifteen Irish acres, much more than the garden which Coote described.[29]

While Coote overstated his case, the statistics which he presented regarding the linen trade in Cavan make it clear that linen did play a major role in Cavan's agricultural economy. At the turn of the century he estimated the sale of coarse linen in Cavan town's market at £70,000 per annum, with an additional £20,000 being exported from the town for sale farther north. In addition, the Killashandra market averaged sales of approximately £50,000 per annum. These price estimates are supported by the figures which Coote gave for the output of Cavan bleach greens, which averaged 91,000 webs per year (each web having a value of about thirty shillings).[30] Coote's claims also receive support from the valuator upon the Greville estates who, writing in the early 40s, stated, "20 or 30 years ago every tenant upon the estate had 2 or 3 looms at work."[31]

The type of fragmentation which Coote linked to linen production was extremely sensitive to changes in that industry's health. By 1820 the competitive strength of the Cavan linen industry was giving way to the more efficiently organized and increasingly mechanized areas of northeastern Ulster. By 1830 the independent weaver, relying primarily on his loom for his family's livelihood, had almost disappeared, although many poor families continued to supplement their agricultural income through textile work. As a result of this decline in the linen industry, the viability of smaller farms and all types of cots declined. Thus, while the size of farms may not have decreased substantially after 1830, the ability of a family to survive on the smaller units did decline. One must keep in mind this changing nature of the relationship between farm size and potential family support when examining the objective figures regarding farm size.

The 1821 census offers the earliest reliable landholding data for Cavan. Although the population statistics for the 1821 census have been questioned due to the understandable suspicion with which the peasantry regarded authorities and the method of compensation for enumeration, there is little reason to doubt the general accurary of the landholding statistics at the local level.[32] In the parish of Lavey, the 625 farms enumerated broke down in the following way when converted to statute acres:[33]

Less than 5 acres	10 percent
Less than 8 acres	21 percent
Less than 16 acres	70 percent
Less than 32 acres	94 percent

As early as 1821 over two-thirds of the farms of this parish were less than sixteen acres, suggesting that the process of fragmentation was already pressing upon the limits of possibility.

A broader and more detailed source of information regarding farm size is available for the 1830s. In compliance with the Tithe Composition Act, the representatives of the Church of Ireland and the tithe payers carried out a detailed survey of the acreage and value of individual holdings. The Tithe Applotment Book for Killashandra parish compiled in 1832 survives in excellent condition and provides the following breakdown of 658 individual farms (the figures have been converted to statute acres):[34]

Less than 5 acres	6.0 percent
Less than 8 acres	17.0 percent
Less than 16 acres	50.7 percent
Less than 32 acres	84.3 percent

The disparity between these two sets of figures may be slightly magnified at the lower end of the scale due to the confusion surrounding the recording of cot and conacre land in the Tithe Applotment Book, but what is most interesting is the apparently greater number of farms of thirty-two acres or more recorded in the figures for 1832. These two sets of figures cannot be compared directly, having been collected for two different purposes for two different parishes, and it is certainly improbable that an actual increase in size took place during this period. Still, with a median (and mean) farm size of approximately sixteen acres in 1841, it is scarcely plausible to characterize 1841 as the end point of a century of rampant subdivision. If we extrapolate back from this point, assuming a very modest 2 percent per annum population growth rate (i.e., about three survivors to age thirty per family), the mean farm size in 1750 works out to nearly 100 acres![35]

The 1821 and 1832 figures receive support from the testimony which the Poor Law Commission took during its investigation into the causes of poverty in Cavan. Testimony received in 1835 covered nineteen parishes in Cavan. The estimate of average farm size ranged from a low of ''2 to 6 acres'' (Irish) to a high and vague ''10 to 30 acres'' (Irish).[36] In some cases, such as that of Enniskeen, observers responded that the farms were ''generally from 7 or 8 acres'' apiece, clearly indicating that they were trying to describe the normal or modal farm size, and thus present a better description of the actual state of land occupation.[37] (The average figure would be inflated by the existence of a few very large grazing farms.) If we convert these figures to statute measure, the average response was approximately seventeen acres. The response for Killashandra, eleven to sixteen acres, corresponds very closely to the mean figure of fourteen acres which the Tithe Applotment Book provides. Still further confirmation of these figures is available through the ordnance survey memoir from Drumlommon parish, which gives the size of the average farm as ten to twenty acres.[38]

The Devon Commission Digest of Evidence, taken immediately prior to the famine, produced a similar range of estimates for farm size. The Devon Commissioners were more interested in this question than was the Poor Law Commission and sought more detailed answers which allow us to draw more precise conclusions. Michael

Kenny, a particularly useful witness who was a tenant of a sixty-acre farm and a deputy agent on the Farnham estate, informed the commission that he thought "20 acres might make the average size of the farms, the most common size would be under twenty."[39] Kenny's conscious distinction between the average and normal size of farms is especially valuable in helping alert us to the problems of interpreting other less specific testimony. Another witness describing the same general area around Bailieborough, Hugh Porter, gave the "general size" of farms as fourteen to twenty acres, adding that "they are considered middling strong farmers that have thirty acres."[40] Other witnesses gave average farm sizes which ranged from "scarcely ten"[41] to "20–25" acres.[42] Clearly there was a wide range of farm sizes, but just as surely there were a considerable number of substantial farms in Cavan on the eve of the famine which had escaped the process of fragmentation.

As noted above, estate papers provide little useful information during this period regarding actual farm size, but at the end of the pre-famine era, provoked by the very crisis of the famine itself, at least two Cavan landowners sought out information on the occupation of their estates. These two reports provide some of the most valuable evidence available on the question of farm size.

On the Hodson estate a single tenant held the townland of Upper Skea. The 208 acres of arable land were actually occupied by 41 undertenants (an average of 5 acres each). The townland of Corleck was held by four tenants and their seven subtenants, again an average of five acres apiece. However, these cases were the extreme; over the entire estate the average holding of direct tenants was twenty acres, and for all tenants approximately nine acres.[43] A similar account from the Pratt estate, also detailing the number of cotters (table 1.2), shows how misleading the estate rental figures (listed in the first column) can be. This account works out to about twelve acres per tenant, but it is worth noting the differences between the four townlands.

The two reports provide detailed information on the townland level of land occupation, and demonstrate the difficulty with averages drawn only on direct tenant evidence. The Pratt information is particularly useful in detailing the ratio between direct tenants and their subtenants. It is clear that the subletting of farms, although substantial, was not nearly as prevalent as is often claimed, and that the cotters were the real source of overpopulation and thus the most vulnerable group in changing conditions.

From the evidence, it is difficult to advance any argument for extreme fragmentation of farms between 1800 and 1845. The two estate surveys, while giving lower averages than any in the official inquiry, are still remarkably close to Coote's 1800 figure of nine acres. Even if we reject his figure as too low, there is no evidence that farms were growing smaller during this period. How, then, can we account for the impressions which so many observers presented of an increasingly fragmented and impoverished countryside? Part of the answer is transparently obvious in the Pratt survey: while the number of tenants remained constant, the number of cotters was clearly far in excess of the number of hands needed to work the few farms involved. Their situation was obviously growing worse, but it was often difficult for the English or urban Irish observer to distinguish between the small farmers and their cotters. Even the officials collecting information for the ordnance survey made the error of confusing cotters with farmers in the Cavan parish of Drumlommon.[44]

In addition, it is important to distinguish between farm size and farm productivity. Changes in crop yields or in alternative income sources such as flax growing and processing and linen production all could lead to a deterioration of the potential of individual families to survive, even if their farm size remained constant.

Table 1.2
Inhabitants on the Pratt Estate

		FARMERS		SUBTENANTS		COTTERS		ACRES PER
TOWNLAND	ACRES	Families	People	Families	People	Families	People	TENANT
Annagh	76	5	20	1	3	24	102	12.67
Lisanstem	82	8	37	2	8	26	127	8.20
Lisaniskee	112	1	6	2	11	25	127	37.33
Donnasee	347	16	81	17	69	112	521	10.52

SOURCE: Compiled from an untitled manuscript report in the Pratt Estate Papers: surveys, accounts, legal papers, letters etc. relating to the estates at Kingscourt and Cabra, Co. Cavan (Ms13.318, NLI).

In any case, the traditional model of the agricultural system of Cavan must be revised to permit the possibility of relatively stable farm size during the first half of the nineteenth century. But how are we to explain this apparent sign of stability in a society which is supposedly tottering on the brink of economic disaster? A reassessment of the process of fragmentation is needed. In retrospect, fragmentation may appear as a disastrous policy, but it could also be seen as a response to the increasing productivity of the land during the eighteenth century, and as partially responsible for this productivity. The limitations which agricultural prices and the productivity of the potato placed upon the family economy checked any further fragmentation during the nineteenth century; or, to put it more bluntly, Cavan's land was already divided into its smallest possible units given the structure of both the market system and peasant society. It was not a progressive set of attitudes of the Cavan landlords or farmers, but the cruel logic of survival, which made subdivision "necessarily less common than before," as one observant critic commented in 1845.[45]

RENT

Arriving at any satisfactory understanding of rents and their movements during the first half of the nineteenth century is problematical on several levels. A perennial problem with the available sources, estate papers, is that they refer only to direct tenants, not to the often large numbers of subtenants. As a result, not only may they present unrealistically low figures for the early part of the period, but the impression of rising rents from 1830 on may be due to the rationalization of holdings through the abolition of the middleman system and the subsequent assumption of the middleman's profit by the head landlord. It is impossible to ascertain precisely how large or small an effect rationalization had in Cavan during the period 1800–1845; however, if judicious use is made of those estate papers which can control for this process, we can arrive at both a detailed knowledge of the experience of the direct tenantry and, through inference, some idea of the experience of the subtenants.

There is an additional problem with the term *rent* itself. Although the concept of rent should be familiar enough to most economic historians to allow for a common understanding, several observations upon the nature of economic relations between landlord and tenant in pre-famine Ireland are in order.

In addition to the normal fixed periodical payment stipulated in a lease or verbal agreement between landlord and tenant, the Irish tenant, like his peasant cousins in most of continental Europe, had to pay substantial additional charges to the landlord and his various agents. The true nature of the price which a tenant had to pay for occupying a holding can only be understood by broadening the definition of rent to include the fines and surcharges which tenants were expected to contribute in addition to the rent stipulated in their rental agreement.[46]

Unfortunately, quantifiable evidence for these charges which the tenants found so burdensome is not readily available. As most of these charges were customary, little evidence remains, other than occasional references from interested observers. While the fines and surcharges often took a semi-legal form and produced some records, the incompleteness of such documentation makes it impossible to draw any hard conclusions regarding the extent to which they increased the tenant's obligations to his landlord. The most that can be done is to catalogue the major charges involved and their effect, if any, upon the tenant's indebtedness to his landlord, and then to speculate on their economic effect. This in itself will help to qualify our faith in estate papers, and may result in a more realistic model of pre-famine economic organization.

In pre-famine Cavan oats were both the major cash crop and a substantial provider of subsistence. As such they were particularly vulnerable to landlord attempts to maintain total control over tenant profits. On many estates landlords owned mills which tenants were required to use if they ground their oats. The prices charged by such mills were often so exorbitant that tenants chose to sell their oats unmilled and buy back oatmeal on the open market.[47] Coote recorded that private mills generally charged one-third more than public ones,[48] and from the Greville estate papers it is clear that the practice continued at least until the famine.[49] This surcharge injured the subsistence farmer most severely, requiring him to pay scarce specie for his food supply. The larger commercial farmers did not escape entirely from this abuse, but they confronted a more serious problem due to the timing of gale (rent) days.

The traditional 1 November gale day fell shortly after the grain harvest, when prices were low and the grain was often still in a green state. As a result, threshing either took place too soon, lowering the quality and price of the grain, or it was delayed and the tenant went into arrears. All stock farmers faced a similar problem with the timing of cattle and pig sales: the glut caused by the universal need for cash with which to pay the rent lowered prices considerably.

The sale of produce on a glutted market had obvious economic disadvantages, but so too did the one alternative. Rents in arrear in Cavan were normally collected through distraint; a bailiff or "driver" seized the stock of the unfortunate tenant and held it until the tenant paid his rent plus a fine in consideration of the bailiff's services.[50]

Tenants also had to pay smaller fees to the driver whenever the gale days approached for his service of "warning" the tenantry of their approaching obligations.[51] As one witness summed it up, "The landlords worry the rents out of the tenants."[52] The largest fines or fees which tenants had to pay were those connected with the granting of a lease. Tenants usually paid a £2 or £3 fine for the privilege of holding a farm worth £17 or £18 a year, plus a solicitor's fee of £3 or £4.[53] In addition, payments to members of the agent's family might be required.

On some estates the incoming tenant was also required to clean up any arrears which the previous tenant had left behind. On others, especially the smaller estates, tenants were required to pay the agency fee (usually 5 percent) out of their own pocket.[54] Finally, a particularly archaic device used to increase the obligation of the tenant to his landlord was the custom of the duty day, which still persisted on some estates in nineteenth-century Cavan. This practice, which was generally limited to the smallest tenants, required individuals to work on their landlord's or agent's property during planting and harvest, thus neglecting their own crops.[55]

In the absence of complete written records, the erratic and sometimes arbitrary operation of these exploitative devices makes it impossible to estimate their impact accurately; still, it is clear from such examples that the rent rolls tell only part of the story of land-lord/tenant economic relations. The picture is further clouded by the occasional favorable action which landlords took toward their tenantry. Among a very few improving landlords, such as Farnham, it was common practice to allow certain credits for construction of new homes or outbuildings or to sell building materials at reduced prices. Also, during times of extreme distress it was common for landlords to offer abatements of 10 to 25 percent. (Unfortunately for landlord/tenant harmony, landlords usually tried first to collect full rents during poor times through the use of distraint or eviction notices, and only when it was clear that distress was general and that other landlords were offering reductions in rent did most take the kinder and wiser course.) Despite these landlord concessions, it is clear that during the pre-famine period the majority of Cavan ten-ants ended most years at a disadvantage to their landlord. Benefi-cent landlords were rare, and their aid was limited to a few special purposes or moments.

The additional payments may have amounted to 5 percent per annum if we amortize them over the length of a twenty-year lease and assume that most tenants had to pay drivers twice a year, as Farnham believed. It is doubtful that they amounted to more, but even 2 or 3 percent of a subsistence farmer's produce would repre-sent a considerable, perhaps critical, sum. This increment must be kept in mind when examining rent. Fortunately for the scholar (but not for the Cavan farmer), the surcharges changed little during the period under study, and as a result we may assume that the direction of change which rent rolls show is accurate even if the figures do not represent the precise cost of holding land under a Cavan landlord.

As already noted, the estate records deal exclusively with direct tenancies and contain no direct information regarding subtenancies and their rentals. However, it is obvious that the rent which direct tenants were charged played a major role in determining the rent which they in turn charged their subtenants. Thus the general move-ment of rents during the pre-famine period can be studied through the estate rentals. But it is also true that the changing nature of estate management—that is, the rationalization of multiple tenant hold-ings and the division of subtenanted holdings among the subtenantry—might affect the rental figures which appear in the rent roll. Therefore we must look closely at the changing number of tenancies on several estates to gain some idea of the changing nature of tenure and, by extension, a more accurate understanding of the estate rentals and the changes which they seem to show.

The rentals and estate papers of the Hodson estate give valuable information regarding the nature of estate rationalization during the period 1816–45. There is no evidence of any significant change before 1830, but during the thirties there were complex and important changes in the composition of the rent roll. These changes were largely hidden on the estate as a whole because of the counteracting nature of the twin processes involved in rationalization. On those townlands where the middleman system was prevalent before 1830, there was a sharp increase in the number of tenants as middleman leases fell in and the land was relet to the occupying subtenants. On the three townlands which show such a process, the number of tenants listed in the rent roll increased by 70 percent.[56] However, it was more common for a decrease to take place: in eight townlands the total number of tenancies decreased by 29 percent. This was due to the consolidation of several small holdings into one farm, usually as the result of eviction and/or emigration. The overall result on the estate was a decrease of 6 percent in the number of direct tenants during the period 1830–41.[57]

Evidence from the Greville estate of Coronary shows a similar but less complicated trend. Here the change began a few years earlier, in 1828, and all townlands gained some tenants (table 1.3). The suddenness of this movement clearly demonstrates that this increase was not due to subdivision and tenant irresponsibility, but to landlord rationalization and confirmation of an already existing situation. When we look at the townland figures this becomes even clearer; although the rentals of all townlands show some increase, several show increases over 200 percent. The highest increase was at Coronary, where the number of tenants jumped 400 percent in thirty years, with most of the change taking place between 1828 and 1833.

From this evidence, it is clear that although rationalization of landholding on these two estates was incomplete, it was well under way during the 1830s. But the results of this process were far from uniform. On some estates the effect of removing middlemen and thus increasing landlord income was offset by the simultaneous consolidation of fragmented holdings. On other estates this led to increased income without substantially raising the rents which indirect tenants paid. On still other estates both the rent paid by the occupying tenant and the rent received by the chief landlord rose sharply. An excellent example of this process took place on the Crofton estate, where a middleman, John Castle, lost his lease in 1811. The landlord relet the land to the occupying undertenants by lease, but the rent which they paid rose from £12/16 to £45/10.[58] This rent was, of course, a reflection of wartime prices, but even so, such a large increase clearly demonstrates that the process of rationalization did not simply imply an assumption of middleman profit by the head landlord; it often meant an additional increase of the real rent. The disparity between these rents also points up an almost incredible case of inefficiency in the middleman system. Indeed, the affairs of the estate were utterly confused until a new agent took over in 1823. Even at that late date, the new agent could not be sure of the rent due on several holdings.[59] For want of contrary evidence, we can only suppose that the comparatively low middleman rates were a relic of the general laxity of Cavan's eighteenth-century estate management. If so, this is one more indication of the relative lateness of Cavan's rationalization.

Because of these variations caused by the changing nature of the

Table 1.3
Greville Estate Rentals, 1808–43

YEAR	NO. TENANTS	RENT DUE (£)
1808	142	1,704
1828	217	1,885
1829	217	1,880
1833	286	2,125
1839	353	1,861 (abatement?)
1840	—	2,247
1843	324	2,335

SOURCE: Greville estate rentals in Greville estate papers (M6178, PRO).

tenure system, the reading of aggregate figures is problematic. However, if one controls for estate rationalization, certain trends in rent movements are obvious. There are four periods clearly visible through the estate papers and various corroborative evidence: (1) a period of inconsistent rents before the beginning of the French wars; (2) the very highly inflated war rents of 1790–1815; (3) the depression rents of 1815–26; and (4) the steadily but slowly rising rents from 1826 until the famine. The timing of these periods is in one sense artificial; although there are fairly clear moments at which market events strongly influenced the level of rents in Cavan, the presence of the lease system on all of the estates under consideration delayed the response of Cavan's rent structure to changing market conditions. But even though this flattens out the curve of rent movements, the changes are clear enough to warrant this periodization.

The evidence for the late eighteenth century is much more scarce than for the other periods, and what evidence there is is less useful due to the rather casual attitudes of eighteenth-century estate management. Before the wartime bonanza prices of the Napoleonic period, Cavan landlords seemingly had little incentive to expend time, energy, or capital in what, to their minds, must have been unproductive and uninteresting work. But the little evidence we do have is fairly consistent, and there is no question of estate rationalization distorting the figures at this early date.

On the Garvagh property leases set between 1772 and 1800 were set either for five, seven, or eight shillings per Irish acre depending upon the quality of the land. There was no change during this period.[60] On the Crofton estate the total rental did not increase between 1784 and 1803 (table 1.4). The average rental for this period was about thirteen shillings per Irish acre.[61] The Crofton figures are average rentals per acre over the entire estate, and thus understate the value of land under new leases. The Garvagh figures are for only those leases issued during the period 1772–1800, and provide a more precise measure of change. It is difficult to reconcile the figures. The most tempting explanation is that there was more subletting on the Garvagh estate, and that therefore the real rents were higher than those reported in the rent roll. However, this seems doubtful, as Garvagh direct tenants held considerably smaller farms than the tenants on the Crofton estate, who were often tenants of entire townlands. This would lead us to expect higher rents on the Garvagh estate, not the Crofton estate. Nor can such a large difference be attributed to different qualities of land; the Crofton property was situated in the less productive "panhandle" section of the county.

Charles Coote claimed that rents during this period (ca. 1780–1800) had "nearly" doubled to an 1801 average of 15s. per acre across the county.[62] There is little reason to challenge his 15s. estimate, as it corresponds closely to the Crofton papers and other information on Napoleonic rentals. His assessment of rental increase is, however, more open to doubt. If it is taken literally, then the estate evidence indicates amazing inefficiency on the Garvagh estate from 1780 to 1800 and a baffling combination on the Crofton estate of inexplicably high rents in the 1780s and a complete collapse of efficient management until 1809. Of course this is all possible, but it is more likely that Coote was actually referring to the rental value of land out of lease than to the actual average rental income. Even so, the picture of these rent increases is confused, and we are left with little choice but to conclude that late eighteenth-century rents varied widely from estate to estate, but not over time on the same estate. Both factors indicate lax control by landlords and considerable undervaluation of some property.

There is no such confusion for the Napoleonic period. Rents on

Table 1.4
Crofton Estate Rentals, 1784–1812

YEAR(S)	RENTAL	RENT PER ACRE
1784	252	13s.
1786	245	13s.
1793	235	12s.
1797	253	13s.
1802	253	13s.
1803	253	13s.
1809–11	371	19s.
1812	453	24s.

SOURCE: Compiled from the Crofton estate papers (Ms8150, NLI)

all estates for which there is information rose dramatically as a direct result of the artificially high prices which the wars created between 1800 and 1815. The quickness with which landlords responded to these prices and the ability of Irish tenant farmers to pay these new rents are proof of the responsiveness of Cavan's agriculture to market conditions and rule out any model of Cavan agriculture which supposes a monolithic subsistence-based agricultural group.

Some idea of the magnitude of these remarkable changes can be gained by way of a few examples: on the Garvagh estate, the prewar and wartime rent levels of leases were 5–7s. and 20–25s., respectively; on the Hodson estate, 7s. and 25s.[63] Evidence from the Greville, Groome, and Crofton estates confirms this increase. On the Greville estate there is no information regarding new leases set during the war years. However, it is known that the average rental in 1808 was about 14s. per Irish acre, an average which suggests that a similar increase was taking place. On the Groome estate leases set in 1809 reached the incredible level of 34s. per Irish acre.[64] On the Crofton estate, where prewar rents had averaged about 13s. per Irish acre, the wartime average rose to 24s. per acre (again this figure represents all tenants, not only those agreeing to new leases).[65]

Increases of 200 or even 300 percent in real rental values seem incongruent with the general image of "subsistence" or even "underdeveloped" agriculture; but as remarkable as these increases are, the most significant indicator of the nature of change in rural economy is found in a claim made by tenants on the Crofton estate that, despite the doubling of the gross rental on their estate, the Napoleonic period was "in the memory of man, the best time for paying rents."[66] These rent increases probably lagged behind the increase in real income of Cavan tenants during this boom period. This was more than a period of "good times" for Cavan farmers; rising agricultural prices and the resulting profits represented the energy that pushed Cavan tenants completely into the market system.

Given the artificial nature of the high wartime prices, it was inevitable that the end of the war would bring the end of the landlords' bonanza. On some estates the inability of tenants to meet obligations undertaken during the war forced Cavan landlords to grant large, permanent reductions in rent. These reductions, how-

ever, were not as dramatic as the wartime inflation of rents. Landlords held them to the minimum possible to insure the payment of
rent, a sort of rack reduction. On the small Shankey estate, reductions in 1818 were limited to 20 percent.[67] On the Hodson estate
reductions ranged from 30 to 60 percent on leases set between 1806
and 1812 (leases which had increased 257 percent when let). Of
course new leases followed suit.[68] On the Garvagh estate, it appears
that there were no permanent reductions during the postwar period.
There, the tenantry had to wait for the slow working of the lease
system. Not until 1826 did large numbers of Garvagh tenants receive new leases and the accompanying welcome relief. Leases set
in that year averaged 13s. per acre (as opposed to wartime levels of
20s. to 25s.).[69] On the Crofton estate we have no information regarding individual leases set after the war, but between 1812 and
1823 the average rent per acre over the entire estate fell from 24s. to
20s. and continued to fall until 1830, when it reached a low of 17s.
per acre.[70] Such sudden declines on this estate would seem to suggest that permanent reductions in existing lease rentals were made.
Still, the process was erratic; as late as 1843 some tenants on the
Royal School estates were fighting to get free of Napoleonic rents.[71]

This boom or bust experience had serious consequences for
Cavan agriculture. Initially it provoked landlords to pay more attention to their estates and consequently brought an end to practices
which led to serious underletting. The depression which followed
the war caused some landlords to lower rents on existing leases, and
all landlords were forced to lower rentals on new leases if they
wished to find tenants; however, their reductions were not nearly as
large as the earlier increases. As a result, on all the estates examined
here, this process left higher rents after the war than before. In
addition, landlords, aware of their vulnerability in long leases, now
watched their estates more carefully, granted shorter leases, drove
middlemen out, and kept a careful eye on prices. This increased
landlord vigilance made it more difficult for the tenantry to profit
from inflation, and it also helps to explain the movement of rents
between 1830 and 1845.

The movement of rents during this critical time was not as dramatic as during either the wartime boom or the postwar depression;
however, the direction of change was clear, and the greater normal-

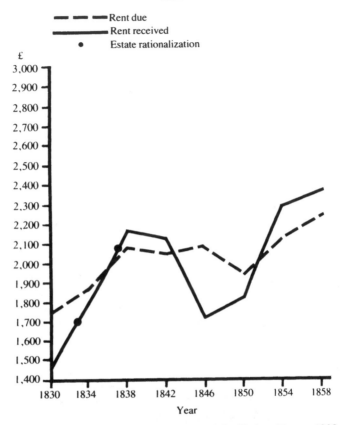

Figure 1.1   Rent Received and Rent Due on the Hodson Estate, 1830–58. Compiled from the Hodson rentals, 1810–66 (Ms16,397–460, NLI).

ity of this period makes this evidence of change in Cavan's agricul- ture particularly important in evaluating pre-famine Cavan's agricultural potential. Figures 1.1, 1.2, and 1.3, which chart rentals for the Hodson and Garvagh estates, present a clear picture of this movement. The Hodson figures are particularly valuable because the availability of complete information on the number of tenants involved makes it possible to control for management rationaliza- tion. As already noted, the change in the number of tenants between

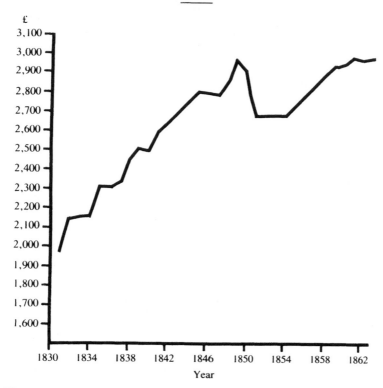

Figure 1.2 Rents Charged on the Garvagh Estate, 1831–64. Compiled from the Garvagh rentals, 1829–65 (M5535, PRO).

1830 and 1841 was small and in a negative direction. Of the two points at which major assumptions of middleman leases took place, obviously the action of 1833 did not raise the rents. That of 1837 may be responsible for the steeper slope of the curve, but considering the rise during the previous and following years during which no such changes took place, it is certain that the overall trend was for rents to increase through the 1830s.

The evidence from the Garvagh estate is remarkably similar. What is most striking is the continued increase in rent charged right through the famine period on the Garvagh estate, and the lack of any abatement on the Hodson estate until 1851. Exactly how many tenants paid these rents from year to year is not known, but the fact that middlemen still existed on this estate in 1860 suggests that there was in this case no vigorous push against the system.[72] Also, it is clear from the size of the holdings on this estate in 1829 that the middleman system was not very prevalent (this may explain the lassitude which the landlord displayed in eradicating it). This too would indicate that no great change in the number of tenants took place before the famine. Thus the figures here should approximate the actual situation of the direct tenants on this estate.

The average rental on the Garvagh estate increased from about 12s. per Irish acre in 1831 to about 17s. in 1845, an increase of 42 percent. The Hodson figures work out to about 16s. in 1830 and 19s. in 1845, an increase of 17 percent. These large increases are substantiated by evidence from the Greville and Royal School estates, where rentals per acre increased from 15s. to 18½s. and from 13¼s. to 18⅓s., respectively, from the postwar period to 1841–45.[73]

The replies which the Poor Law Commissioners received to their inquiries provide important corroborating qualitative evidence for this period. Their correspondents reported the average rentals of small farms in Cavan as ranging from 20s. to 30s. per acre (presumably Irish), with the majority of estimates falling around 25s. per acre.[74] The difference between these figures and the estate paper figures may be due either to the bias toward smaller holdings in the report or to the variation between the average rents of direct tenants (which the estate papers recorded) and the average rents of the entire tenant population which the Poor Law Commission figures reflect. Most likely the discrepancy derives from both of these factors. Finally, immediately before the famine the Devon Commission compiled its evidence on rents in Cavan, and its information coincides fairly closely with that of the Poor Law Commissioners. One particularly well-informed and explicit witness placed the average rental at 20–30s. per Irish acre depending upon the quality of land.[75] All of this qualitative evidence supports the case for generally rising rents from 1827 until the famine.

Having traveled these confusing waters and arrived at a fairly accurate understanding of exactly how the rents charged by Cavan landlords changed over time, we are still left with two interrelated and immensely important questions: What did the undertenants pay as their rent? and (the perennial and polemical question) Were rents too high? The answers to both of these questions are uncertain and complex. A good deal depends upon how the terms involved are understood. Some of the additions and subtractions which might be made to rental figures have already been examined. How "just" the rents were also depends on who was paying them: the direct tenant holding twenty to thirty acres or the subtenant holding a few acres which he used as a partial source of income to supplement his wages from the loom or the spade. What was the relationship between these two inhabitants of the Cavan countryside, and how did their rent payments compare?

On a general level, part of this question is easily answered. Of course the undertenant paid a higher rent than did his overtenant, and this relationship allowed the system to operate by giving the direct tenant an incentive to relinquish direct control over a part of his holding. But it is much more difficult to arrive at any precise relationship between the two rents. There were no leases involved and no reason for any of the participants to keep records. Indeed, both parties had reason to keep their arrangement as covert as possible, lest a landlord or his agent discover just how much the direct tenants' property was really worth per year and raise the primary rent. We have only the declarations made before the Poor Law Commissioners and the Devon Commission, which stated that the rents charged by middlemen were noticeably higher than those of the head landlord, and one piece of evidence from the Nicholson survey of the Greville estate in Knockbride:

John Shannon has lived with his family under James Reilly of Crann for the last 7 years and has been charged nearly £2 per acre for 3 plantation acres of land not worth £1 per year. . . . Neither the agent nor the bailiff knew that Shannon was an under-tenant. . . . [Other land is] let at from £2 to 2 guineas per Irish acre although it is only worth from 22s. to 24s. per acre.[76]

Even this evidence must be taken with some caution. As events later proved, Nicholson had much to gain by drawing as bleak a picture as possible of the estate, especially where the current agent could be implicated as responsible.[77] But it seems likely that these statements are based at least in part on truth, as the agent did not attempt to refute them. If representative, this ratio of 2:1 between direct and subtenant rents explains both the poverty of the latter and perhaps the origin of the common assertion that Irish peasants were mercilessly exploited.

What numerical relationship existed between these two types of tenants? Were the subtenants the "real" peasantry, vastly outnumbering the direct tenants, or were the subtenants a subordinate group both socially and numerically? It is impossible to be very precise for the county as a whole, but once again the documents allow for a rough appraisal of the situation. On the Greville estate on the eve of the famine, Nicholson reported that there were "but few undertenants compared with the number of immediate tenants,"[78] and we have already seen that there was little action upon that estate to prevent subletting. On one part of the Pratt estate in the mid-forties there were twenty-two subtenants for every thirty tenants.[79] On the Hodson estate in 1847 there were 126 subtenants holding from 106 direct tenants.[80] This fragmentary evidence indicates that in pre-famine Cavan anywhere from a few to over one-half of peasant farmers were subtenants, but there is no evidence to suggest that they greatly outnumbered the direct tenantry. It would appear that there was considerable variation from estate to estate and probably from region to region.

There is no evidence allowing an objective decision on the exploitativeness of rents; that is a value judgment based not only on social ethics, but on the understanding of the economic system itself.[81] But from the information regarding rent movements, tenure change, and the prevalence of subletting already discussed and the data on arrears presented in figure 1.3, a few observations can be made regarding the economic viability of agriculture under the rent levels prevalent during the pre-famine period. On the Garvagh estate between 1830 and 1845, arrears never amounted to more than 10 percent (in 1843) and generally were closer to 5 percent of the rental. On the Hodson estate, pre-famine arrears peaked in 1843 at 20 percent of the total rental, but they generally averaged 15 percent. Perhaps more important, these arrears generally were cleared without recourse to eviction.

The ability of the direct tenantry during normal years to pay their

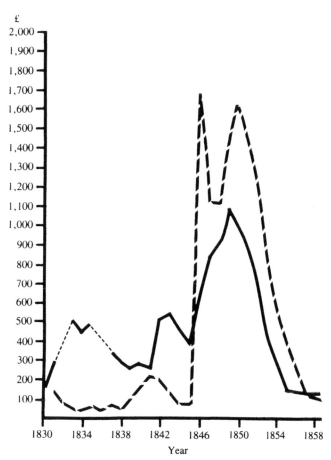

Figure 1.3 Arrears on the Hodson and Garvagh Estates, 1830–58. Compiled from the Hodson (Ms 16,397–400, NLI) and Garvagh (M5535, PRO) estate papers.

rent regularly and fully suggests that the rents which they were charged were not so high as to cause extreme hardship. During years of crop failure or personal disaster these tenants could be pushed to extremes, but this is endemic in any rental situation. More problematic is the high degree of variation from one estate to another. For example, as already noted, the tenants of the Hodson estate received reductions of 30 to 60 percent during the postwar depression, but on the Crofton estate, in a more poverty-stricken area, a tenant named O'Brien wrote to his landlord in 1822: "The land I occupy under you in Glyn is by the one half too dear, and unless you are kind enough to consider me and give an abatement I cannot occupy it any longer."[82] But even this picture can be misleading. Despite the extreme hardship of the year 1822 to 1823, O'Brien was able to pay his rent plus a large arrears bill.[83]

The undertenants with their much higher rents were the most vulnerable members of the land-occupying community during hard times. Unprotected by lease from arbitrary removal or rent increase, these individuals were generally less able to benefit from rising prices, and during times of distress they could not expect an abatement from their overtenant, who himself was struggling to pay rent. Nicholson felt that the undertenants on the Greville estate were "really the most industrious persons upon it."[84] They had to be in order to meet the rents which they were charged. Most of them did manage to pay exorbitant rents through great self-exploitation and through the abuse of the soil and other resources at their disposal. During poor times they possessed no reserve of either capital or labor, and their suffering was extreme. It was often difficult or impossible for outsiders to distinguish between these undertenants and agricultural laborers. Indeed, the line between the two groups was very fluid, for many undertenants hired themselves and their children out as day laborers on the farms of their overtenants. (Movement in the opposite direction was extremely rare.)

The situation of the direct tenantry was radically different. While it would be absurd to suggest that the average direct tenant paid a "low" rent, it would be fair to imply that relative to undertenants, and outside of crisis years, the direct tenantry paid a "workable" rent. Given the fact that many direct tenants had subtenants of their own who paid the truly "racked" rents, and that many of them enjoyed the use of extremely cheap labor, a case might even be made that for such entrepreneurial tenants, rents during normal times were "rational" on most estates. However, they too were vulnerable in poor years, especially if they relied heavily upon their subletting income for making up their own rent. For these tenants, often the largest, the insecurity of the undertenant "backed up" along the rental system and made agriculture an even more speculative venture then it ordinarily was.[85]

There were considerable variations in the prosperity of the direct tenantry. Different landlords, different estates, and different qualities of land all affected the ability of the individual tenant to prosper under a given set of agricultural conditions. But by far the most important factor was farm size. The tenant of thirty acres or more was in a strong position. He could organize his production to best take advantage of market conditions while at the same time producing his entire food supply, thus relieving himself of the burden of entering the market as a buyer, as his smaller neighbor was often obliged to do. The strong farmer also had the option of subletting when both tillage and animal prices were low, thus removing himself from the agricultural market when conditions were especially unfavorable and reaping his reward from the ever favorable land market. Finally and perhaps most important, the large farmer's more diversified productivity and his ability to save during good times enabled him to ride out distress when others could not.

At the other end of the scale there were direct tenants with farms as small as those of the smallest undertenants. In Killashandra parish, among 625 tenants, 25 percent had holdings of less than ten statute acres, and 11 percent held six acres or less.[86] These direct tenants had the advantages of lower rents and a direct relationship with the head landlord (and were thus protected from arbitrary removal), but their overall economic security and viability, especially during poor times, was little better than that of the undertenants.

Between the strong farmers and these very small tenants, the great majority of Cavan tenants occupied an uneasy ground. It was here that individual farming families were most vulnerable to family or market misfortunes which might upset the delicate equilibrium between productivity, consumption, and rent needs. Unable to put aside significant surpluses in good harvest years and justifiably cau-

tious in following new market trends, they were the bellwether of
the agricultural community. Generally their farms were too small to
permit either significant degrees of subletting or to allow grazing
activity, yet were large enough to require very large labor inputs for
their highly intensive tillage operations. The economic health of this
group helped to determine the general economic conditions for the
county; when they experienced difficulty, laborers found it difficult
to find employment, beggars their alms, and the church its dues.

The effect which the rising rents of the 1830s had upon these
different groups of tenants ultimately depended upon the reasons for
such increase. If the rising rents were due to increasing demand for
agricultural products operating through the local market system, the
result would be to increase the viability of the commercially oriented farms which could take advantage of such changes. These
farms, primarily held by direct tenure and at least ten acres in size,
would feel few negative effects of the steady but gentle rise in rents
taking place during the 1830s. The undertenants of such farmers and
the smaller direct tenants would become increasingly uncompetitive
as they could not participate in the positive movement behind the
rent increases, and consequently they would find it increasingly
difficult to survive as independent farmers. The farming community
would become increasingly surplus-producing and diminishingly
"Chayanovian."

On the other hand, if the rise in rents in the 1830s was due to
opportunistic landlords taking advantage of the increasing competition for land caused by a rapidly increasing population, we would
expect to find that all sectors of the community suffered. In fact, we
should find that the larger tenants found it increasingly difficult to
compete for their own land against a desperate pauper population
seeking access to any parcel of land. This situation would have led
to increasing fragmentation as both landlords and perceptive strong
farmers rushed to profit from an economically irrational hunger for
land. But in the long run even this would be only a short-term
solution to the problems of capitalistic agriculture faced with a
crisis, for this new drive toward subdivision would only further
increase the concentration of population upon the land.

This last scenario is the common model of pre-famine developments. The evidence here, however incomplete, does not support it.

Judging from available sources, subletting appears to have been decreasing, not increasing, after 1815; and as the arrears information suggests, direct tenants were having little difficulty paying the increasing rents of the 1830s as long as harvests were reasonable. But is there any evidence to support the more optimistic interpretation? Was there increased market activity with increased prices?

The next chapter will present evidence which suggests that within certain critical limitations, Cavan's agriculture was reorienting itself along more commercial lines.

Agricultural Structure: Markets, Capital, and Production

2

The information concerning rents, tenure, and farm size suggests that agriculture in pre-famine Cavan was providing rising profits for landlords and the substantial tenantry. We need to identify the source of this increasing profitability and assess its economic and social costs and its long-term potential before we can determine if it was the first stage of agricultural modernization or a temporary ripple in a subsistence economy headed towards inevitable destruction.

Agricultural modernization for most Western European countries consisted of two stages: market integration, followed by regional specialization and rural depopulation. These stages were not necessarily either discrete or continuous; but market integration was, by necessity, the first stage in the process. Because of this, an area such as nineteenth-century Cavan, which (there is reason to suspect) was beginning agricultural modernization, should show clear signs of an increase in market activity.

For Cavan, as for all of Ireland, the demand of British industrial cities would ultimately supply the stimulus for agricultural commercialization. But before British demand could be translated into an Irish response, markets were needed to connect the centers of supply and demand; and before individual farmers could participate in these markets, the necessary factors of agricultural change had to be locally available.[1]

CAPITAL

One of the most crucial elements necessary for the organization of agriculture along competitive market lines during the nineteenth century was ready capital. From the acquisition of additional land, seed, or stock to the ability to withstand poor harvests or prices, the availability of capital determined the potential for success of the individual farm family. For the community as a whole, the presence of capital helped to determine the overall economic potential of the area. Without it, the ability of the community to reorganize its agricultural system along commercial lines depended upon greater exploitation of the few resources within the control of the actual occupiers of the soil. The evidence at hand indicates that there was a severe shortage of capital in pre-famine Cavan; that what capital was available was not equally available to all members of the farming community; and that it was seldom easily accessible to any member of the community.

For the potential farmer, the practice of tenant right created the greatest need for capital. This custom, especially strong in Ulster and almost universal in Cavan, recognized an interest in occupation of a piece of land which a departing tenant could sell (usually subject to landlord approval) to an incoming tenant. It was also possible in some areas to mortgage this right as the need arose.[2] Much has been written about the supposed good or evil of this practice. Contemporaries often thought that the security which it afforded the occupying tenant helped to account for the relative prosperity of Ulster, but recent scholarship has rejected this favorable view as simplistic. Raymond Crotty has argued quite convincingly that the arrangement was not necessarily a beneficial one.[3] It acted as a barrier to a free market in land and severely limited the mobility of laborers and small tenants. Furthermore, as the sums required were considerable, incoming tenants were often forced to borrow heavily at exorbitant interest rates in order to gain access to a new farm, thus severely limiting the needed capital and credit which they could devote to production factors. In this sense, the existence of tenant right was testimony to the inadequate development of the cash economy. The practice of mortgaging tenant right illustrated how limited opportunity was, both for the rural capitalist (invariably another farmer) and for those seeking capital. Yet despite these qualifications, tenant right did fill an important role as a means of storing capital which the individual could call upon in time of individual (although not communal) need.

Whatever the overall effect of the tenant right system upon tenant prosperity was, it did represent an opportunity rent upon land, and the scale of this rent can give us some idea of the productivity of Cavan farmland during the pre-famine period as well as some idea of the level of capital investment in agriculture by the tenantry. The magnitude of tenant right payments during the 1830s and their subsequent collapse during the crisis of the early '40s (beginning before the famine) would seem to indicate that either farmers were desperate to gain land during the '30s or agriculture was profitable even with the increasing rents of this period. The facts that the available figures are generally for the larger farms and that prices collapsed at the moment of highest population pressure suggest that such pressure was not responsible for these extremely high payments.[4]

The Devon Commission recorded figures for tenant right payments on two Cavan farms. In the mid-1830s one farm of between eleven and twelve Irish acres cost its new tenant £96 for the privilege of occupation.[5] Another witness testified that in two different cases about which he had certain knowledge tenants had paid £100 and £150 respectively for farms of twenty Irish acres.[6] These figures, which are approximately equal to five to ten years' rental value, might appear beyond belief, but there is additional evidence which suggests such payments were not unusual. The Report on the Coronary Estate estimated the tenant right value per Irish acre at about £6 on fairly let land, but the author added the proviso that it might go much higher. He reported a case in the townland of Glassdromin where "£40 was paid for two Irish acres though let at a full rent. This was almost equal to the fee simple value of the land."[7] These extremely high payments represent a tremendous investment for the opportunity to take land on a short lease at a high rent. There was obviously great pressure upon the land, but those tenants who could compete at such high stakes were few and were relatively immune to competition from the increasing pauper population, as long as the market provided a favorable outlet for their surplus production.

Even those who could enter into such competition could not under normal conditions have such large sums available for immediate expenditure. One means of financing these tenant right sales was through the local money lender. These usurious figures, who were often the most hated members of the community, charged interest rates of 5 percent per month.[8] The involvement of substantial tenantry in the usury system is a clear indication of the serious shortage of free capital which inhibited the development of Cavan agriculture. Other farmers depended upon the sale of stock at favorable moments in order to finance their new acquisitions. This in turn indicates that those involved in the tenant right market had substantial resources (by local standards) and that the stiff competition which kept tenant right prices up was most likely motivated by the belief that such transactions would eventually produce profits.

The extent of this investment by farmers in their land increased the vulnerability of the farmer to changes in both market and crop conditions. Not only did poor conditions make it difficult to meet rent payments out of current income, but they depressed the competitive price of tenant right by dampening the demand for land at the very moment when many farmers were forced to offer some of their land on the market. This was precisely what happened during the very poor years of 1839–41. The witnesses before the Devon Commission were unanimous in pointing out that the prices of tenant right had decreased drastically during the preceding years and that finding takers for property was becoming more and more difficult.[9] The famine, of course, would completely destroy the market for land until 1850.[10] This inability to gain access to their fixed capital may explain why the emigration of tenant farmers during the famine years did not peak until 1850.

In addition to tenant right payments, the incoming farmer had to provide for the initial stocking of the farm. This expense was considerably lower for Irish agriculture than for other parts of Europe, since Irish tenants did not need plows, plow horses, or other costly equipment or buildings. The spade replaced the plow, agricultural

laborers the horse, and with Ireland's mild climate and small farms
there was little impetus to build substantial outbuildings. Even so,
seed and stock could come at a stiff price, especially if they had to
be purchased on credit. Nicholson estimated that £100–£120 would
be required to fit out a twenty-acre farm.[11] Inputs were highest on
dairy or cattle farms, which helps to explain the resistance to any
rapid movement in that direction. Established tenants usually saved
part of their crop as seed for the coming year, decreasing prospective yields but saving scarce capital.

There was another potential use of capital in regions with wet
soils, particularly in the Lough Erne basin area around Killashandra:
permanent drainage promised enormous increases in productivity,
particularly on grasslands. The costs of such projects, however,
were clearly beyond the means or the economic self-interest of a
tenant without at least a lifetime interest in the land. A sad example
of both the modern economic orientation of the tenantry and the
pernicious nature of landlordism's effect on capital availability is a
futile plea by the tenants of the Greville estate to their landlord in
1848. They urged their landlord to undertake a drainage project on
the land they occupied; in return, they agreed to accept a permanent
rent increase.[12] It was the landlord, not the tenants, who was un-
willing to underwrite the major improvement that Cavan's agriculture required. Nicholson also found that the tenants were willing to
"bear half the expense in labour" to build decent roads upon the
estate.[13] Their desire to offer labor rather than cash underlines the
central issue here: a severe lack of capital.

One additional form of capital expenditure should be mentioned
under the heading of agricultural capital, even if its relation to
agricultural production may appear remote. The dowry system,
which was such a prominent part of the Irish marital system, had
some very real economic functions. The system, which was almost
universal among the substantial tenantry in Ireland throughout the
nineteenth century,[14] often required the payment of large sums,
usually part cash and part stock, by the bride's parents to the husband's family. The operation of this system necessitated the acquisition of capital in specie or kind with which to enter the marriage
market. This was not a casual affair draining needed capital away
from the farm; it was necessary to form the essential interfamily

alliances which would allow the new couple to establish their own family and farm, and it served as a means of controlling both access to land and full membership in the farming community. Unfortunately, no information about the scale of dowry payments has yet come to light. Written records were rarely kept, and the practice was so universally accepted that it elicited very little comment from contemporaries.

The picture, then, of the credit situation in Cavan during the pre-famine period was not very bright. There were substantial needs for capital but very undesirable means of satisfying these needs. Yet Cavan farmers spent large sums for tenant right and the general operation of their farms. In the absence of commercial banking, there would seem to have been only one means of securing such capital—through recourse to the local usurer; but there is one facet of the credit problem which this discussion has thus far ignored and which may have been of considerable importance in the operation of the Cavan tenant farm system. Arrears are normally treated as indicators of distress and, in Ireland, of the general ill health of the land system. While such a treatment is certainly understandable and useful, there is an alternative viewpoint. It is possible that arrears were less of a problem to tenants than is generally believed. In the first instance, upon assuming a farm it was the custom in Cavan to allow a tenant to withhold the payment of rent (the hanging gale). Such a system was inevitable in an area where tenants had to expend large sums on tenant right, lease fines, and stock. As the tenant established himself and began to receive a return from his efforts, this deficit could be gradually overcome, but without having to square accounts with the landlord. As Coote put it, "one-half of the yearly rents of Cavan are left with the tenants to trade on."[15] The time and expense required to collect arrears made it the normal course on most estates to wait at least one additional gale day (six months) before taking legal action. This would allow the tenant to use his landlord as a sort of de facto creditor. There would be fines for late payment of rent, but fines were small compared to the interest charged by the gombeen-man. There is some evidence to support this alternative view of the arrears situation. When commenting on individual tenants in arrears, estate agents often acted very much like bank officers, appraising the stock and other resources which the tenant might use to discharge the back payments. These financial assessments went into minute detail, considering every animal and tub of butter and sack of oats.[16] Nicholson observed tenants intentionally falling into arrears in order to purchase the tenant right to additional land.[17] The speed with which tenants paid off large arrears, often amounting to several years' rent, seems to demonstrate that it was not always the most desperate tenants who were involved in the arrears situation. This is not to suggest that arrears on an aggregate level do not represent an indication of agrarian distress, or even that the calculated use of an estate's arrears policy indicates less landlord-tenant friction, but it does suggest that the nonpayment of rent does not necessarily indicate the inability to pay rent. Tenants could use the cash return from a harvest for purposes other than paying the rent and gamble on being able to recover the sum needed for the rent before the landlord took serious action. Like all financial maneuvers in Irish agriculture, it would be risky, but no more so than recourse to the gombeen-man.

MARKETS, PRICES, AND PRODUCTION

Ultimately any economic development in Cavan depended upon the expansion and development of market opportunities. Cavan's location, straddling the country without touching the sea, made her market position vis-à-vis British demand tenuous. The production of Cavan farms during the middle of the eighteenth century was geared largely toward domestic consumption and only secondarily toward a limited intraprovincial trade in linen, butter, pigs, and calves. As long as transportation between Cavan market towns and Irish and British ports remained haphazard and expensive, there was little hope of developing a permanent and vigorous market economy. It was partially for these reasons that Cavan had missed out on the prosperity of the mid-eighteenth century. However, there was another serious obstacle. Gentle increases in agricultural prices, even as prolonged as those of the period 1738–70 (see table 2.1), failed to break this geographic barrier because of the key relationship between rent and free capital noted above (page 15). Increased market activity during this phase of economic organization created a negative feedback loop centering on the relationship between capi-

tal, agricultural productivity, land pressure, and rent: as market
activity increased profits and the availability of capital, which stimulated overall productivity, it also encouraged an increase in rent,
which in turn reduced the amount of free capital available for further
investment. Unless a dramatic increase in market activity could be
sustained over a considerable period of time (a decade at the very
least), the system would be unable to overcome this self-limiting
device.

For Cavan, as for much of Ireland and peripheral Europe, this
sustained and dramatic activity began in the late eighteenth century
and culminated in the extraordinary grain prices of the Napoleonic
period. For the nation as a whole the trend is clear enough (see table
2.1). An unprecedented increase in prices from 1786 to 1815 provided the necessary "push" for tenants to increase their net income
even while the landlords increased their rental charges.

Price figures for Cavan before the war years are not available, but

Table 2.1
Irish Oat and Butter Prices, 1738–1840

| | AVERAGE PRICE PER HUNDREDWEIGHT | | | |
| | Oats | | Butter | |
YEAR(S)	s.	d.	s.	d.
1738–48	3	4	21	5
1749–58	4	10	25	3
1759–68	5	7	25	7
1769–78	5	1	38	11
1781–85	4	10	47	3
1789	7	8	41	9
1800–05	8	4	89	9
1806–10	9	6	100	0
1812–15	10	2	108	2
1816–20	9	10	87	9
1821–25	6	11	83	8
1826–30	8	10	66	11
1831–35	6	4	73	3
1836–40	7	9	93	2

SOURCE: Crotty, *Irish Agricultural Production*, table 4, p. 21; table 67C,
p. 283.

it is fairly safe to assume, given the high cost of transport to a port
(see p. 82 below), that Cavan prices must have been lower than
those quoted for Dublin and other ports (it is worth commenting that
the very absence of specific data on either the volume or price of
agricultural produce from Cavan before 1800 may itself be evidence
of the county's peripheral relationship to the market economy at this
early date).

Fortunately, we do have price figures for Cavan's major exports
during the wartime period. It is clear from these figures (table 2.2;
figures for other counties are included for comparison) that Cavan
was strongly affected by the wartime boom prices. According to
these estimates, both oat and butter prices in Cavan were competitive with the major eastern markets. Cavan's geographic position
did keep those prices slightly below those of her major coastal
market targets—Dundalk for oats, Newry (best represented by
Down in the table) for butter; but it is significant that under this high
price regime Cavan oat prices were close to those of Dublin, and
Cavan butter prices actually exceeded those of Dundalk and Dublin.

Clearly, despite Cavan's geographic and transport problems vis-
à-vis the British market, the price surge of the Napoleonic period
had a significant effect. This becomes even clearer when Cavan
prices are compared with those for Clare and Galway, two west
coast counties. Even though Cavan was landlocked, her prices were
considerably higher.

These figures need to be treated with some care, as they are

Table 2.2
Local Oat and Butter Prices, 1811

COUNTY OR TOWN	OATS, CWT.		BUTTER, CWT.	
	s.	d.	s.	d.
Cavan	9	3	5	5
Dundalk	10	1	4	10
Galway	5	9	3	14
Clare	4	10	4	11
Dublin	10	3	5	0
Down	8	10	6	5

SOURCE: Wakefield, *Ireland*, 2:208–30.

(except for Dundalk and Dublin) the figures supplied to Wakefield as local prices of the various counties. They are not necessarily identical to the prices received in the major market town of the particular county, such as Galway city or Ennis. Fortunately the actual oat market prices for several of these market towns are available (table 2.3). These figures confirm that the highest prices were offered in the northeast ports of Louth and Newry, and the lowest in the western towns of Ennis and Galway. As expected, the prices of the western ports are higher than those Wakefield cited for their respective counties. The figure for Dundalk is somewhat lower than that Wakefield reports, because the market town figures are twelve-month averages whereas Wakefield's report from Dundalk was collected in December 1811, the month during which oat prices reached their year-long high in all of these market towns. The figure from the *Freeman's Journal* for December 1811 is also 10*s*. 7*d*. per hundredweight.[18]

Although there are no figures for Cavan's individual market towns, there is no reason to suppose that the difference between town and county figures would be any greater in Cavan's case. Indeed, given the absence of a port town in the county, it is much more likely that county figures and market town figures would be closer in Cavan than in a county such as Galway, where there was

Table 2.3

Twelve-Month Average Oat Price in
Several Major Market Towns, 1811

	PRICE PER CWT.	
TOWN	*s*.	*d*.
Cork	8	3
Dundalk	9	1
Drogheda	9	4
Newry	8	10
Ennis	6	6
Galway	7	3

SOURCE: *Freeman's Journal*, Jan.–Dec. 1811. Averages were calculated from the weekly average of the first week reported in each month (where available). The average for the nearest alternative week was substituted when necessary.

considerably more variation in market accessibility. As in table 2.2, what is most significant here is the very high price offered in the port towns of Dundalk and Drogheda, through which Cavan's oats were exported to Britain.

These very high wartime prices were followed by a peacetime price collapse which was sharp and long-lasting, and which affected all agricultural commodities. It was so severe and protracted that it represented a very serious challenge to the survival of commercial agriculture in many areas of Ireland. The response which Cavan's agriculture made to the difficult postwar period reveals the deep foundations which commercialization had already established by 1815. There are no known surviving records of local Cavan prices from 1811 until the 1840s, but as nothing had been done to improve the overland transport system during that period, a pretty fair idea of Cavan price movements can be gained by looking at the Dublin price figures in table 2.1.

The decade 1816–26 was one of the most difficult periods in Irish agricultural history. Tenants were forced to endure the scissors effect created by their recently increased rents cutting against rapidly falling prices. The situation was so serious that even some landlords recognized the danger of inaction and granted unprecedented permanent rent reductions; but as noted above (chapter 1), these reductions did not keep pace with the price decline.

Oats began to recover in the late twenties but slumped badly again in the thirties; and except for the famine years, they would never recover their wartime competitiveness. Butter prices began their recovery later, in the 1830s, but in this case the recovery was generally well sustained and long-lasting. Detailed comparative price information exists for the years 1849–51 which shows that the relationship between Cavan and her port market towns was similar to what it had been thirty years earlier. The three-year average (1849–51) of oat prices lagged behind Drogheda by 5.6 percent, and the three-year average butter price lagged behind Newry by 3.5 percent. [19]

In summary, during the period 1780–1850, Cavan experienced price movements that lagged slightly behind those of her major port markets, but that were consistently and substantially stronger than those of selected western coastal counties and ports. Most important, despite lacunae in the evidence, available data for the critical wartime period of expansion demonstrate the deep penetration of British market forces into Cavan.

The experience of the 1790s is much less certain. Charles Coote did report that at the turn of the century high oat prices were causing Cavan tenants to "ignore" flax and linen production.[20] He also indicated that the hillsides were "entirely under oats."[21] Finally, he offered a local estimate of the oat market price of 13s. 4d. per cwt.[22] This figure is very high by any standards, and it is difficult to accept it without some corroborating evidence. Still, given what we know of Cavan's prices a decade later and Coote's many comments on the high local price of oats, it is probably safe to assume that whatever the precise figure was, the Cavan local prices did rise with the national price. A similar deductive argument can be made regarding the postwar prices from 1818–45: given what is known about prices in 1811 and 1849, there is little doubt that Cavan prices followed the national trend. Indeed, there is no alternative logical supposition.

The impact which these wild price fluctuations had on the volume of Irish exports provides vivid evidence of just how responsive Irish agriculture in the pre-famine period could be. It also provides an interesting example of the complexity of the price/export relationship. Table 2.4 illustrates the nature of the revolution taking place in Irish agriculture.

Table 2.4
Irish Wheat, Oat, and Butter Exports, 1745–1845

YEAR(S)	AVERAGE (LONG TONS)		
	Wheat	Oats	Butter
1754–58	861	6,193	9,878
1794–98	812	34,138	15,008
1813–17	28,906	71,855	21,109
1824–28	106,037	264,950	—
1830–34	115,090	226,871	—
1835	—	—	41,350
1835–39	58,134	266,914	—
1843–45	63,789	263,990	—

SOURCES: Crotty, *Irish Agricultural Production*, table 2, p. 19; table 3, p. 20; Donnelly, *The Land and the People*, table 3, p. 32; table 4, p. 33.

Even these figures do not indicate the potential for change during
the Napoleonic era in marginal production areas such as Cavan.
Some more advanced areas, such as Kilkenny and Cork, were already producing large quantities of wheat and butter for export in
the early eighteenth century, and it is therefore unlikely that they
contributed large amounts of additional outputs in the pre-famine
era. Conversely, other areas, such as Mayo and Connemara, played
only a minor role in exports before 1850. In this light, it is probable
that Cavan and other marginal areas contributed disproportionately
to this increased productivity. It is worth noting that oats, the predominant grain of the less fertile areas such as Cavan, led the way in
this rapid expansion of exports.[23]

Whatever detailed records of the local production and export of
pre-famine tillage once existed are probably lost forever, but we do
have some rather interesting stray notes on Cavan's tillage productivity during this critical period (table 2.5). These figures are truly
surprising, given the liabilities under which Cavan farmers worked
and the general image of pre-famine peasant agriculture as "ineffi-
cient." They are, of course, only estimates; but given the diversity
of sources, the knowledge we have of the rental yields of this land,
the very labor-intensive tillage, and the comment which the witness
before the Devon Commission made that the estimate of average

Table 2.5
Oat Yields per Statute Acre (cwt.), 1776–1895

YEAR(S)	CAVAN	IRELAND	ENGLAND/WALES	DENMARK
1776	10.87	—	—	—
1802	14.2	—	—	—
1811	13.0	—	—	—
1845	17.3	—	—	—
1850–59				
(est. av.)	—	13.4	—	—
1869–95	—	14.5	13.8	12.4

SOURCES: 1776. Arthur Young, *Arthur Young's Tour in Ireland*, ed. Arthur
W. Hutton (London: George Bell & Sons, 1892), 2:20. 1802: average of
Coote's estimates, *Cavan*, pp. 33, 95. 1808, 1811: Wakefield, *Ireland*, 1.369.
1845: Devon Commission, xx, p. 110. 1850–95: Crotty, *Agriculture*, pp. 25,
118.

yield per acre in 1845 only represented a "fair crop,"[24] they can be viewed with some cautious confidence.

Of course these figures do not by themselves permit an assessment of the efficiency of Cavan oat production in terms of yield per man-hour, the measure that Western economists often prefer, but whatever reservations are made, it seems that Cavan's farmers, despite methods that outsiders often found "slovenly," were able to produce high yields of their preferred tillage crop. Furthermore, if these figures have any accuracy, productivity appears to have increased significantly during the critical years in question, a conclusion which would be quite compatible with what we know regarding prices and rents. In addition, Cavan farmers matched the high yield of their tillage with high quality. Even Nicholson, a suspicious Scot who had little positive to say about the method of production, grudgingly admitted that the local oat crop was "of excellent quality, scarcely surpassed in quality anywhere."[25]

Far less is known about butter production during the war period. There are no local estimates of production or exports before 1835. However, Coote and Wakefield both noted the importance of butter production to Cavan farms. Coote believed that at the turn of the century butter was one of the major staples exported for cash income by the smaller farmers,[26] and Wakefield reported in 1812 that substantial quantities of butter from Cavan passed through Newry en route to England. He estimated that Cavan supplied twice as much butter as the neighboring county of Armagh.[27]

What may be the most significant and surprising trend which table 2.4 illustrates has yet to be mentioned. If a simple and positive correlation existed between prices and export volume, we would expect a drastic decrease in exports after 1815. Not only did this not occur, but as prices fell by a third between 1815 and the early 1820s, oat exports, despite an increased demand for food at home, more than trebled. The market impulsion model supplies an explanation of this conundrum.

The scissors effect caused by the upward trend of rents and the downward spiral of prices cut deepest into the most commercialized tillage operations. With their higher variable input costs, these operations were extremely vulnerable to rapid price decline.[28] Unless landlords were willing to index rents to prices, the larger tenants would have to increase their output and, if possible, cut their variable input costs. One possible solution might have been to cut wage labor inputs by shifting significantly more land to pasture. However, there were two obstacles to this: a shortage of capital, and a high rent regime which favored intensive over extensive use of land. In a sense, once "launched" on the path of market integration and commercialization, it was very difficult (though not impossible) to reverse course. In order to survive, many Irish tillage farmers had to increase their production for export. In this way the market, even with falling prices, impelled Cavan farmers towards higher productivity.

Defaults in rent payments did occur with increasing frequency in Cavan during this period, and (as noted above) some landlords did offer some rent relief. This unusual landlord action was a clear signal of the nature of the crisis of the 1815–25 period; many landlords could see the necessity of granting reductions because they recognized that it was the most productive of their tenants who were in the most difficulty. Yet these reductions were one-time events which were not in proportion to the decline in prices, and by the 1820s, rents had begun to increase again. The pressure to produce was very strong indeed: the yearly average export of oats in 1824–28 was over three and one-half times greater than in the price boom period of 1813–17 (table 2.4). There is probably no single fact which underlines the strengths (and vulnerability) of Irish agriculture as sharply as does this paradoxical increase in exports at a time of price depression.[29]

Like it or not, many Irish tenants were now locked into market production, and the farmers of this era had many reasons not to like it. On the individual level, the new forces probably appeared in rather traditional terms: the landlord had returned to the old policy of "rack renting" his tenants and "stealing" the profits which had come their way through their exertions and risk taking. It is hardly surprising that from the start of this period up to the famine, Irish rural people both mobilized for an aggressive constitutional agitation and carried out a bloody campaign of agrarian violence seldom equaled in European history.

All was not darkness and difficulty, though. There were some changes taking place during the 1820s and 1830s which partially offset the soft prices of this period. Two developments stimulated Cavan's commercial agriculture during the twenties and thirties: improved transportation and an ever-increasing demand in Britian's western market cities, especially Liverpool. The introduction of regular steamship service between the Irish ports of Dundalk and Drogheda and the major western urban centers of Great Britain increased the competitiveness of all Cavan produce; but more important, it meant that certain perishable articles, such as eggs and live pigs and cattle, could be transported more safely and with much less weight loss. Paralleling this improvement in transportation, the demand for all agricultural products was increasing with the size and, eventually, the prosperity of the British population.

During the pre-famine period the impact of these changing conditions was often difficult to perceive. The deep and widespread rural poverty which undeniably existed in Cavan prevented all but the most sensitive and knowledgeable observers from noting any real improvements in the conditions of the strong farmers and a rising potential for most mid-sized farmers as well. Fortunately, there were several such observers, as well as some statistical evidence of the nature and extent of this improvement.

The Poor Law Commissioners were not interested in the conditions of the more prosperous tenantry, yet in their study of agricultural laborers' dietary conditions and employment opportunities they did record some evidence relative to the market situation in Cavan during the mid-1830s. Their most important evidence recorded for Cavan was the relationship between tillage and pasture on larger farms. The commissioners were concerned with this because they feared that in the country as a whole, the decline of grain prices in the postwar period was driving many larger farmers toward pasture, thus further reducing the opportunity for agricultural laborers to find work. In Cavan they found that no such movement away from tillage was taking place. One witness reported that "no land, formerly in tillage, has been of late years converted into pasture; the reverse has been the case."[30] Further testimony of this witness connected this trend with the changing market conditions. He stated that many of the local mills were idle because farmers were selling their grain unmilled on the open market, presumably for export.[31]

Much more detailed evidence on the market structure of Cavan

was collected by the Parliamentary commission established to inquire into the feasibility of railroad construction in Ireland. This
commission's report, published in 1838, constitutes one of the most
comprehensive contemporary studies of the pre-famine Irish economy. The commissioners found that "the quality of Irish produce has
considerably improved; Irish butter, Irish pork and Irish beef bring
greater prices in the English market, than they did some few years
ago: while the quantity produced and exported has much increased."[32] What was true for Ireland was also true for Cavan; the
commissioners noted in the mid-thirties that "great improvements
have taken place within the last ten years; and during that period the
produce in corn has increased more than fifty percent and that of
butter and cattle and pigs &c. has also increased, though not to an
equal extent."[33] They also noted that the trade of Cavan town was
"annually increasing"[34] while the grain markets at Killashandra
and Belturbet were supplying the brewery and distillery located in
these towns.[35]

Cavan's economic situation was by no means unique in Ireland,
but there were several factors which separated the experience of
Cavan and other midland areas from those counties such as Wex-
ford, Louth, or Cork which had a long history of market experience
throughout the eighteenth century. In Cavan some forms of produce, such as poultry and eggs, had never been exported due to their
perishability and the unreliability of transport by sail; and while the
most important cash crops of the county, oats and butter, had a
history of success, they both suffered from the costs of transportation. Cavan's roads were terrible. Nicholson reported in 1845:

> With the exception of the new road between Bailieboro and Coote-
> hill they are all hilly and a heavy load could not be drawn upon
> some parts of them. . . . The farm roads are invariably bad—sever-
> al of the townlands have scarcely a passage at all . . . nearly inac-
> cessible with a load except by horse back.[36]

The common charge for transport on roads by horse car was 5d. per
ton per mile, and the average carrying distance from Cavan market
towns to the major ports involved in Cavan's trade (Newry, Dundalk, Drogheda) was forty miles.[37] This works out to an average
transport cost to an Irish port of approximately 16s. per ton. The

impact of this high cost of transportation on the profitability of produce exports varied with the type of produce. Butter, with an average value of £90 per ton in 1835,[38] required a transportation surcharge of less than 1 percent, while the cost for a ton of oats worked out to a 13 percent surcharge.[39]

Given this differential between the transportation costs of butter and oats, it is not surprising that butter proved to be a major export item for Cavan. Yet Cavan's butter trade was not well developed and certainly lagged far behind the major butter-producing areas such as Cork, Tipperary, and Kilkenny. About 200 tons of Cavan butter (with a value of £18,000) passed through the two major butter ports of Newry and Dundalk each year, with an unspecified (although surely smaller) amount passing through Drogheda.[40] The Drogheda trade is of particular interest in regard to market development. Drogheda merchants accepted orders from English dealers which they in turn forwarded to Cavan town. This would appear to be a sign of a developing market which had not yet formalized its own mechanisms for responding to external demands. There were no local agents responsible for negotiating export sales, nor was local activity sufficient to attract buyers to Cavan town itself.

In 1835 the total value of the Cavan butter trade to Newry and Dundalk was about £18,000 per annum. Allowing an additional twenty-five tons for the Drogheda trade, the total butter export trade was about £20,000. This figure, although modest when compared to the national trade in butter centered on Cork city,[41] was tremendously important to Cavan's economic development and represented an even greater potential as English demand increased and Cavan market and production practices improved.

Cavan's major export commodity was its principal crop, oats. The Railway Commission estimated the volume of oats handled by the Cavan market at 7,500 tons per annum and that of the Arvagh oat market (in Killashandra parish) at 7,500 cwt. (about 375 tons). The total value of the oats sold in these markets would have been approximately £55,000 on the export market, and we do not have figures for other Cavan markets such as Cootehill, Shercock, and Bailieborough. This extensive oat production kept the demand for labor as high as possible in Cavan, but the demand for labor could not keep pace with the rising population dependent upon wage labor. For this reason, oats produced for local consumption could not provide the cash income that tenants required in a time of soft prices. Only the export market offered the potential for large increases in production, and only such increases could permit the more commercial tenants to continue to pay competitive rents. In fact, Irish producers did dramatically increase their exports (table 2.4).

There is more evidence of the oat export orientation of the county on the eve of the famine. Nicholson noted that Cootehill had an "extensive exportation" of oats and that carmen from Drogheda were now regularly traveling to Bailieborough to buy oats. He also noted with interest that Shercock, because of its proximity to Drogheda, offered the best prices for oats.[42] A local clergyman, R. M'Collum, also noted the rise of the Bailieborough oat market, calling it "one of the best" in the county, and he reported a steady supply of oats at Shercock.[43] There were other signs as well of increasing economic activity on the eve of the famine. The Belturbet distillery reported the production of £20,000 worth of whiskey in 1845,[44] and Cavan's new newspaper, the *Anglo-Celt* (itself a sign of increasing prosperity), could proudly announce the completion of a new oat mill in Cavan town, "where there is one of the best Markets in the North of Ireland,"[45] and the growing interest of tenants in agricultural improvements, noting with great optimism the presence of 10,000 spectators at a plowing demonstration in February 1846.[46]

The continued strength of tillage is a bit puzzling. Butter production, after all, would seem to have offered a solution to many problems. Its primarily export orientation meant that it added considerably to the income of the county. There was also potential for a dramatic increase in the demand for this product with the continued growth of British cities and the gradual improvement of conditions for industrial workers. Serious competition from outside of the European market still lay in the future, pending breakthroughs in long-distance transportation. Butter production offered the possibility for middling farmers to participate in the benefits of the export market while cutting wage labor inputs. The close attention needed for dairy production favored small-scale operation. (Herds of ten or more cows were beyond the resources of the normal family farm and

were exceedingly rare in Cavan until the twentieth century.) The
reduction of wage labor requirements would, in addition to saving
scarce specie, permit the tenant to narrow the gap between variable
costs and gross income and thus make himself more secure in a time
of declining or unstable prices. With such advantages, the most
puzzling question would appear to be, "Why didn't Cavan farmers
turn more strongly towards dairy production?" The answer involves
several factors, but they can ultimately be reduced to two common
denominators: the landholding system and overpopulation. As long
as rents remained competitive—and we have seen that despite the
postwar depression they did—and as long as tenant right prices
remained very high, farmers had to return as much as possible from
each acre of land which they controlled. As he had little control over
the size of his farm, the tenant could increase his profit only by
greatly increasing the labor input per acre through greater self-exploitation or through the increased use of hired labor. This need to
maximize production per acre through the use of the only expand-
able resource, labor, strongly favored the retention of the traditional
tillage system with its oat/potato rotation system. Economic and
social inertia could be said to have played a part, inasmuch as an
already established tillage orientation made conversion difficult: it
would have required a high fixed capital expenditure (cattle) and a
socially provocative policy (agricultural laborers had resort to a
secret society). But *momentum* played no less a role. The expanding
laboring population kept wages low, or even reduced them, and thus
removed some of the rationale for such conversion.

CROP ROTATION

Cavan farmers did not have the opportunity to choose the single
crop they believed would yield the greatest harvest or the highest
price. Individual crops were not so easily interchangeable as many
improving landlords believed. The turnip, which played such a
large part in Britain's agricultural development, was of little use in
Ireland, which lacked large sheep walks. Cavan, with its wet climate and undrained fields, could not have produced sheep successfully even had farmers desired it. Without the sheep needed to
complete the grain/root animal complex which the turnip facili-

tated, Cavan farmers had no incentive to experiment with the British wonder crop. Furthermore, the turnip could not be used as fodder for milch cows, its only other conceivable use in Cavan, without tainting the milk produced.

Fortunately Cavan tenants, like all Irish farmers, had a more efficient animal/root crop system. The potato filled an almost magical combination of needs for the Cavan farmer. It brought rough land into tillage, provided a major part of the farm's vegetable food, served as the major form of animal fodder, and acted as a restorative root crop which replenished land exhausted by successive cereal crops. It cannot be stated too strongly that the potato, when grown by farmers, was not solely or even largely a subsistence crop in Cavan. The persistence of the potato in Ireland after the famine was not due to some perverse pleasure which the Irish tenants took in difficulty, but to their inability to find a crop which could fulfill the multiple roles which the potato served. Potato acreages would not decline until the general tillage acreage declined. A witness before the Poor Law Commission noted the connection in discussing the economic attractiveness of oats. "In potatoes and grain much more is raised now than formerly because there is much more of the land worked and nearly the whole attention of the farmers is devoted to this description of produce."[47]

The relationship between the general tillage acreage and potato acreage was due to a general but fairly flexible complex of agricultural relationships. In areas with adequate farm size, grass and clover were often included in the oats-potato rotation. This grassland, commonly referred to as "meadow," was part of the rotation system and quite distinct from "pasture"—permanent grassland which was often of inferior quality.

By the nineteenth century this system of rotation had become fairly regular in Cavan. Ley ground was normally brought into cultivation with an unmanured crop of potatoes, which was almost always followed by a manured crop of potatoes. The following year a crop of flax or oats would be taken, depending upon the relative prices of these crops and the food needs of the family. In the following three years tenants would plant oats. In the seventh year the field would either be put out to grass, or be manured and returned to potatoes to begin the process again.[48]

This system, with its built-in ratio of 2:1 of cereal and flax to potatoes fit the multiple needs of the Cavan farmer. Despite the natural problems of tillage in Ireland, he was able to engage in highly intensive tillage which permitted him, in good times, to meet the demands of both his landlord and his family. The pig which was reared on potatoes and dairy waste, the butter produced in the dairy, most of the oat crop, and the extra calf all provided for the landlord's requirements. The remainder of the oats and potatoes and some of the fresh skim milk provided the diet of the farm family.

Both oat and potato crops were cultivated by spade. The spade was the traditional agricultural implement of Ireland. Although requiring more effort than the plow, it was better suited to traditionally Irish conditions, and this was especially true in Cavan. Rocky soil was a problem for plowmen here as in most of Ireland, but in Cavan there were additional and more substantial problems. The small farm size made the maintenance of a horse a luxury, not a sound economic venture. Most important, the extremely wet climate and the poorly drained fields of Cavan encouraged the ridge system of farming, which in Ireland was ironically known as "the lazy bed." The ridge system, which was traditionally used for oats, was also adapted quite readily to the potato.[49] In this method, the farmer laid manure (if he were using any) directly on the surface of the sod. The seed was then placed upon the surface and covered with an inverted sod dug with the spade from a trench paralleling the seed row. This was repeated across the width of the field to create a series of troughs and ridges which provided for the drainage of the field and kept the potatoes or oats high and dry. This system, although considered archaic by outsiders, produced the excellent yields already noted.

Quite obviously the lazy bed required enormous physical efforts by those planting. Even on the small Cavan farms, with half their land in grass, the labor requirements were beyond the means of most families. Coote, remarking on the tremendous dexterity and strength of the Cavan men, stated that it took "but twelve men to dig an acre in a day's work."[50] Women and children preceded the men with the seed, but even with their help, it would have been necessary to call upon outside labor when planting more than a few acres. It was this tremendous requirement for labor which allowed

Table 2.6
Agricultural Statistics of Bailieborough, 1845

DIVISION (ARABLE ACRES)	PERCENTAGE OF ACRES IN:											
	Wheat	Barley	Oats	Rye	Flax	Potatoes	Nips	Vetch	Clover	Meadow	Pasture	Cabbage
Bailieborough (5,858)	0	.2	27.4	.2	1.3	16.5	.7	.5	2.0	7.8	43.0	.7
Skea (5,132)	0	0	27.9	0	.9	14.1	.3	.1	.5	3.6	51.7	.5
Termon (6,304)	0	0	24.2	0	.3	11.9	.2	.1	.2	3.5	58.9	.5
Shercock (5,041)	0	0	33.8	0	.6	18.7	0	.3	1.3	2.7	41.4	.6
Kingscourt (8,600)	0	0	25.4	0	.2	15.0	.5	0	.4	3.6	53.1	.6
Ardagh (4,192)	.2	.1	21.5	0	0	14.9	0	0	1.3	1.9	55.3	.4
Newcastle (2,930)	.7	1.2	19.4	0	.3	13.8	0	0	1.9	2.9	58.8	0
Maybologne (3,616)	0	0	26.2	0	.6	15.7	0	0	2.8	2.8	53.2	0
Tullyarren (2,730)	0	0	21.7	0	0	16.7	0	0	.8	1.6	58.2	0
Crossbane (3,902)	0	0	26.7	0	0	14.6	0	0	0	2.0	55.4	0
Killenkere (3,224)	0	0	24.5	0	0	13.2	0	0	.7	3.2	57.2	0

great numbers of agricultural laborers to survive, and its seasonal nature that insured their poverty.

The actual pre-famine relationship between the various crops within this system can be studied more carefully for Cavan than for any other area in Ireland. It was a Cavan Poor Law Union, Bailie-borough, which served as the pilot area for agricultural statistics in Ireland. Under the direction of Sir Charles Young, M.P. for Cavan and a local agricultural improver, detailed statistics were gathered for the planting of 1845, the last normal planting before the chaos of the famine swept away "normality." These statistics are especially important because they covered the union on an electoral division level. Ranging between 2,700 and 6,700 acres, these units permit a view of local variations which might be masked on a more aggregate level (see table 2.6).

The observer with only a casual knowledge of Ireland would undoubtedly be surprised by the seemingly low figure for potato acreage. Only 15 percent of the agricultural land in the Poor Law Union was in potatoes. Of course, a good deal of the land listed as pasture was unsuitable for tillage of any sort, but even discounting pasture entirely, potatoes account for only 31.6 percent of the total tillage acreage, as compared with 54.3 percent for oats. It is clear from the distribution across the electoral districts that this is not a statistical impression created by a few extremely large estate farms.

These figures for oats and potatoes reflect the rotation system just described. The potato acreage was largely determined by the total tillage acreage. The rotation system of two years of potatoes and four of oats would lead us to expect a ratio of 2:1 of cereal to potatoes. The ratios which actually existed were very close to this, and remarkably consistent across the divisions. Of course the ratio was not exact; there were farmers who, for various reasons (such as an attempt to take advantage of market fluctuations), altered the system of rotation. However, there was another factor involved which was more important in keeping the potato acreage consistent-ly above the anticipated acreage. Laborers, who had garden plots or who hired conacre, grew potatoes exclusively. But even with this proviso, it is clear that potatoes were not the primary agricultural interest of the Cavan farmer.

The fixed nature of the relationship between oats and potatoes is even more apparent in post-famine years. During normal years, the ratio of oats to potatoes in Bailieborough Union remained constant from 1845 until 1901. This helps to explain both the persistence of the potato in Irish agriculture and the cautious response of Cavan agriculture to market pressures. It was very difficult for Cavan farmers to increase or decrease the acreage in either tillage crop without a corresponding change in the complementary crop. Thus as long as oats were profitable, potatoes were inevitably produced: and as potatoes served as a fodder crop for pigs, the oats/potato complex facilitated pig production. Individual agricultural products did not compete with one another (pig production, for instance, was quite compatible with dairy farming, as post-famine Cavan agriculture demonstrates), but as long as one of these related forms of produce played an important market role, it was difficult for Cavan tenants to increase the acreage under grass at the expense of one tillage crop without affecting the other. In essence, pasture had to compete with these crops as a system and not independently; and as the Poor Law Commission witnesses testified in the mid-1830s, tillage was holding its own or even expanding at the expense of pasture.[51]

Of course, farm size had a great influence on the use of resources. In 1841, the smaller farms seem to have been more pig and poultry oriented, and the larger more cattle oriented (table 2.7; the figures do not distinguish between dairy and beef cattle). Twenty-nine percent of the cattle of the county were on farms of over fifteen acres, while only 15 percent of the poultry and pigs were found on these farms. However, because the census figures do not permit the calculation of the numbers of livestock per acre, they do not provide a complete picture of the land usage by farm size. Table 2.8 represents an estimate of animals per acre produced by the following calculation:

$$\frac{\text{Number of animals on farms of this category}}{\text{(estimated mean farm size in this category) x}}$$
(number of holdings in this category)

The estimate of mean size was derived by calculating and rounding the mean size of farms within these same categories from the tithe applotment figures in the Killashandra File. These estimates differ from the "literal" mean calculated by averaging the high and low

Table 2.7

Distribution of Pigs, Cattle, and Poultry by Farm Size in Cavan, 1841

	FARM SIZE	PIGS	CATTLE	POULTRY
ANIMALS PER	1–5 acres	.9598	.8490	5.66
FARM	5–15 acres	1.75	2.02	8.90
	15–30 acres	2.63	4.29	14.57
	30+ acres	2.63	9.52	17.04
	Total	1.51	1.90	8.18
PERCENTAGE OF	1 acre	16.3	3.6	20.3
TOTAL ANIMALS*	1–5 acres	22.5	18.2	23.26
	5–15 acres	46.3	48.93	41.33
	15–30 acres	11.2	16.63	10.85
	30+ acres	3.8	12.59	4.3

SOURCE: *Census of 1841*, table 3, pp. 454–55.

* Totals for all farms were: pigs, 46,123; cattle, 50,533; poultry, 262,926.

Note: I have not attempted a comparative review of these statistics because the reliability of the results of measurement is suspect: see P. M. A. Bourke, "The Agricultural Statistics of the 1841 Census of Ireland: A Critical Review," *Economic History Review* 18:2, 2nd series (August 1965): 377–81. Bourke believed that these figures were collected without proper regard for the type of acre (statute, Irish, or plantation) which was in local use. This makes the comparison of counties quite risky. However, within a single county for which we know the normal unit of measurement (the Irish acre in Cavan), the figures can be used with confidence.

Table 2.8

Stocking Index: Estimate of Animals per Acre on Farms of Different Sizes, 1841

FARM SIZE (ACRES):				
Range	Est. Mean	PIGS	CATTLE	POULTRY
1–5	4	.2400	.2123	1.4149
5–15	8	.0714	.1448	.6364
15–30	20	.0190	.0817	.2774
30+	35	.0753	.2722	.5087

SOURCE: *Census of 1841*, pp. 454–55.

parameters of the size categories, as they inflate the mean size of the smallest farm from about three to four acres and slightly deflate all of the other means. In essence, they approximate the "small" farm norm in Cavan, assuming that above five acres farms tend to cluster at the lower end of these size categories. It is fairly certain that these estimates are better than the "literal" means because the total number of arable acres obtained by summing the product of mean and farm numbers for the literal mean, 392,397, exceeds the total arable land of the county (375,473). The sum of the estimated means, 340,212 acres, falls below the total arable figure. This is reassuring, as the census figures exclude holdings of one acre or less. At any rate, however accurate or inaccurate this method may be, the use of the "literal" mean would actually noticeably increase the strength of the relationship between farm size and livestock per acre.

That relationship is striking. Farms of one to five acres had the highest numbers of pigs and poultry per acre by a wide margin over all other categories. Only on those very small farms did pigs exceed cattle. Farms over thirty acres had the highest cattle stocking figures. Yet there is no simple linear relationship here; the 15–30 acre category has the lowest level of stocking for all three types of livestock.

The picture that emerges from this evidence is fairly logical. The 1–5 acre farms are clearly the most intensively stocked, a sign, no doubt, of their inability to exploit the cereal market with such small units of production. In addition, the very high pig figures confirm that the smallest farms were heavily involved in potatoes for use as pig fodder. The middle range, and especially the 15–30 acre farms, have low stocking ratios, which most likely mark them as the primary cereal producers of the county. The largest farms can be seen as the most pasture oriented, with over three times as many cattle per acre as the 15–30 acre category. The moderate pig stocking figure (second highest) would indicate the compatibility of dairy and pig production on these larger farms. There are two possible explanations for the sharp difference in land utilization between the 15–30 and the over 30 categories. First, very large farm size often indicates poor or marginal land, such as rough mountain pasture which had no other use than grazing. Second, the highly labor-intensive nature of tillage in Cavan probably created certain upper limits on the extent of land an individual producer could efficiently control.

Taken in conjunction with the figures on land usage in table 2.6, these figures confirm the evidence which the Railway Commission and other sources of trade information gave regarding Cavan's agricultural orientation during the late pre-famine period. As oat, pig, and dairy production received the greatest land resource, Cavan's agriculture was in a position to profit from improving trade conditions and the consequent higher prices for these commodities. It is also evident that there was a rough balance between tillage and pasture and that any increase that was taking place in the area under tillage was due to a balanced expansion and not to the expansion of a subsistence crop at the expense of commercial agriculture. The large extent of pasture, the significant extent of clover and meadow (noted in table 2.6), and the potato's use as a fodder crop confirm this.

The significant acreage in meadow and clover, 9 percent of tillage acreage, is an indication of the importance of ley farming and the dairy production that went with it. As part of the permanent rotation, these fodder crops are evidence of Cavan farmers' desire to respond to the growing demand for dairy products. The clover acreage is particularly interesting, as it shows a significant interest in adopting "modern" agricultural practices which fit into the local system. There is also evidence that new varieties of grass seed were being sown in this meadowland.[52]

Pigs and chickens also played an increasingly important part in Cavan farm organization as a direct response to market conditions (Drogheda being the largest pig exporting port in the country)[53] because they fit especially well within the traditional tillage system.

In this light, it is interesting to note that it was during the decade before the famine that the older breed of Irish pig gave way to heavier breeds,[54] while the traditional breed of cattle successfully resisted attempts at replacement. The new pig breeds could fit into the traditional system and provide more efficient use of available foods. The new cattle breeds, although bigger and more efficient meat producers, could not replace the local breed, which was exceptionally hardy, able to produce milk on poor feed and able to ride out the winter without the need for expensive winter fodder which did not exist within the traditional system and which would have required the complete reworking of the tillage system. Local conditions—not blind acceptance of, or resistance to, change—determined which improvements tenants would adopt.

Within certain limitations, Cavan farmers were able to participate in the changing market situation. That much established, it is possible to approach the question of "improvement." I have already argued that prices, rent, productivity, and exports were all increasing in the period 1800–1815 and that exports and productivity remained high even after the decline of prices (indeed, exports may well have *had* to increase after the price collapse in order for Cavan agriculture to survive). What can be said more specifically about the situation of Cavan's farming class?

All three of the major pre-famine Parliamentary inquiries into Irish agriculture and social conditions offered observations on the improving conditions of tenant farmers in Ireland in general and some comments specifically on Cavan's tenantry. Unfortunately, due either to the historian's need to find indications of impending doom in pre-famine conditions or to Irish suspicions of British government–sponsored reports, these comments are seldom given the attention they deserve.

George Nicholls, in his Report on the Poor Laws in Ireland, went to great pains to stress the improvements which had taken place in Ireland:

> The investigations and inquiries in which I have now been engaged have led me to the conviction that the condition of Ireland has, on the whole, during the last thirty years, been progressively improving. It is impossible to pass through the country without being struck with the evidence of increasing wealth, which is everywhere apparent. Great as has been the improvement in England within the same period, that in Ireland, I believe, has been equal.[55]

Nicholls attributed the great suffering and misery which still existed in Ireland to a population increase so rapid that it outstripped the economic gains of the rural community. Unfortunately, because the work of the Poor Law Commission was to study poverty and not the entire community, Nicholls did not go into more detail in his discussion of overpopulation. However, as the inquiry was clearly focused on the agricultural laboring population, he could not avoid the observation that the growth of population had its major impact upon this class.

The witnesses from Cavan also provided evidence of the ambiguous nature of "improvement." When asked to state whether conditions of the poor had improved or deteriorated since the Napoleonic wars, fifteen of the thirty-three who responded said that conditions had worsened, while twelve said they had improved.[56] Close examination of their responses reveals a slightly clearer picture. Most of those who cited improved conditions either spoke in very general terms of their community or made clear references to "farmers," not "laborers." For example, Henry Gibson of Munsterconnaught felt conditions were "rather improving, for the farmers are industrious, and obliged to be so from the badness of the soil and high rent charged." Others, such as John Young, M.P. for Cavan, and the Reverend Samuel Crookshanks, Church of Ireland rector in Knockbride, simply stated that conditions had improved noticeably without identifying whether they spoke of the "poor" or of the entire community.[57]

Those who believed conditions were deteriorating were generally more specific and identified the "poor" or "laborers" as their subjects. For example, Rev. Henry Martin, Church of Ireland rector in Killashandra, not only answered the general question, but explained why conditions were "much worse": "employment [is] much harder to be found amongst farmers." The Reverend Matthew Webb concurred: "Their condition is worse and principally from want of employment." The Reverend John King of Killinkere added yet another reason for the laboring employment crisis: "Our landlords charge very high rents, and therefore farmers cannot pay labourers as they should, nor give them sufficient employment." Less specific comments were that "the poor have every day declined by poverty and wretchedness," and, succinctly but eloquently, "population increasing but by no means improved."[58]

Considered as a whole, the local evidence supports Nicholls's general observations. Those with substantial resources seem to have been holding their own or even improving their lot during these difficult years; those without access to land, and therefore without the opportunity to utilize their labor, were "much worse in every respect." Nicholls himself identified the proximate cause of the crisis as unemployment and underemployment. His analysis of this period closely resembles that offered here; he even used the phrase "transition period" to describe the painful phenomenon which he witnessed in Ireland:

> By the term "transition period" I mean to indicate that season of change from the system of small holdings, allotments, and subdivisions of land . . . to the better practice of day labour for wages and to that dependence on daily labour for support. . . . This transition period is, I believe, generally beset with difficulty and suffering . . . and every aid should be afforded to shorten its duration and lessen its pressure.[59]

This Poor Law evidence does not stand alone. The Railway Commission, which reported in the following year, was more detailed in its description of improvement and more specific in its explanations of the continuation of massive social problems. The Railway Commissioners echoed Nicholls's overall characterization of Ireland, but went further in detailing the specific nature of the problem.

> The present social aspect and condition of Ireland is an anomaly in itself. Whilst the country is making a visible and steady progress in improvement, and signs of increasing wealth present themselves on all sides, the laboring population . . . derive no proportionate benefit from the growing prosperity around them. In many places their condition is even worse than it has been.[60]

The commissioners found that what was true of Ireland as a whole was true in Cavan. They found that "the general trade of Cavan is annually increasing," but that there was "considerable distress among the poorer classes of the people."[61] The principal explanation given for this "anomaly" was the same as that cited by Nicholls:

> These signs of growing prosperity are, unhappily, not so discernible in the condition of the laboring people, as in the amount of the produce of their labor. The pressure of a superabundant and excessive population (at least, with respect to the resources as yet developed for their maintenance and occupation) is perpetually and powerfully acting to depress them.[62]

Even on the very eve of the famine, the report of the Devon Commission struck an optimistic tone when discussing the situation of the tenant farmers of Ireland:

> Another general remark which our tour through the country and an extensive intercourse with the farming classes enables us to make, is that in almost every part of Ireland unequivocal symptoms of improvement, in spite of many embarrassing and counteracting circumstances, continually present themselves to the view; and that there exists a general and increasing spirit and desire for promotion for such improvement. . . . Indeed, speaking of the country generally, with some exceptions which are unfortunately too notorious, we believe that at no former period did so active a spirit of improvement prevail, nor could well directed measures for the attainment of that objective have been proposed with a better prospect of success than at the present moment.

But once again the condition of the agricultural laborers made complete optimism impossible:

> We regret, however, to be obliged to add that in most parts of Ireland there seems to be by no means a corresponding advance in the condition and comforts of the labouring classes (who endure) suffering greater . . . than the people of any other country in Europe has to sustain.[63]

The witnesses reporting on Cavan stressed the evident but selective nature of this improvement. One noted that there had been "very considerable" improvement in his district and that "money is returned back into the country, to the hands of the farmers; and not only is there a considerable improvement in the agriculture of the country, but in the houses also."[64] Kenny, the agent on the Farnham estates, believed that conditions for the "large farmers" were improving; but he was careful to point out that laborers and small tenants were not participating in the economic improvement of the county.[65]

These reports identify the real dangers to Irish rural society. It was not a case of a subsistence oriented society crashing to the ground under the weight of an endogenous population explosion. Rather, Cavan and most of rural Ireland suffered from a growing imbalance between the labor requirements of commercializing agriculture and the labor supply, between the farming and laboring population. This increasingly dangerous situation was, of course, the direct result of the tremendous population growth of the late eighteenth and early nineteenth centuries; but it was not a development of the subsistence system in Ireland, but a response to the increasing commercialization of agriculture in Ireland—specifically, a direct response to the growing demand for Irish agricultural produce in Great Britain.[66]

The answer to the great conundrum of Cavan's "selective" pre-famine prosperity centers on the nature of agricultural organization. The rent system, coupled with the absence of ready capital, encouraged intensive rather than extensive use of land, because Cavan farmers could only benefit from the market through the greater exploitation of the one factor of production over which they had direct control: labor. It is here, in the relationship between market integration and agricultural productivity, that the true heart of most Irish problems lay. Poverty and overpopulation were not linked in a causal way; both were the result of a serious defect in the nature of Irish economic integration with Great Britain. Irish economic development within the constraints imposed by the landlord system and the British government's ideology could only take place at the expense of part of the rural population.

In more precise terms, Cavan farmers of the pre-famine era had to balance the relative profitability of "corn" and "horn" on a scale which also controlled for quality and quantity of production input. Not until after the famine, when butter prices soared, grain prices plunged, and agricultural labor was decimated (and much worse), did the Cavan farmer face a different and less restrictive situation. Until that time, the agricultural laboring population would have to provide the "human" accumulation of productivity.

Agricultural
Labor
3

The social structure of most rural communities has one great divide: the occupation of land. Those who have control over the use of land, however it is obtained, have obvious social and economic advantages over the landless. This was true in Ireland before the arrival of the Normans, and it remained true into the twentieth century. However, dramatic changes took place in the numbers and the function of the landless population during Ireland's colonial period. In the Gaelic landholding system, the landless had certain rights along with their responsibilities. Under the English landholding system they had no rights, not even that of survival. It was this complete "rationalization" of the laborers' relationship to the land that prepared the way for Cavan's agricultural development during pre-famine times, and which in turn produced both the dramatic demographic explosion of late eighteenth- and early to mid-nineteenth-century Ireland and the appalling poverty and tragedy which these people would suffer.

The family and demographic experiences of farmer and laborer diverged widely, and must be examined separately. Before such an examination can begin, however, the social boundary lines must be

drawn—a preliminary that many nineteenth-century British observers overlooked and many subsequent historians have also neg-
lected.

TYPES OF LABOR

In pre-famine Cavan, as in most of peasant Europe, specific occupational categories were very loosely defined. Individuals who
lacked sufficient land to provide for all of their family's needs were
forced to undertake many different activities to earn a living. They
took work job by job, and thus might pass through several "occupations" during the course of their lives, or practice several
simultaneously, This temporary nature of employment and the
simultaneous practice of two or more occupations makes the drawing of clear demarcation lines between social groups difficult, and it
is also difficult for the historian to reconstruct an occupational profile for the purposes of comparison and analysis. For example, many
"weavers" were actually small farmers who used their looms only
during slack periods on the farm. These farmer-weavers employed
agricultural laborers themselves and often occupied farms above the
average acreage for their district.[1]

The weaver, like most artisans, became a field hand during harvest and planting times. The agricultural laborer would rent a tiny
piece of land and become a "farmer." The farm servant would take
conacre ground and become a speculator in the potato market.

The difficulty of assigning occupational titles in pre-famine
Cavan is reflected in the labor account book of a Cavan entrepre-
neur, Alexander Faris, who, in addition to being a substantial land
occupier, operated a bleach green. Owen McCabe, a laborer who
earned £8/9s./9d. in 1829, also rented a farm from Faris in
Drumeron for £9; took concacre in Farinseer for £17/3s., in Cloggy
for £1/5s./6d., and in Drumcrow for 17s./1d.; and ran up a further
debt for potatoes and oats. In all, with his income of £8/9s./9d., he
owed Faris £27/15s. He paid the difference in cash, presumably
earned through conacre speculation. Thus McCabe was a tenant
farmer, a wage laborer, and a conacre tenant; and Faris was his
overtenant, his employer, his conacre landlord, and his creditor.[2]

Despite this confusion, the distinction between laborer and

farmer was very real. In a society as dependent upon agriculture as Ireland was before the famine, there was an enormous divide between the two great classes, the landed and the landless. While many fell from the more privileged situation, very few were ever able to move in the acending direction. A witness from Cavan before the Poor Law Commission stated that "no one could recollect a case of a day-labourer raising himself up to the condition of a farmer."[3] The very high price of tenant right and the precarious nature of the laborers' income had combined to create this situation. On the eve of the famine, the social differentiation implied by the Cavan witness was well advanced.

Yet at the turn of the century Coote had believed that there was "no great demand for labour, the family on the land being generally fully adequate to all the work; nor for the same reason have they cottiers, as in Leinster and Munster."[4] Even as late as 1811 Wakefield reported that "it is not the custom to hire labourers for any rural work; when it becomes necessary to plough, to dig . . . , the neighbors assemble."[5] Nevertheless, the Poor Law commissioners of the 1830s were convinced that the poverty of the county was directly related to the large and constantly increasing population of agricultural laborers.[6] It is likely that Wakefield, assembling a vast amount of information from diverse sources, reported impressions that failed to note recent and rapid developments (the same is possible in Coote's case, though less likely, as he was at least a resident of the county). In any case, sometime between the 1790s and the 1830s the number of agricultural laborers began to increase rapidly; and by 1841 the landless were the majority in Cavan's rural society.

Table 3.1 provides the best available outline of the size of the various occupational groupings within Killashandra in 1841. Household heads are used for this breakdown because the children and spouses of farmer-headed households often were listed as "laborer," "spinner," etc., and thus their inclusion would artificially inflate the "landless" category. From this information, it is quite clear that a homogeneous peasant world had long since ceased to exist. Farming families account for only 34 percent of the rural households. The other large group, the agricultural laborers, account for 27 percent of the total. If "laborers" are added to the "other employment" category (which takes in specialized agricul-

Table 3.1

Occupational Classification of
Heads of Household in Killashandra, 1841

OCCUPATIONAL GROUP	MALE	FEMALE
Laborers	601	22
Artisans	191	5
Weavers	153	0
Spinners	0	87
Other employment	296	22
"None"	17	106
Total landless	1258	242
Farmers	757	16
Total	2015	258

SOURCE: Killashandra Study File.

tural labor such as herding and threshing), their combination represents the largest single group in this community.

Despite the unenviable position of laborers as a group, there was
considerable variation in the conditions of individual laboring families. These differences were due in part to the various forms which
the relationships between farmer and laborer took. There were three
main types of labor exchange in Cavan: farm service, cotting, and
wage laboring. These types of labor represent different solutions to
the problems of incomplete monetization and underemployment.
Only wage labor completely represented the new modernizing
forces at work within the market economy; but as we shall see, its
efficiency as a means of winning sustenance was severely limited by
overpopulation and the seasonal nature of agriculture work.

Farm service was the most secure but the most restrictive form of
labor in Cavan. Farm servants (male and female) lived in the cabin
of their employer and often shared his meals. They worked as servants and were bound for a year to their employer. Wages were paid
at the end of the year, giving the employer considerable power over
his servants. There is evidence from another South Ulster community that farm servants had to ask permission to leave their employer's holding, even at night;[7] but as servants were often youths
(in Killashandra their average age was 21.9 years) and always
single, these restrictions were not considered unnatural.

Although farm servants had little personal freedom, they did have the security of full-time employment and sustenance. In addition, because they were single and had few obligations, they were often able to save a large part of their meagre salary, and this allowed many of them, after three or four years of careful saving, to accumulate money for passage to North America. One of the witnesses before the Poor Law Commission went so far as to class the unmarried farm servants as a distinct and privileged class of laborers because of their security and opportunity to emigrate. Another witness claimed that the farm servants were the only laboring people who drank, because they were the only laboring people who could afford it.[8]

The second type of labor agreement, cotting, was the direct result of the twin problems of undermonetization and underemployment. The cot system enabled farmers to circumvent the need for liquid capital, while allowing the laborer and his family to utilize their surplus labor. In this arrangement the laborer received a cottage and a small potato plot in return for his labor on the tenant's farm. A dry-cot take consisted of potato land only, while a wet-cot take contained additional land to support a cow. This agreement was normally for a year, but it often developed into a longer-term arrangement.

To the tenant farmer, the major attraction of this agreement was his release from cash responsibilities. The small laborers' cabins were cheaply erected on poor land, and in return the farmer received the necessary labor to till his land. Many laborers were attracted to this relationship because it offered some security in an insecure world. As long as the potato crop was plentiful, the cotter on his cot was better off than his neighbor who worked for a cash wage. Also, the potato plot allowed the cotter's family to utilize its surplus labor. Women and children had little opportunity for employment on farms except during harvest, and even the head of the family was often not fully employed. The cot gave the family a means of turning this surplus labor directly into food without the need for cash with which to rent land.

Cotters, like farm servants, were extremely dependent on their employers. Their agreements usually were not written; in any case, the cotter was anxious to be retained for the coming year. Further-

more, in times of distress the cotter would have to seek assistance
from his employer. Cotters were subject to the usual restrictions
upon labor, such as fines for absence from work, and Cavan tenants
even imposed economic restrictions upon their cotters. For example, many Cavan tenants forbade their cotters from keeping
chickens to reduce competition with them in the growing egg trade.[9]
It would be difficult to find better evidence of the conflicting economic interests of these two groups, or of the economic power of the
tenant vis-à-vis the cotter.

The third type of laborer, the daily or wage laborer, was a semi-
modern economic man. He was modern because he worked for a
daily wage and was independent of any social or economic restrictions outside of his labor contract. However, this modernity was
tempered by overpopulation and the incomplete rationalization of
the region's economy. The absence of a well-developed retail food
market prevented him from functioning as a market consumer,
while the extreme competition for employment and the daily nature
of this employment combined to make him insecure.

The wage laborer was not tied to any particular farmer for employment, but he was not totally independent of the farming class.
He had to rent his house and his garden from the tenant farmer. The
rent for a cottage and half-rood was generally around £2 or £3, a
large sum for a man earning 8d. or 9d. a day. Wage laborers were
also indirectly dependent on local tenant farmers for their food
supply. Because of the imperfectly monetized economy of the
region and the long periods of unemployment, wage laborers were
forced to rely on a system known as *conacre* for their subsistence.

Conacre was a highly specialized form of land rental whereby one
party offered land prepared for potato planting for a period of eleven
months only. The laborer taking conacre agreed to rent a small
parcel of land, a rood or half-rood, at an extremely high rent and to
pay all sums owed before removing the potato crop in the fall. In
1811 Wakefield recorded conacre rent for Cavan of £7/12s. per
acre, while the Poor Law Commission placed the Cavan average at
£8–9 per acre on land for which the farmer paid 25s. to 30s.[10] The
laborers were willing to pay these rents because they could generally provide themselves with potatoes below the market price as
well as procure waste fodder with which to fatten a pig.[11] Just as

important, conacre allowed the laboring family to utilize the labor of women and children who otherwise would be idle and the surplus labor of underemployed males. Nothing could indicate more clearly the lack of employment opportunity for Cavan laborers than this system in which laborers literally had to bid against one another for the opportunity of working.

Conacre was almost universal among Cavan wage laborers because, as long as the potato harvest was good, it placed a supply of food under their direct control. But there were several problems with the system, even in good years. The high conacre rents required a fairly steady income, something which the laborer could not be assured of in Ireland. Conacre tenants often had to leave the country to find cash wages in England or Scotland in order to meet their conacre rents. Furthermore, the conacre tenant was not allowed to remove his crop until he had paid his rent, and he was legally responsible for the rent even if the potatoes produced were not worth the sum owed. This situation led to frequent conflicts between laborers and tenant farmers who let conacre. Yet despite these problems and the ever-present danger of total failure (in which case the laborer was still responsible), every rood of ground offered for conacre was eagerly taken. One tenant in Loughtee let thirty acres in rood parcels; each rood was bid for competitively.[12] Laborers were so anxious to get conacre land that when the laboring witnesses before the Poor Law Commission were asked if they would like to be able to remove their potatoes before paying rent, they responded negatively because they feared that such a change in custom would decrease the attraction of conacre for the farmer and lead eventually to the end of a system which served as the lifeline of the wage laborer.[13]

Although conacre was primarily the preserve of the wage laborer, many other types of landless people participated in the system. The artisans of Cavan faced many of the same problems as the wage laborers. They too could not rely on the market to provide them with potatoes and needed to employ the entire family in order to survive. During long periods of high potato prices, such as the late twenties, farm servants often took conacre land as a form of speculation, offering the produce of their plots for sale to cotters and day laborers who could not produce enough food for their own families.[14] This gave farm servants still another economic advantage over their more independent neighbors.

Ironically, the personal freedom of the wage laborer bound him to this system. The ease with which laborers found conacre land during the first three decades of the century increased the certainty of survival, and as a Cavan witness before the Poor Law Commission noted, "The conacre system, from the certainty and facility of procuring provision which it affords, has undoubtedly a tendency to increase the population." [15] It opened the way for early marriage and the subsequent larger families. As already noted, single farm servants often participated in the conacre market for profit, and it was an easy step to exchange farm service for wage labor and keep the conacre produce for the provision of a new family.

The rapidly rising population of the early nineteenth century, which was at least partially due to the conacre system, in turn increased the demand for conacre and drove conacre rents higher, encouraging farmers to let more land through this system, thus reinforcing a spiral which seemed endless. Although there is no way to measure the relative distribution of land utilization within individual tenancies, the high conacre rents and the increasing demand for conacre certainly must have affected the relative competitiveness of the subletting system. Subtenants who paid their rents largely out of their farm produce could hardly compete with cotters and laborers who in essence subsidized the productivity of their conacre land with the cash earned on the farms of large tenants. In this way, the rising laborer population most likely contributed indirectly to the decrease in subletting which took place during the 1830s. This in turn led to an increasingly differentiated social structure as a larger and larger percentage of the population was forced into the laboring category, further increasing the pressure of the spiral toward higher conacre rents and more conacre land (see table 1.1 for an example of the numerical relationships between cotters and subtenants on an individual estate).

This process was dependent on the continued success of the potato, which required little attention once it was established and which could easily be left in the ground without damage while its cultivator worked on the harvest of a large tenant. Most important, the potato was extremely prolific and provided the maximum return for the acreage and labor required. Although flax was occasionally grown on conacre land (presumably by speculators), conacre production of oats, the dominant tillage crop in Cavan, was unknown.[16] This was because the careful cultivation and precise timing of harvest which oats demanded could not be guaranteed by the laborer, who had other obligations. The potato—and in Irish conditions, only the potato—fit the needs of the laboring population.

Of course, the famine would devastate all those who depended on this system for survival, but even without the famine there were certain limits which kept the conacre system from totally differentiating rural society into two opposing groups, the conacre takers and the conacre letters. The primary retardant to the expansion of the conacre system was the very engine that kept the system operating: the high conacre rents had to be paid by wages earned from labor on tillage farms. The increase in the laboring population and the decrease of land tilled by the tenant farmer led to increased competition for employment with a consequent drop in wages and a rise in underemployment. Together, these developments helped to form a ceiling on the rents which laborers could offer for conacre.

The full effect of this ceiling was delayed for a time by the increased seasonal migration of labor either within Ireland or to England and Scotland, which allowed the tenant to supplement the work locally available. But this external income was largely inelastic, and once it became common for many wage earners, its effect was diminished. This seems to have happened in Cavan by the mid-thirties. The Presbyterian minister of Killashandra reported to the Poor Law Commission that in his parish 191 laborers left the county for seasonal labor, and of that number 187 were married men whose "wives and children live on conacre potatoes." The wages which they brought home paid the conacre rents.[17] Similar accounts came from Drumlane, Castleterra, Belturbet, Drumgoon, Enniskeen, Knockbride, and Kildrumferton.[18]

After 1821 the one other alternative source of income which a laborer might resort to in order to meet his conacre rent, linen production, was in decline. As remarked earlier, Coote believed that weaving was the major ancillary occupation in Cavan at the turn of the century. While his claims were certainly exaggerated, the

importance of the linen industry in Cavan before 1825 was considerable. The families of many small farmers and laborers had
looms and spinning wheels. When farm duties were not pressing, or
when there was no other employment, the men would turn to the
loom and the women to the spinning wheel. For some laborers (and
even for some small farmers), the income from the wheel and loom
could pay the rent. But after the demise of the linen industry in
Cavan due to northern competition, families could not depend upon
linen to supply their cash needs. In a completely monetized economy, Cavan's linen industry (as distinct from flax production)
would have disappeared in the altered situation. But the choice for
Cavan textile workers was not between two full-time employments,
but between a failing supplementary source of income and no
income at all. The Reverend Bernard Brady, parish priest of Killashandra, pointed out that, except for linen, there was no employment available for women.[19] This explains the persistence of
spinning and weaving in Cavan against all economic rationale. Rev.
Henry Martin, the Church of Ireland rector of Killashandra, testified
to the Poor Law Commission in 1834 that two-thirds of the laborers
"have looms at home and earn something by weaving."[20] He estimated family yearly income possible from linen to be two and a half
pounds, enough for the rent of a cottage or a rood of conacre, but
not both.

As late as the census of 1841, 9.1 percent of heads of households
listed their occupation as either weaver or spinner. But as the age
breakdown for male heads of families in table 3.2 indicates, weaving was on its way out (spinning survived longer because of the even
more limited opportunities for employment for women).

LABOR SUPPLY AND DEMAND

Nothing could have been more obvious to even the most casual
observer of pre-famine rural Ireland than the horrendous conditions
of the Irish agricultural laborers. As we shall see, it was equally
obvious that the conditions of this group were deteriorating during
that time. Yet, once again, observation does not explain either the
cause of this misery or its effects upon the society as a whole. As

already suggested, the horror of the conditions under which the laborers existed often blinded observers to signs of improvement in the tenant population and also tended to deter most contemporary observers from dwelling too long on the subject. Only by closely analyzing the reasons for the decline in laborers' living and working conditions is it possible to unravel the problem of the whole society and to fully appreciate the significance of the famine.

The conditions of any laboring group are closely tied to the level of wages which they receive for their work; but excessive reliance on agricultural wages as an indicator of laborer conditions is dangerous for three reasons. First, in an incompletely monetized economy there is no valid way of estimating the value of labor in purely monetary terms. As Chayanov observed, "Any attempt to evaluate [the value of labor] at the rate of agricultural wages is arbitrary."[21] Wages offered by farmers in an incompletely rationalized economy reflect subjective value judgments based on family needs, family work abilities, and perceptions of the market economy. In such a system farmers have the option of determining the extent of their

Table 3.2
Age Breakdown of Adult Textile Workers
in Cavan, 1841

AGE	TEXTILE WORKERS IN EACH AGE GROUP AS % OF TOTAL TEXTILE WORKERS
21–25	2.5
26–30	3.4
31–35	8.1
36–40	6.9
41–45	9.0
46–50	10.5
51–55	12.1
56–60	11.5
61–65	9.2
66–70	14.3
Over 70	13.0

SOURCE: Killashandra Study File. N = 153.

involvement in the commercial market, and hence their need for labor.

A second problem with interpreting the level of agricultural wages is directly related to the underemployment which plagued the Cavan laborer. For the majority of wage earners, work and wages were offered on a daily basis. While daily wage levels may not have fluctuated much, the yearly income of laborers could gyrate wildly according to the demand for labor and the individual's ability to work during the peak agricultural seasons. Finally, agricultural wages in Cavan were strongly influenced by local custom. They did not respond quickly to other economic changes, because the community was culturally committed to offering a living wage. Laborers, as a large proportion of the community, had various means available for insuring the maintenance of this situation, the ultimate being the physical threat of the secret society.

Given these three reservations, the most that can be said about the level of wages is that any change which occurred between 1800 and 1845 was more significant for its direction than for its magnitude. Detailed wage evidence is difficult to come by, but the direction of change in Cavan is clear enough. Even though rents and prices generally rose during the pre-famine period, daily wages fell. There seems to have been a rough correlation between wages and prices during the boom and bust years of the wartime period, but when prices and rents began their recovery, wages stagnated and remained below their earlier levels.

The detailed evidence of wage levels at the turn of the century is unfortunately limited to Coote's survey. While some corroboration would be helpful, it should be pointed out that Coote is probably more reliable on this subject than on others. He employed laborers himself and was familiar with the general trends of agriculture in his county, and as we shall see, wages were remarkably constant across the county. Coote gives both average and specialized figures for daily wage rates (see table 3.3). We can see from these figures that there was considerable variation in the wages which laborers could earn, but it should be recalled that individuals would be forced to alter their activity according to the vicissitudes of season and fortune. Obviously mowing and reaping were highly seasonal; these could be engaged in only for a few weeks each year by the strongest and healthiest laborers. Turf cutting was also a seasonal activity, undertaken during the slack periods of the growing season when the weather was dry. At other times these individuals would have to hire out, if able, at 9d. per day as general laborers.

Although these agricultural wages compare favorably to those of the ensuing decades, Coote still considered that they were "not in a fair proportion to the increased value and rise on the produce of the land."[22] Laborers were living in poverty, with a poor diet and wretched living conditions.

The wages of the weaver and other craftsmen were high at the turn of the century, reflecting the general prosperity of the community and especially the health of the linen industry. The high wages of the turf cutters were also due to the linen activity in the country. The great demand for turf which the bleach greens created provided one of the few alternatives to agricultural employment for the unskilled laborer. The demise of these sources of income would have a devastating effect on the laboring population.

Wakefield believed that agricultural wages had nearly doubled during the period 1779–1811, but that textile wages had remained stagnant.[23] Of course the reason for this was the growing marginality of South Ulster domestic textile production as the industry increasingly concentrated in the Lagan Valley. As early as 1801 Coote was noting with alarm the "extraordinary emigration of linen

Table 3.3
Some Late Eighteenth-Century Wage Levels
in Cavan

TYPE OF LABOR	RATE PER DAY
Mower	2s.
Reaper	1s.
Artisan	2s.
Turf Cutter	1s./4d.
Journeyman Weaver	1s.–1s./6d.
Master Weaver	2s.–5s.
General	9½d.
Women	4d.–6½d.

SOURCE: Charles Coote, *Cavan*, pp. 61, 78.

weavers.''[24] By 1824 the linen industry in Cavan was in great difficulty, though still surviving. On Alexander Faris's bleach green, workers were earning an average wage of 9*d*. per day. By 1828–29 the effect of the competition from the Lagan Valley was clear;[25] the average daily wage had fallen to 7*d*. Not only did wages decline, but Faris began to hire laborers by the week rather than by the month.[26] Actually, because they pertain to the linen industry, these figures are only partially relevant to the agricultural wage. Faris was employing these workers for a strictly capitalistic enterprise which he watched carefully and which we can assume responded in a more economically rational way than the average tenant farm. Therefore it is unlikely that agricultural wages fell as quickly or as drastically. Yet these figures clearly show the nature of the problem which was developing: the leveling of wages outside of agriculture and the increasing uncertainty of employment in those spheres made competition among agricultural laborers that much more frantic. This in turn not only decreased the bargaining power of the agricultural laborer vis-à-vis his wage, but also decreased the length of his working year. Thus real wages declined more precipitously than the daily wage, creating a severe crisis for agricultural laborers beginning in the mid-1820s.

It is not possible to follow the exact development of the crisis of the 1830s and 1840s created by the increasing pressure of competition for work, but the evidence of the Poor Law Commission and the manuscript census forms for the parish of Killashandra for 1841 convey a strong impression of the nature of that crisis.

The Poor Law Commission, attempting to find the reasons for endemic poverty and distress in Ireland, was interested in the employment potential of the Irish countryside and asked questions to find out specifically how many laborers were fully employed. Table 3.4 summarizes the responses for nine Cavan parishes. While these figures are certainly imprecise (the Killogher figures are probably as accurate as any of the others), the general agreement is clear. Except for Kingscourt, with its large estate farm, constant employment was beyond the hopes of most agricultural laborers.

The census form of 1841 asked each family to record the number and length of employment of laborers which it hired. Most of those surveyed did not respond (even in the negative), so the answers cannot be used to ascertain the exact demand for labor in the parish for which these forms survive. However, the responses which were made allow some assessment of the nature of partial employment. In the 47 farm families answering the question completely and who hired agricultural laborers, the average length of employment for the 114 male laborers hired was 72 days per year. Only six females were employed, with an average period of employment of twenty-nine days (four of the six were employed for less than a week).[27] These figures vividly illustrate the term "underemployment"; only 27 of the 114 male laborers were employed for more than 90 days, while 60 were employed for less than a month. It is possible that some of these laborers were employed on several farms, thus increasing their real length of employment; but given the strong seasonality of this sort of labor and the competition for employment, such cases are unlikely to have been very common.

The wages paid to those working less than a month (11½d.) were much higher than the wages for those employed for periods longer than one month (8¼d.). This probably indicates that reaping, mowing, and potato digging were the primary forms of short-term labor, and by implication that a large portion of the laboring class worked only during planting and harvest time. These were certainly the

Table 3.4
Incidence of Full Employment in
Selected Cavan Parishes, 1836

PARISH	NUMBER OF MALE LABORERS	NUMBER IN CONSTANT EMPLOY
Shercock	400	100
Enniskeen	600	200
Kingscourt	150–200	All
Kilbride	323	150
Killesherdiny	770	170
Killogher	80% male pop.	Very few
Kinawley	105	5
Anney and Annageliff	240	72
Drumlane	310	12 or 14
Total	2,948	911 (31%)

SOURCE: Compiled from *First Report of the Commissioners, Supplement to Appendix D*, H.C. 1836, xxxi, pp. 295–300.

periods in which women were hired by the week or less. When these wage levels are compared to those cited by Coote, they confirm the impression gained from the Faris figures. The differences between Coote's figures (from 1s. to 2s. for mowing and reaping and 9½d. for general labor) and these figures are slight but consistent. Still, the significant variable here is the length of employment.

The highly seasonal nature of this work was due to a tillage system which required very high labor inputs for two short periods, planting and harvesting, and almost no wage work for the remainder of the year. The paradoxical result on Cavan farms was a demand for large numbers of laborers during the peak spring and fall seasons, with women and children finding work easily, and a labor famine during the remainder of the year. During the slack summer and winter months, only a few seasonal laborers could find employment building ditches and hedges, reclaiming rough land, or doing other heavy work which was not part of routine farm operation. Such work was very difficult to find and low paying. Women, children, and older men had no opportunity for employment during the off season, while able-bodied men were often forced to work for their diet only.[28]

The "idleness" of the Irish "peasants," which the English considered proverbial, was not due to choice; chronic underemployment lay at the base of the poverty and misery of the agricultural laborers in Cavan. The dependence on a few months' earnings for a year's sustenance was fraught with the worst kind of risk. The illness, injury, or death of the laboring male in a family could mean starvation. The need to depend on usurers or a truck system for survival during the lean months meant that even the healthiest, most robust worker would not be able to put money aside for a calamity or old age. One witness before the Poor Law Commission reported that the call of every male beggar in Cavan was, "I am past my labour."[29]

We have already seen that the laborers who worked for William Faris often ended the year in debt to their employer due to his position as a supplier of grain, potatoes, and land. This was common among large employers of labor, who generally charged the same interest as the moneylender, "so much for instance as from 4s. or 6s. on the price of a single cwt. of oatmeal"[30] or 1d. on a stone of potatoes (about 25 percent). This credit trade with the laborers was a significant economic activity because of the dire need of the laboring people. Just across the Monaghan border, a farmer testified about another farmer, "[he] gives out potatoes and meal at a profit; he is the best man for the poor in this part," whereas the local Catholic priest said of the same man, "[he] is worth 8,000 or 10,000 pounds, that he has made in this way from the poverty of the people."[31]

LIVING CONDITIONS OF AGRICULTURAL LABORERS

When dealing with the living conditions of agricultural laborers in Cavan, we are confronted with the same problem of perspective which hampered most British efforts to understand the Irish problem. Just as many contemporary observers could not distinguish between farmer and laborer because the disparity between all rural Irish people and the observers was so vast, it is difficult for the residents of contemporary Ireland or other modern countries to discern the change in the conditions of the very poorest section of pre-famine Ireland.

When wages are measured in pence and there is no concrete evidence of consumption other than general statements of poverty, it is difficult to measure change. Likewise, with conditions as poor as they were at the beginning of the nineteenth century, it is difficult to believe that they could deteriorate substantially in the following half-century. Yet there is no doubt that conditions grew more precarious for the laboring population of Cavan during this period. The rapidly increasing population, the failure of the linen industry, and land rationalization which removed subtenants combined to increase the need and decrease the opportunity for employment.

The best available source of particular information about laborers' living conditions is the Poor Law Commission Report. Unfortunately, there is little specific evidence from the earlier part of the half-century. In some areas it is only possible to speculate on the nature of change during this pre-famine period, but fortunately many of the witnesses before the Poor Law Commission commented on the nature of change during their lifetime, and their comments agree overwhelmingly.

For the laborers of Ireland, food was always the major source of anxiety. Clothing and entertainment were so rudimentary that an acceptable level was fairly easily obtained. Not so for the absolute necessities. While the diet of the laborer was based on the potato, it would be foolish to suppose that laborers ate nothing else. During the summer most of them could afford milk, although not butter.[32] During the winter a herring occasionally would cross the laborer's table.[33] Even the poorest were acquainted with other types of food out of necessity. In Cavan the supply of potatoes began to taper off in June and never lasted beyond 1 August. Between the disappearance of the old potatoes and the first potato harvest (the "hungry months"), laborers had to survive on grain, usually oatmeal. This simple diet was nutritious, especially when milk was available, and satisfying when in adequate supply. Late summer was the normal crisis period when the laborers were forced into the market to find an alternative to their dwindling and rotting potato supply. If meal was short or if the laborer had been unable to find work during the spring, hunger could change from an annoyance to a threat. If the fall potato harvest was delayed by poor weather, the situation could become critical. If the harvest was small, the laborers would enter the winter under a sentence of hunger for the coming spring.

To the outsider this diet did not seem all that different from the farmer's. Both relied mainly on the potato supplemented with oats, milk, and herring. The great difference lay in the proportions of these different foods in the diet. The farmer may have had an occasional egg and some bacon; but the great difference between the two groups was that the farmer had oats, milk, and fish available at all times, whereas the laborer had them only sporadically, either when these foods were in great supply or during the "hungry months" when the old potato crop was no longer usable and the new one not yet available. There were small farmers who ate as poorly as the laborers, but as a group the laborers were far more vulnerable to any change in the supply, condition, or price of both potatoes and oats.

Like the potato, turf has a reputation for being readily available in Ireland. But it too was subject to shortage, and even occasionally to "famines." Turf bogs were plentiful in Cavan; but as in other cases, property rights often prevented those in need from sharing in the abundance. Farm leases often carried provisions for cutting turf on the bogs of an estate, or a farmer could lease a small piece of bog for 4s. or 5s. a year. But laborers had no such privileges or opportunities, and in most areas had to purchase turf from a tenant farmer. This was a particularly difficult problem for the wage laborer who did not have a special relationship with any one farmer.

In some areas where bog was extensive, this was not a serious problem. In Munsterconnaught parish, turf was so cheap that laborers from Meath and other parts of Cavan often traveled there for the winter months.[34] But as this migration indicates, where bogs were scarce, or where there was competition from industry such as brewing or bleaching, turf shortages could be a serious problem. On the eve of the famine in Cavan, a long wet summer prevented the proper drying of the turf and drove the price of usable turf sky-high. The situation was so serious for the laboring population that Lord Farnham had to begin a subscription to prevent the death of laborers and their children.[35]

The costs of food and housing consumed most of the laboring family's budget, leaving little for clothing and other personal necessities. A comment by the parish priest of Killashandra, Rev. T. Brady, reveals both the wretched state of the laborers' wardrobe, the shame which this caused the laborers, and the obvious social differentiation which was taking place: "The clothing of the labouring classes is of such nature, that to my knowledge many of them are kept from prayers on Sunday."[36] Protestant laborers suffered from a similar problem. The parish register of the Killashandra parish Church of Ireland shows that many laborers had their children baptized at home because they could not attend church in their clothing.[37] Most of the laborers' garments were castoffs from the farming classes which were patched and mended until the original fabric was unrecognizable. One suit of clothing generally had to serve its owner winter and summer, day and night. Not all laborers could afford coats for the cold weather, and women and children seldom had the luxury of footwear. The one laboring witness from Cavan who was asked by the Poor Law Commissioners about his expenditure for clothing replied: "If I get one pair of shoes, that is the chief cost; you need not count anything else."[38]

The entertainments of the laborers were, by necessity, simple and inexpensive. The only noticeable expenditures were for tobacco and alcohol, neither of which was consumed in large quantities. A local J.P. told the Poor Law Commission that "labourers often drink on Saturday night," but laborers present were vociferous, in denying this, stating that "if they drank on Saturday night they should be without dinner on Sunday" and that only unmarried laborers could "occasionally" drink. According to these witnesses, the drunkards came from among the tradesmen and most especially from among the cattle jobbers.[39] The Poor Law Commission found that tobacco use had increased, most likely due to its falling cost. Some laborers were said to consume a halfpenny's worth a day, but this probably referred to the same farm servants who could afford drink.[40] Tobacco played an important role in the laborers' social life, as visiting their neighbors for a smoke and a talk was their most common form of entertainment and filled the void of the unemployed days, weeks, and months. The talk revolved around all topics imaginable; any "news that may be going" could serve as the focus of discussion and disputation.[41]

The limited means of the laborers were so severely stretched by their modest needs that they were often unable to resort to the normal refuges of the poor. Not only was Sunday church beyond the hopes of many of the poor; in Cavan the pawnbroker was also beyond their reach. With no furniture or clothing of any value, they were unable to patronize that questionable friend of the poor.[42]

There is overwhelming evidence of the poor diet, clothing, and general living conditions of agricultural laborers, and a dismal litany could be extended at will; but one critical aspect of the laborers' poverty has special relevance to this study. All observers agreed that the housing of laborers was universally miserable. Whether a laboring family lived as cotters or wage laborers, they invariably inhabited a sparsely furnished, one-room mud cabin. There was seldom a chest of drawers or bedstead; a chair or stool with a rough table was the most that the average laborer could afford. Beds were usually straw laid on the dirt floor of the cabin. Bedclothes ordinarily consisted of the daytime apparel of the family, or occasionally a single blanket for the entire family.[43] In general, the cabins were built to let either as cots or as cottages by tenant farmers who made a tidy profit through the laboring families' need for shelter. Some idea of the scale of exploitation is indicated in the testimony of a small landlord named Renny, who constructed some decent cabins at a cost of four pounds each. He testified that they paid off his expenses in two years at the going rate, and his cabins were far superior to those normally available to the laboring family. The "normal" cabins were considered so distasteful by the farmers that they were "always located at the outside parts of the farm, that the farmers may not be annoyed by them."[44]

As unpleasant as this housing was, there was a great demand for it. Connell has remarked that the ease of housing construction in Ireland contributed greatly to the population increases during the period in question.[45] This was true for tenants, but one must note that laborers were dependent on farmers for housing. They did not have the opportunity to throw up their own cabins because they did not have access to even a tiny plot of land, except at the favor of the tenants. Thus, as long as it was in the tenants' interests to build cabins to meet the demand of the laboring population, the number of houses available would continue to increase; but should the tenantry as a group decide that there was a better use for their land, the ease with which laboring families could establish themselves would be greatly diminished. This is precisely what appears to have happened during the 1830s. Although there probably was no decrease in the number of laborers' cabins in Cavan during this period, the rate at which they were built seems to have slowed considerably, and as the large birth cohorts of the 1790–1820 period reached marriage age, a crisis emerged. The Reverend Bernard Brady, who testified before the Poor Law Commission in 1835, noted that "owing to the dense population it is more difficult for a poor man to procure a site for a house now than formerly."[46]

Several forces lay behind this reaction to the growing laboring population. Certainly there was a limit to the amount of land which farmers were able to let to their laborers. As explained above, the rent for the laborer's cabin had to be earned through labor on tenant farms. As the number of cabins grew, the ability of the laborer to pay these rents decreased as work became harder to find. In the case of the cotter the situation was even simpler: a farm could only absorb so much labor, and each additional cot reduced the available acreage while increasing the hands working.

In addition to these structural limitations on the spread of laborers' cabins, a significant voluntary change was taking place during the period. With the increased dairy prices which Cavan farmers received between 1830 and 1840, the economic attractiveness of building cabins faded beside the promise of increasing market profits. Tenants were encouraged in this direction by the many Cavan landlords who began to insert clauses in their leases prohibiting the erection of cabins without landlord permission. The landlords obviously believed that the laboring population was already too large and that further settlement would prevent the rationalization of their estates (landlords were also responsible for the poor on their estates through the county rates). This case of landlord involvement in farm management is especially interesting in light of the general lack of landlord action during the pre-famine period. Amazingly, these same landlords who forbade cabin construction did not prohibit subdivision, the normal prohibition in the lease of concerned Irish landlords.[47] The only possible interpretation of this unusual combination of action and inaction is that by this date landlords no longer considered subdivision a serious problem, but could not ignore the grave dangers which the overpopulation of laborers represented for the survival of their system. Their unusual action, coupled with the dynamics of labor demand and a rapidly growing population, created a housing crisis for the rural poor which would have an important impact on Irish population dynamics; but the housing problem was only one aspect of a catastrophe of unimaginable proportions.

It is clear from the evidence which the Poor Law Commission found in the early 1830s that the conditions of the laboring population were abysmal. The commissioners were anxious to discover if these conditions had been improving or deteriorating during the preceding decade or so. The evidence which they collected and the conclusions which they drew from that evidence were sobering; there had been a steady and apparently irreversible decline in the already precarious position of the agricultural laboring population.

John Young of Bailieborough noted that farmers holding from ten to sixty acres had "improved both in external appearance and actual comforts," but Reverend Bernard Brady of Knockbride noted that the smallest farmers and the laborers had "every day declined by poverty and wretchedness."[48] The Catholic parish priest of West Annagh, Hugh Fitzsimmon, described the cause and timing of the laborers' decline. He testified that while food had become "cheaper and more plentiful since 1815," the destruction of the linen trade "put the weavers and others into the field of labour (with) no (other) means to pay rent, to find food or clothing, . . . all being thrown upon the land for support."[49] The Reverend Patrick McCabe, parish priest of Drumlane, described the same situation but gave slightly different causes:

> I believe the condition of the poorer classes is much deteriorated since 1815; high rents, losses, taxes and c. render the farmer, with bad markets for their commodities, less able to employ the poor, or otherwise contribute to their support; hence arises a scarcity of money and a difficulty of procuring it, and of course, a corresponding difficulty of providing the comforts, and very often the necessities, of life.[50]

While the reasons cited by McCabe for the increasing difficulty of finding employment are at variance with those offered here, his identification of the problem of underemployment and its effects coincides with the picture of a rural society with increasing competition for survival among its poorest members.

The conclusions which the commissioners drew for the entire country echo those put forward by the Cavan witnesses. They identified the lack of work for the agricultural laborers and the consequent low wages as the causes of Ireland's general distress and recurrent crisis. They stated that because of the lack of employment opportunity "it is impossible for the able-bodied, in general to provide against sickness or the temporary absence of employment, or against old age or the destitution of their widows and children in the contingent event of their own premature decease."[51] The commissioners believed that the problem was so serious and so enormous that only government-supported emigration would solve the problem: "It is thus and thus only, that the market of labour in Ireland can be relieved from the weight that is now upon it, or the labourer be raised from his present prostrate state."[52]

The question of emigration of laborers during the pre-famine period is clouded. Most existing literature on this question is on a national level and generally ascribes pre-famine migration to the movement of tenant farmers.[53] There is, however, much evidence, at least for Cavan, that laborers played a significant part in the pre-famine exodus. Reverend Bernard Brady stated: "During the last five years [1830–35] emigration among all classes, but especially servant boys, farmers, and weavers has increased; the servant boys have been induced to emigrate by the accounts received from those who went out to America [because] of the high rate of wages in that country."[54]

As we have already seen, these single laborers had the means available for such a step, and the reports of high wages hit directly upon the most responsive chord in a county beset with low wages and underemployment. The questionnaire responses which the Commission received from Cavan make it clear that the movement which Reverend Bernard Brady described was not limited to his parish. The parish of Denn had sent twenty unmarried laborers and only three families (occupation not specified) to seek a new life. From Kilbride came 45 to 50 "middle farmers and servant boys," from West Annagh 116 "labourers and small farmers," from Drumlane 110 "mostly young labourers," and from Annagh an unknown number, all of the "working classes."[55] In several cases the correspondents attributed emigration chiefly to the farming classes. Reverend Henry Martin of Killashandra stated that emigrants from that parish were "chiefly snug farmers."[56] But it is clear from other sources that Killashandra was sending large numbers of laborers to America and other destinations. Of the laboring families in Killashandra in 1841, at least 10.6 percent had sent children out of the county (as compared to 13.2 percent for farmers).[57]

Still, the evidence of the emigration of large farmers is convincing. Actually there were two types of emigration: one by a fairly substantial tenantry who wished to take advantage of open lands in North America, and the other by a young, single, laboring population anxious to avoid the desperate conditions of their married cousins.

Laborers undoubtedly had every possible incentive to emigrate. There were only two forces preventing a full-scale exodus: the lack of cash which afflicted most married laborers, and the natural reluctance to leave family and community for an unknown and unalterable alternative. Both of these forces were less significant to the young farm servants who had already made the first step of cutting family ties by going into service. In addition, the servants had no spouse or family responsibilities of their own, ready access to the passage funds, and, as one Poor Law Commission witness put it, the youth, health, and disposition needed for such an adventure.[58]

The restrictions on other types of laborers were substantial and probably prohibitive during the pre-famine period. The irregular nature of employment and the high costs of survival made any type of saving impossible, or at least irregular. Family responsibility prevented all but the most adventurous or reckless heads of laboring families from leaving the country. There is some evidence of married male laborers migrating without their families, presumably to earn the passage money with which to bring their families over at a later date; but such a course of action was filled with uncertainty for family members on both sides of the Atlantic and certainly was not common. That such a process took place at all, however, indicates the deteriorating conditions of the laboring population and the growing desire on the part of laborers to emigrate.

By the time the Devon Commission was collecting its information, the witnesses from Cavan were talking of a rapid emigration which had developed during the period 1840 to 1845. The Reverend Robert Sargent, agent to the Marquis of Headford, noted that "the principle of emigration has been increasing rapidly in the last few years" and that this was particularly true for the Catholic population and for single women.[59] The increase in the number of single women leaving is particularly interesting. Single females in agricultural laboring families suffered an even more extreme form of underemployment than their male counterparts. They could hope to find day work only during the few frantic days of planting and harvest when all hands were welcome. At other times they were forced out of many jobs traditionally performed by farm women by the vast numbers of unemployed laboring males. Other aspects of female unemployment are dealt with below; but it is worth noting here that the unique Irish pattern of single female emigration began well before the famine and was most likely a reflection of the laboring population's special problems.

By the eve of the famine, conditions for the agricultural laboring family had not improved, and perhaps had grown even more desperate. One witness from Cavan stated that, although willing to work, the laborers were "coming very near to the poor house."[60] This short statement serves very well to indicate both the state of the agricultural laborer and the nature of the problem of poverty in Ireland. The recommendations of the Poor Law Commission, which had centered on the creation of employment through the development of resources and assisted emigration, were passed over by the Liberal administration for ideological reasons. Instead, Ireland received a Poor Law modeled on that of Britain, which created a system of workhouses (not poorhouses) which were supposed to act as buffers between the poorest and starvation. These buffers, which were intended to be a means of last resort for the most desperate, were by 1845 but a breath away from serving as charnel houses for much of the laboring population of Ireland. This disaster was not accidental, but was owing to the increasingly marginal existence of the agricultural laboring family. Again, however, the growing desperation of the laboring population must be placed in relief against the waxing market orientation of Cavan agriculture and the relative prosperity of the middle and strong tenant groups which other witnesses proclaimed.[61]

Family
Structure
4

Since its origins, the historiography of the European family has centered on the concept of the "stem" family. The early arguments, many of which were ideological at best and polemical at worst, proclaimed the universality and superiority of the extended patriarchal family.

The contemporary debate that began with Peter Laslett's convincing critique of the "myth" of the stem family in England has persuasively confirmed the dominance, past and present, of the nuclear family in Europe. Lutz Berkner, who has made an important contribution by insisting on an understanding of a family dynamic, has challenged the "nuclear" school. Still, as the evidence accumulates, Laslett's early, provocative argument appears more and more to be the new orthodoxy. [1]

Although this debate is already better articulated than most in the historical domain, there is much more to say about family structure. Preoccupation with the "dominant" family type, necessitated by the almost theological beliefs of early commentators, may have deflected attention from other issues of critical importance to the broader demographic discussion. We need to know more about the forces behind family formation, development, and extinction—the forces which generated the interaction between family structure and social and economic change, and which are the focus of this exploration of Irish family structure.

Whether the subject of study is a Chayanovian subsistence community or a commercialized, socially differentiated community, much can be learned from the size and structure of family/producer units and from the means by which family structure "fits" the changing composition of family and farm into the larger social matrix of townland/village and nation. Indeed, the evidence below suggests that family—or more precisely, "household"—formation may be a critical element in population control and in the general economic/demographic function.

The dispersed settlement pattern of the Irish countryside might lead one to expect a preponderance of nuclear family households greater than in those areas of Europe where village settlement prevailed.[2] With the lack of rigid physical boundaries around inhabited areas, and of village control over land and housing allocation, and the relative ease of acquiring building space and materials, the Irish countryman of the pre-famine period should have been able to form new nuclear family units with relative ease, especially in comparison to his continental neighbors. However, this appears not to have been the case.

In his study of Austrian peasants of the late eighteenth century, Berkner found that roughly 25 percent of peasant families were in some way extended. The figure was identical for the peasants of Killashandra parish in Cavan.[3] The implications of this coincidence are wide-ranging. Not only does it suggest that many Irish peasants were living under social or economic restrictions which retarded the formation of independent family units, but it also raises serious questions about traditional interpretation of the Irish demographic experience. Kenneth Connell, in *The Population of Ireland, 1750–1845*, argued that the Irish peasant, always eager to marry young, created the pre-famine population explosion because the spread of potato farming provided the opportunity for subdivision and, hence, for easy and early marriage.[4] The parallel between Irish and Austrian figures for family extension, however, suggests that, at least on the eve of the famine, the opportunity to form independent nuclear units did not differ significantly between Ireland and Austria, nor, perhaps, between Ireland and other parts of Europe.

The figure of gross family extension tells us nothing about the nature of family formation or family experience. For Berkner this calculation was only the beginning of a complicated analysis of the family experience over time, or what he called the family cycle. In challenging Laslett's emphasis on the nuclear family as the historical norm for Europe, Berkner argued that the family moved through various stages which were related to marriage and child-rearing. Young couples planning to marry often found it difficult or impossible (depending on the social necessity for domestic independence as well as on economic conditions) to establish households of their own and therefore had to begin their married lives as secondary family units in the parents' homes (usually the parents of the husband). The stem family thus created the first and critical stage of Berkner's family cycle. A classic nuclear stage followed, beginning with the parents' deaths and the birth of children to the new couple. Finally, that couple's eldest son married and brought in his wife to create a new stem family.[5] Because the nuclear stage of child-rearing was the longest phase of this cycle, at any given time (such as a census day) the family structure of a community was primarily nuclear even though the majority of its families and individuals lived within some sort of extended family during their lifetime.

Using a similar but more complicated family cycle model, it is possible to examine the family experience of the people of Killashandra parish during the pre-famine period of the nineteenth century and test the hypothesis of easy and early marriage which Connell proposed and others have modified.[6] The major difference between the family cycle suggested here and Berkner's is an added emphasis on child-rearing, child support, and child contributions to the household economy. The Chudacoff/Litchfield family cycle employed here consists of the following stages:[7]

1. Beginning: a couple with the wife under the age of fifty has no children.
2. First stage of fertility: children of the head are under the age of seven.

3. Second stage of fertility: children of the head are both above and below the age of seven.
4. Completed fertility: the youngest child of the head is over age seven but under the age of twenty.
5. Elder children: the youngest child at home is over age twenty.
6. Empty nest: the wife of the head is age fifty or over with no children at home.

Because this cycle does not contain nuclearity as a variable, the nature and frequency of family extension can be measured along a scale which approximates the experience of family maturation. This method is particularly useful when dealing with data based on census enumeration, as it permits extrapolation from a single instant to a schema illustrating a lifetime of family changes.

Because it rests on a researcher's parameters and assumes a certain continuity over time, this procedure cannot be used categorically to interpret past experience, especially in a society like pre-famine Ireland, which manifests such dramatic demographic changes. The age parameters, although consistent with observed experience in Ireland and other European countries, might be adjusted to produce slightly different results.

Yet despite these limitations, the six-stage family cycle is an invaluable tool for examining social structure in Ireland. And, though it precludes precise description of family structure during the earlier part of the century, it illuminates with unusual accuracy the relationship between family organization, fertility, child-rearing, child contributions to the family, and the social and economic pressures which weighed on the community during the late pre-famine period.

Most important, the six-stage cycle facilitates scrutiny of the differences between farming and laboring households. Comparison of family structure at each stage of the cycle reveals the pressures under which each group functioned and the influence of family organization on each group's response. Without this approach we would be limited to the aggregate data for these groups, which would obscure much of the household complexity in the community and would tell very little about the forces behind extension by occupational classification of the household head. (See table 4.1.)

My categories are compatible with (but not identical to) those Laslett has proposed. *Vertical extension* combines the "upwards," "downwards," and "stem" categories of his system.[8] In Killashandra, the difference between "upwards" and "downwards" generally is an arbitrary distinction; hence, to avoid misleading precision, the two are combined. True "stem" families also are included to complete the identification of those families which are (1) vertically extended because of family succession, or (2) laterally extended because of labor demand or other forces. For comparative purposes, the Appendix provides a table of family structure using Laslett's criteria (table A.6).

These figures indicate a considerable difference in the family experiences of laborers and farmers. Farmers' families were more likely than those of laborers to be extended in every direction, and they were also more likely to consist of a single member. This might suggest that farmers experienced greater difficulty in establishing new nuclear families than did their laboring neighbors. However, these figures are specific neither to age nor to family cycle stage. They combine familial extension during mid-life and old age with that of the newly married, making it impossible to measure the relationship between marriage, family structure, and economic class. This relationship lies at the heart of the Irish demographic debate and would help to test my suppositions regarding pre-famine agricultural and laboring conditions.

Actually I am attempting to document the reemergence or readjustment of social limitations upon family formation and hence upon

Table 4.1
Household Structure of Killashandra in 1841 (a)

FAMILY TYPE	FARMING FAMILIES (%) (N = 815)	LABORING FAMILIES (N = 588)
Head alone	3.19	2.72
Nuclear	65.40	76.53
Vertical extension	9.57	6.80
Lateral extension	18.53	12.10
Complex extension	3.31	1.87

SOURCE: Killashandra Study File.

population growth. It would be tempting to call these limits natural, but they clearly depend on the social organization of the community and its reaction to the economic climate of pre-famine Ireland.

The number of families a given area of land could sustain was not determined by a rigid relationship between the productivity of the soil and the food needs of a community. The community could alter the inputs of time, energy, and natural resources of agricultural production. Unfortunately for the laboring population, the decisions on these issues were not reached by a democratic or even paternalistic process. Market forces, totally beyond the control of Cavan farmers, laborers, or landlords, determined the parameters within which Cavan producers could negotiate the best possible return. The rent structure and the shortages of capital and land drove pre-famine farmers to work their land as efficiently and intensively as possible.

The resultant emphasis on tillage in Cavan, facilitated by the potato, aided the initial subdivisions, subletting, and increase in population of the late eighteenth and very early nineteenth centuries. But by 1841 the practice of subdividing had nearly disappeared. Furthermore, just as labor requirements for smaller farms were decreasing, the children of couples who married in the 1820s reached maturity, increasing the labor supply. Consequently, family formation became more and more difficult for both farmers and laborers, but the problems of each were different, controlled by different forces.

Two separate but related reasons for their familial extension are discernible. Because farming families participated in the economic life of the community as both producers and consumers, their labor requirements were important in determining the timing of marriage and the type of familial extension. With impartible inheritance (an increasing probability in the pre-famine period),[9] the formation of a new family meant the replacement of an established one. Thus prospective farmers and their spouses had to await the death or retirement of the family head. The inevitable prolonged adolescence was to become the main feature of the post-famine demographic landscape, and by 1841 it was already well entrenched among the farming classes. The land already held power over the children of the farms.

Labor requirements also affected the structure of farming families throughout the family cycle. Smaller Cavan families responded to the constant demand for labor by turning to unattached relatives outside the nucleus for help on their farms. Thus, families were likely to be extended during the early years of marriage, when children were still too young to help in the field or barn. Likewise, older couples with only one or two children at home were likely to take in other relatives. The demand for labor was so strong that many larger farmers extended their families to include non-nuclear healthy young relatives throughout most of their lives.

Both the inheritance and labor requirements are aspects of the relationship between the peasant family and its land. Chayanov laid out an inverted scenario in which the peasant family increased the size of its holding so that everyone in the household could maximize his labor contribution. According to Chayanov, peasant families unable to expand their holdings either planted more labor-intensive crops or turned to the production of linen and other local necessities.[10] In Cavan, as in most of Ireland, all three of Chayanov's alternatives had become irrelevant by the 1840s. Clearly there was little or no additional land; further agronomic intensification was impossible on the tillage farm (Chayanov himself cited the potato as a classic factor in the intensification decision);[11] and finally, the rural linen industry had long since lost its viability in Cavan (though it played a minor rear-guard economic role). Although Chayanov did not deal with such a circumscribed situation, his theory predicts the direction that the farming family would have to take to adapt to it: the family would have to adjust its own size, instead of its holding size, to achieve the most efficient use of the limited land supply. During early fertility and old age the family had either to extend beyond nuclear membership or increase the use of wage labor. Likewise the optimum time for a couple to marry was before the parents of the inheritor had become unable to work the farm and before all the inheritor's siblings had left the family.

Agricultural laborers living within the farmers' household obviously fulfilled a role similar to that of adult children and other relatives within the farm families' labor equilibrium, providing additional hands when the farming family could not meet its labor needs. But laborers generally worked only seasonally, and then usually on the larger farms. The mechanisms of family formation

and survival were less complicated for agricultural laborers, but
their family units, once formed, were far more vulnerable to external forces than those of their farming neighbors. As suggested
above, new couples were hard-pressed to find housing as tenants
and landlords began to resist the use of farmland for buildings. But
the most severe problem confronting all laboring families was underemployment and its consequence, poverty. There were no significant inheritance restrictions to retard marriage for laboring couples, but the fine line between subsistence and starvation made too
cavalier an attitude dangerous. As a result, although laboring couples found marriage "easy," they found the formation of an independent family unit difficult.

Consideration of the forces affecting both laborers and farmers
during the late pre-famine period reveals how the relationships
among their family formation, family structure, and the economic
climate of the community differed. Although farming families were
sensitive to radical changes in market conditions, their control over
their own food supply cushioned the effects of normal economic
change. A moderate fluctuation in certain prices or rents might alter
their labor requirements, but such changes were usually gradual.
Furthermore, as Chayanov argued, any small change in productivity
would most likely either be absorbed or compensated for by farm
consumption patterns rather than through an alteration of the labor/
production equilibrium.[12] Such changes would have little, if any,
immediate effect on the inheritance pattern on which marriage and
new-family formation were founded. On the other hand, laborers
were subject to direct pressure from economic variations. Employment and housing depended both on the reading of economic conditions by farmers and on the demographic structure of the laboring
population. During hard times farmers invested less of their scarce
capital in hired labor, depriving laboring families of their liveli-
hoods. Even during good times, the farmers' reluctance to turn
profit-making land over to laborers for use either as conacre or
garden land inflated the cost of land that was available. During good
times laborers would also find food costs higher and housing scarce.
While the farming community could continue to transform slowly to
meet modern conditions, laborers were vulnerable to the play of an
increasingly complex market system over which they had no con-

trol. Between 1821 and 1841, laborers paid the price for the great population increase of the previous half-century through higher marriage age, higher emigration and infant mortality rates, and a general decline in living standards. The famine itself would select them for special and horrible treatment.

THE FAMILY CYCLE

The details of the relationship between family structure and the pressures discussed above can best be demonstrated by a close examination of the family cycle, and the differences between farmers and laborers reveal the differences between their family structures and economic pressures.[13] Before presenting the results of my study of the family cycle, I should discuss the measurements attempted and the complications encountered.

My aim is to measure the degree of difficulty the members of the two groups had in marrying and establishing independent households, and the nature and causes of family extension throughout a family's existence. Age suggests itself as a variable for studying both questions. However, as figure 4.1 demonstrates, the information can be confusing. From this graph of the percentage of married males living in nuclear households, two generalizations follow. First, as expected, nuclearity follows a certain logical progression for both groups: low during early adulthood, increasing during middle age, and falling off during old age. Second, it is clear to see that the experiences of the groups differed considerably. Laborers appear to have had either a more flexible or a more vulnerable family experience, with greater extremes of early extension and middle-age nuclearity. This is useful and important information, but because it cannot be easily related to data on childhood and fertility, not much can be inferred about the causes of these observed differences.

Another point is worth noting before invoking the six-stage family cycle: the definition of our unit of measurement is crucial to the interpretation of evidence. Because we are following the formation of families as well as their existence, the conjugal unit serves as the basic unit of analysis. A comparison of figures 4.1 and 4.2 will help to clarify the reasons for this strategy. The differences between figure 4.1, which includes all married men, and figure 4.2, which

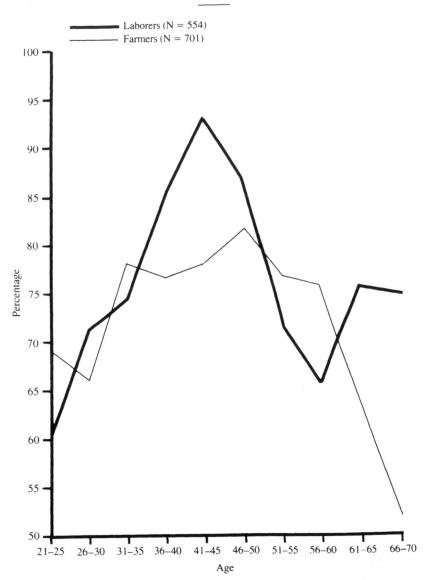

Figure 4.1 Percentage of Married Farming and Laboring Males in Nuclear Families, by Five-Year Cohort. (From the Killashandra Study File; see
Appendix.)

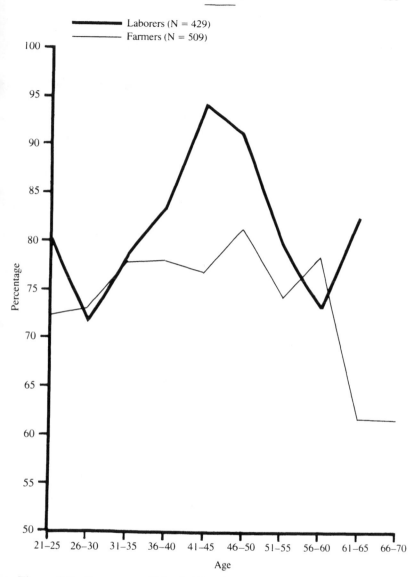

Figure 4.2 Percentage of Married Farming and Laboring Male Household Heads in Nuclear Families, by Five-Year Cohort. (From the Killashandra Study File.)

examines only married males who were heads of households, are extremely important: the experience of farmers appears generally the same in both graphs, with the important exception of the age cohort twenty-five to thirty; but the experience of laboring males appears significantly different. Laborers appear far more nuclear in figure 4.2 than in figure 4.1, and those over age sixty-five are too few to consider statistically. The differences are attributable, of course, to the exclusion from figure 4.2 of married males who were not heads of households. The young people attempting to start a family under privation are the major concern of this examination. Thus, to track the experience of laborers through late adolescence and early adulthood, we must deal primarily with the individual couple rather than larger family aggregates.

Finally, a few words about occupational identification: the 1841 manuscript census forms requested individual occupational titles for all family members, permitting the classification of individuals according either to their own occupations or to those of the heads of the households in which they lived. While at first it might appear that a more precise study could be made using individuals' occupations, careful consideration of the problem with which we are dealing and of the nature of pre-famine society suggests the need for a familial approach to this classification question. For example, farmers' sons normally were classified as laborers and their daughters as spinners, the same occupations listed for most children of laboring households. Clearly, to categorize married farmers' sons living at home and likely awaiting an inheritance as ''laborers'' would skew the analysis. Therefore, except where noted, I have categorized individuals according to the occupation of their family head.

Another potential source of misunderstanding (discussed in chapter 3) is that the term "laborer" applied to several occupations in pre-famine Cavan. The wage laborer, the cotter, and the farm servant all occupied separate niches in Cavan's agricultural economy, and therefore they should be examined separately for significant differences between their experiences. Because they always lived with their employers, farm servants are easily distinguishable from other laborers, but this is of little use in family analysis because few farm servants married or lived with relatives. Because wage laborers and cotters cannot be distinguished on the basis of the manuscript census, they must be studied as a single group. This is unfortunate, but hardly a handicap. Both cotters and wage laborers suffered the economic hardships of underemployment, insecurity, and poverty, and though the degrees of their suffering may have differed slightly (depending on the relationship between grain and potato prices), there is no evidence of great differences in living standards. More important, there is little reason to suppose that the children of cotting and wage laboring families faced different problems in forming new households; each competed for the same housing and employment opportunities.

The situation is slightly different for farmers. The file contains information on landholding, gathered from the Tithe Applotment Book of 1832 and from Griffith's Valuation of 1855; thus, groups of farmers can be identified by the size of their farms. However, because not all farmers could be successfully linked with the landholding information, and because this information pertains to either a decade before or a decade after the date of the census, I have used the occupational title only in the main analysis (this also increases the number of cases involved). A separate analysis of the major differences among farmers according to the sizes of their holdings follows the laborer/farmer comparison.

The first stage of the six-stage family cycle is the most critical in the study of both family formation and the relationship between economic and family structures. The time before the birth of the new couple's first child is the best focus for analyzing the difficulty in creating a new household and determining the devices by which the young family coped. Also, by comparing the experiences of farmers and laborers during this stage, we can assess the relative difficulty of marrying.

Figures 4.3 and 4.4 show a nearly identical cycle of nuclearity for men and women within their respective groups. The only noticeable difference is between males and females of farming households during the first stage. But the absence of the wife in five households created a difference in the total number of men and women (fifty-six males and fifty females) in this stage. If the missing wives could have been returned to their families, 73.2 percent of males and 74.5 percent of females would have been counted as living in nuclear

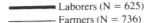

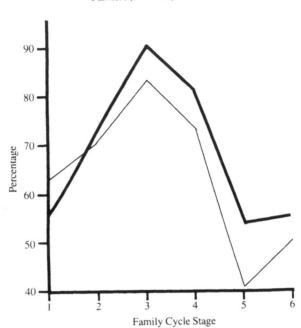

Figure 4.3 Percentage of Married Farming and Laboring Males in Nuclear Families, by Family Cycle Stage. (From the Killashandra Study File.)

households—rendering a truer picture of family formation among farming households. In either case, however, the crucial relationship of the first stage of the family cycle remains unchanged. Laboring couples were far less likely to form nuclear families between the time of their marriage and the birth of their first child: only 55 percent of married laboring males and females without children had established households of their own, compared with 63.2 to 74.5 percent of farming couples.

The reason for the delay can be seen in figures 4.5 through 4.8, which show the type of family extension characterizing each stage of the family cycle for the two groups. Laboring couples were three

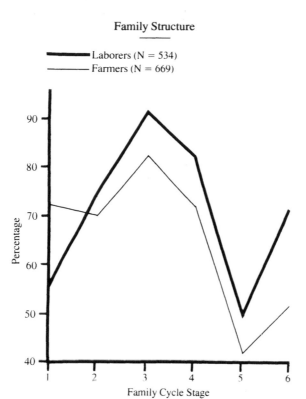

Figure 4.4 Percentage of Married Farming and Laboring Females in Nuclear Families, by Family Cycle Stage. (From the Killashandra Study File.)

times more likely than farming couples to be living in a family with vertical extension (normally, married children living with an ascendant relative), but considerably less likely to be living in a laterally extended family (i.e., a married couple living with a sibling of either spouse). This is an important indicator of the forces behind family complexity in pre-famine Cavan. The high incidence of the vertically extended family among laborers is a symptom of the economic uncertainties of the laboring household. The insecurity of temporary employment hindered the hopes of laboring couples for a constant level of income. By moving into the established household of a parent, a laborer reduced his risk of catastrophe by increasing

140 Family Structure

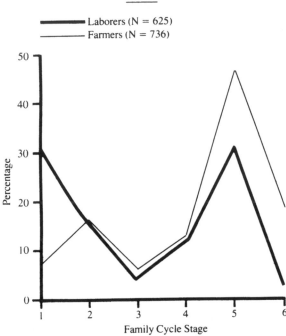

Figure 4.5 Percentage of Married Farming and Laboring Males in Vertically Extended Households, by Family Cycle Stage. (Killashandra Study File.) The presence of vertical extension in stage 6 is due to the presence of grandchildren, nephews, and nieces of the household head.

the number of able bodies contributing to the family's income. An additional adult did not substantially alter the consumption/production ratio of the household. Indeed, considering the alternative loss of a healthy young male's potential wages, the decision was probably beneficial to both the old family unit and the newly formed one.

The extension of farming families was totally different during this stage. The minimal incidence of vertical extension and the relatively high incidence of lateral extension are signs of the land/labor equilibrium at work. Young farming couples could establish families independent of their parents, but the labor requirements of the farms

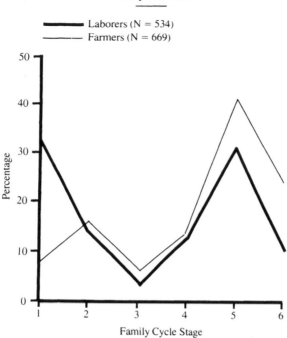

Figure 4.6 Percentage of Married Farming and Laboring Females in Vertically Extended Households, by Family Cycle Stage. (Killashandra Study File.) The presence of vertical extension in stage 6 is due to the presence of grandchildren, nephews, and nieces of the household head.

they controlled far outstripped their capacity for work and created a need for additional hands. Statistics on full-time farm labor (i.e., servants living with a farm family) confirm that labor demand had more to do with the extension than did economic hardship. During the first stage, while lateral extension was at its peak, farming families employed a high proportion of outside agricultural labor; on the average, they employed 80 percent more labor then than during the peak stage of fertility.[14] Their households also contained a high proportion of lodgers and other unrelated co-residents.

Several aspects of the first stage of the cycle tell much about the social and economic structure of pre-famine Cavan. Laborers found fewer social barriers to marriage than did farmers. Establishing

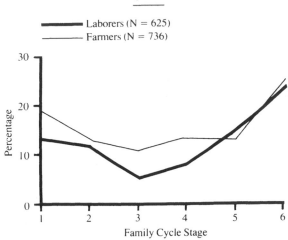

Figure 4.7   Percentage of Married Farming and Laboring Males in Laterally Extended Families, by Family Cycle Stage. (Killashandra Study File.)

independent households, however, was more difficult because of the relationship between the individual and economic productivity. The laborer, lacking all control over property, had neither immediate nor long-range prospects for economic security and, therefore, no real incentive for delaying marriage. Yet once he had married he had every reason to seek an alternative to the nuclear family—one in which the entire responsibility for survival would not fall upon the strength and good fortune of two individuals.

Farming children tended to delay marriage until they had control over a farm. Such control did not guarantee security; there was still the landlord to deal with. Once they had established themselves on their land, however, they entered into full economic membership in the peasant community, participating as consumers and producers, workers and employers.

The second stage of the family cycle represents the early years of marital fertility. A family moved from the first to the second stage with the birth of the first child and remained there until that child reached the age of seven. Certainly the most dramatic of the changes attending childbearing and rearing was the rapid nuclearization of laboring families. Among both farmers and laborers at this stage the

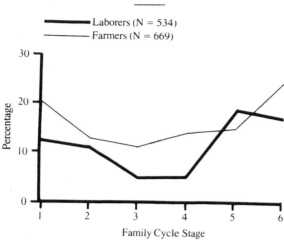

Figure 4.8 Percentage of Married Farming and Laboring Females in Laterally Extended Families, by Family Cycle Stage. (Killashandra Study File.)

percentages of individuals in nuclear families increased, but the dramatic movement of laboring families from 55 percent to 73 percent nuclear dwarfs the inconsistent 3 percent change for farming couples. Still, over 25 percent of laboring families failed to form independent households.

This decrease in extension for laboring households was due to a rapid decline in the number of vertically extended households (see figures 4.5 and 4.6). The percentage of couples in laterally extended households remained fairly constant (figures 4.7 and 4.8), while the percentage living in households both laterally and vertically extended fell dramatically. Although a new baby brought little additional economic strain (its consumption was negligible and could not upset even the precarious balance of the laboring economy), laboring couples apparently were pressed to leave the parents' household when the first grandchild was born. My data do not show how they were pressured, and other evidence is scarce.

The reasons for their expulsion were most likely tied to the logic of family experience itself, and to the physical conditions of the household. The birth of a child signaled the beginning of a biological process which (in this non-contraceptive society) would last for twenty years or so and create a new, large familial group. This in itself would have marked the second stage as a logical point at which to seek independence; but as we have seen, compelling economic reasons for remaining may have outweighed the logic of departing had it not been for certain reinforcing factors. First, there was the physical crowding.[15] Almost invariably, laborers lived in single-room cabins, usually of mud, to which the addition of the new spouse at the outset of marriage must have required quite an adjustment for all concerned; the arrival of an infant could only have recharged the tensions.

There were also younger siblings to consider. Laboring children could not expect an impartible inheritance, and there were usually younger children awaiting their opportunities to marry, opportunities which may well have depended on the departure of their elder sibling and his spouse from the household.

The conflict between two generations of women under one roof is an integral part of post-famine Irish folk wisdom and sociology.[16] However, although this conflict certainly existed in some pre-famine families, it would be an egregious error simply to transpose post-famine conditions into the earlier period. For pre-famine farming families such conflict is understandable. In these households the arrival of the new couple signaled the end of the parents' reign as undisputed heads of the family, and in symbol and fact marked the irreversible beginning of their old age and dependency. Considering the uncertainty of authority and the emotional difficulty parents must have had in accepting a declining role in the family and society, it is hardly surprising that this period was one of potential family conflict.

Among laborers, family extension was not part of a long-term life experience. It was a way of dealing with the temporary problems that confronted the poor when they tried to establish new family units. Young laboring couples came to live with their parents not to usurp their households; they came seeking survival. The very rapid decline of vertically extended laboring families visible in figures 4.5 and 4.6 indicates that laboring, secondary nuclear units were leaving rather than succeeding their primary units. This is made especially clear by the different experiences of farmers and laborers during the transition from the first to the second family cycle stage. Among farming families the percentage of stem families actually increased during this period. Perhaps more important, throughout the first four stages of the family cycle (encompassing all the fertile years) the experience of farming families evolved much more gradually than did that of laboring families. This reflects the basic biology of the farm cycle: the vertical farming family waxed and waned with the survival and death of the older parents, whereas laboring families were condemned by economic constraints to lives of great uncertainty and constant poverty. Their parents' households could not sustain them long enough for them to achieve succession.

The third stage of the cycle, representing later fertility (children both above and below the age of seven), shows the continuation and climax of the trends discussed above. Although laboring couples surpassed farming couples in the percentage of nuclearity by stage 2, the percentage continued to grow—and grew more quickly—in stage 3 (figures 4.3 and 4.4); and once again, the rapid decline in vertical families accounts for the change. The percentages of nuclearity for both groups rose to their peaks, 90.0 percent for laboring males and 82.7 percent for farming males. For both groups the process of child-rearing clearly dominated this third stage: all family extension decreased for both groups. The percentages of laboring couples in vertical families fell to the lowest points of the entire cycle. Also, in farming families the number of farm servants continued to drop (from .26 per household in stage 2 to .20 in stage 3), while in laboring families the number of lodgers and visitors dropped (from .35 per household to .30).

All these factors reflect the common experience of child-rearing. In both farming and laboring households the growing number of children made familial extension increasingly rare. By the age of twelve or thirteen, farmers' children had begun working on the farm, which explains the decrease in lateral family extension as well as in the number of farm servants living in farm households. These factors were of little consequence for the average laboring family; certainly the help of elder male children with the tending of the cot or conacre land and the help of elder girls with child care eased the burdens of the laboring parents, but the children were still too young (averaging an age of 8.15 for boys and 7.55 for girls) to hire themselves out and make a real economic contribution to the family. For the laboring family the continued decline of familial extension was due to the completion of the exodus from the vertical household. The forces behind this exodus were the same as during stage 2, only greatly increased. The continued coexistence of two families was no longer possible unless the young husband or wife was the last child of the heads of the household.

The fourth stage signals the completion of fertility and in many ways reflects the experiences of the first stage of the cycle. With their youngest child between seven and twenty years of age, the couple could begin to count on their elder children for an increasingly adult contribution to the family economy. During this phase, laboring children started thinking about marriage, and vertical extension among their families began to rise once again (see figures 4.5 and 4.6).

Because of the inheritance process, farming families do not yet show a similar increase in vertical extension. In stage 4 the head of a farming family and his wife were still young and vigorous and not prepared to hand over family control to their elder children. The average age of farming husbands during this stage was 53.65 years and that of their wives was 48.03. The fact that the average age of sons (13.26 years) was considerably lower than that of daughters (16.44) would seem to indicate that the older sons were leaving home, perhaps to marry and form the high percentage of nuclear households observed for young farmers in stage 1 of the cycle.

The fourth stage was a time of maturation. Figures 4.9 and 4.10 show the percentage of children at each age working as laborers or spinners or attending school. Farmers' children of both sexes were more likely to contribute economically to the family than were their laboring counterparts. Farmers' sons between ages ten and fourteen were twice as likely as laborers' sons to work as laborers. This statistic probably represents work on their parents' farms and not outside wage labor, but it clearly signifies a difference between the family organizations of the two groups. As early as age ten, 13.7 percent of farming boys worked to sustain their family farms while only 2.2 percent of laborers' children worked to help support their families. Not until age fifteen were the sons of laborers more likely to be identified as laborers than the sons of farmers. The percentages

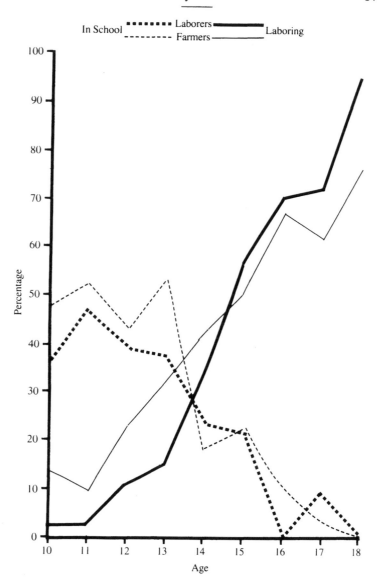

Figure 4.9 Childhood Work and Education Experience: Farming and Laboring Males. (Killashandra Study File.) Farmers' children: N = 488. Laborers' children: N = 314.

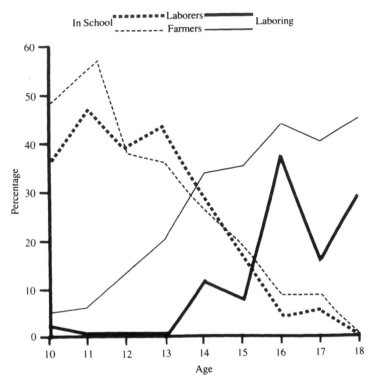

Figure 4.10 Childhood Work and Education Experience: Farming and Laboring Females. (Killashandra Study File.) Farmers' children: N = 490. Laborers' children: N = 260.

of male children in school confirm this, although they reveal an unusual side effect of economic difficulty. While farmers' sons were more likely than laborers' sons to attend school at every age but 14, a surprising number of laboring males obtained a formal education for a considerable period of childhood.

The experience of female children is even more surprising. Laboring girls, too, remained in school because there was no income-producing work at home. They were actually more likely than farming girls to be in school between the ages of twelve and fifteen, and only slightly less likely before and after that time. Once again, farming children leaving school to work at home made the difference. The number of farmers' daughters employed at home as spinners rose steadily from age ten on, reaching 20 percent by age thirteen, 35 percent at age fourteen, and peaking at 60 percent at age nineteen. Remarkably, the daughters of laboring couples did not even begin spinning until age fourteen, and their numbers never rivaled the farming girls'. This is difficult to explain, given the acute poverty of the laboring population. According to Coote, the most likely explanation was that laboring families never became involved in textile production because looms and wheels were so costly.[17] When the linen industry declined during the 1830s and farming families could neither pay workers to operate their equipment nor commit an adult male's labor to such activity, women and girls (for whom there was no paying work) continued to operate the otherwise idle wheels, producing some financial return. But for laboring females to have invested in the necessary equipment would have been irrational. Whatever the explanation, laboring girls were rarely able to help out financially at home.

Other evidence of the differences in childhood experience lies in the age structure of the child population. Figure 4.11, showing the children in each two-year cohort as a percentage of all children between ages ten and nineteen (two-year cohorts are used to correct for the overrepresentation of even-numbered ages), reveals that both laboring boys and girls left home at younger ages than their farming counterparts. The critical time for laboring boys seems to have been their fifteenth year. Between age fourteen and fifteen the number of laboring boys dropped by over 50 percent, and that of laboring girls by 35 percent. This exodus began at precisely the same moment that laboring parents began classifying their children as workers (see figure 4.9 above). Another measure of this phenomenon is the average age of the oldest child in the households of each group: 15.65 for farming households and only 12.23 for laboring households.

Thus, economic hardship had some unexpected effects on children of the poor, laboring population. Their lack of work and the resultant opportunity for education appear as strange corollaries of poverty; but the early expulsion of children from their parents' homes hints at the less positive aspect of economic pressure on laboring families: the difficulty of maintaining family units.

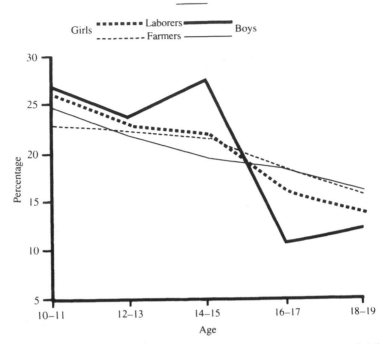

Figure 4.11   Children in Each Two-Year Cohort as a Percentage of All Children Aged Ten to Nineteen. (Killashandra Study File.) Farmers' children: N = 516 males, 517 females. Laborers' children: N = 334 males, 269 females.

The experience of farming children also reflects the major economic relationship between their parents and the community. Although education was an important part of childhood on the farm, it appears to have been subordinate to the needs of the land. In a similar manner, the ability of the farm to absorb labor and the role of the farming child as potential inheritor of the rights to the land enabled and encouraged the children to remain at home longer than laborers' children.

The farm families' ability to provide support past adolescence helps explain the persistence of lateral extension among farm families throughout the family cycle. It also helps explain the major differences between laboring and farming families during the final stages of the family cyle. Stages 5 and 6 signify the end of the original family unit and either its extinction or its rejuvenation. Households with all children at home over the age of twenty comprise stage 5; those of married or widowed persons over the age of fifty with no children living at home comprise stage 6. When I first applied these stages of family development, I believed that they would follow one another; but my study shows that, at least for pre-famine Cavan, stages 5 and 6 seem to represent different end points for the family, requiring that these stages be considered together.

Figures 4.12 through 4.15 demonstrate once again a difference between the experience of farming and laboring families. For both elder males and females, farmers were more likely than laborers to share a household with their mature children. This was particularly true for widows. Ninety-one percent of farming widowers in stages 5 and 6 lived with their children, compared with only 66.6 percent of laboring widowers. The figures for women were 60 percent of farmers' widows and no laboring widows.[18] These figures, like the others already cited, reflect the greater difficulty laboring families had in accommodating additional family members.

Figures 4.3 through 4.9 make clear how the difference in family composition affected family extension. Farming and laboring groups had similar experiences during these stages, but there was significant difference in the magnitude of change. Figures 4.5 and 4.6 demonstrate a jump in vertical extension during stage 5 for both groups; however, the increase in vertical families was nearly twice as great in farming families. Surprisingly, considering the high level of vertical extension for laboring couples in stage 1, far fewer laboring children who lived with their aging parents were marrying. The timing of vertical extension in laboring families is responsible for this phenomenon. Young laboring couples co-resident with an ascendant relative were much more likely to have siblings under age twenty within the household. Thus, stage 1 extension was balanced by extension in stages 4 and 5. A similar predictor of stage 5 extension for farmers appears in the bulge in vertical extension during stage 2. The vast difference in the number of cases (123 in stage 2, 34 in stage 5) accounts for the difference in magnitude between these two points of the graph. Thus, for both groups, stage 5 reflects

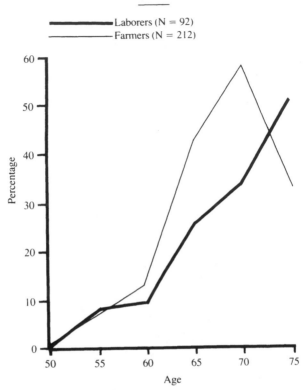

Figure 4.12 Percentage of Married Farming and Laboring Females in Family Cycle Stage 5, by Age. (Killashandra Study File.)

the earlier stages. The significantly higher percentage of farming families who ended their family experience in this stage reflects their greater ability to withstand the forces which led to family disintegration as the household heads reached old age.

The sixth and final stage of the family cycle, the empty nest, is more difficult to interpret. For most farming couples just over age fifty and in good physical and financial health, it might have meant independence from the pressures and problems of the stem family. The great majority of individuals in stage 6 were part of a couple living together (94.4 percent of males, 93.1 percent of females). As

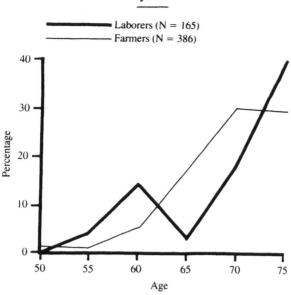

Figure 4.13 Percentage of Married Farming and Laboring Males in Family Cycle Stage 5, by Age. (Killashandra Study File.)

Table 4.2
Old Age and Co-Residence

CATEGORY	PERCENTAGE WITHOUT CHILDREN	PERCENTAGE WITH CHILDREN
Farming Couples	50.0	50.0
Laboring Couples	90.9	9.1
Farming Widows	40.0	60.0
Laboring Widows	66.6	33.3

SOURCE: Killashandra Study File.

the couple or surviving member grew older, the isolation of nuclear existence became burdensome and even unsafe. Obviously the outlook was more ominous for laborers, whose income depended on their physical well-being. For them, life after age fifty was uncertain unless they could count on their children's support. In this light, table 4.2 gives still more evidence of the laboring population's vulnerability. Laboring couples and widows were unable either to

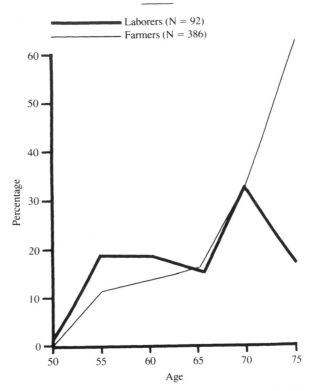

Figure 4.14 Percentage of Married Farming and Laboring Females in Family Cycle Stage 6, by Age. (Killashandra Study File.)

maintain or to reestablish habitation with their children with the same frequency as farmers.

Figures 4.3 and 4.4 give further evidence of the same phenomenon. The disparity between farmers and laborers increases considerably during the sixth stage. Here again, economics prevented many laboring families from taking in their elderly parents.

FARM SIZE AND FAMILY STRUCTURE

Thus far I have dealt with the farming community as a group, ignoring economic differences which might have existed within the farming class. As noted above, I took this approach because I could

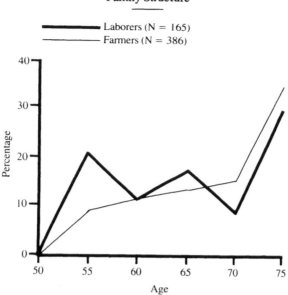

Laborers (N = 165)
Farmers (N = 386)

Figure 4.15 Percentage of Married Farming and Laboring Males in Family Cycle Stage 6, by Age. (Killashandra Study File.)

not identify the land-holding status of all farmers. Furthermore, the results of my research suggest that the different economic forces which affected the laboring and farming groups are the major determinants of pre-famine family organization and that, as such, a dual-group comparison would be the most straightforward and useful.

Still, the tremendous importance of farm size in the debate over the modernization of agriculture[19] and in the contemporary debates over Ireland's condition require that I analyze the impact of farm size on family structure and, eventually, fertility. Also, the variations in family experience due to farm size help to confirm my general argument regarding the relationship between land and family organization.

From a theoretical perspective, one might expect that if the relation between family extension and farm size were due to the labor-equilibrium needs of the family during its various stages of development, the relationship between farm size and familial extension would be linear and in a positive direction. However, several intervening variables affect the relationship. Inheritance also affected the type and timing of family extension in rural Ireland. Because the importance of inheritance to all phases of family life increases with the amount and value of property held, a reasonable prediction is that its influence will be greater among the larger farmers.

In a similar way, the labor equilibrium itself varies according to farm size. Although labor requirements and, often, the responses to them vary directly with the size of the farm, the relationship usually is not linear. Two independent factors are responsible. First, soil quality influences land use. Larger farms might indicate more rough pasture and less tillage, which require less labor per acre. Second, even on land of uniform quality, the economies of scale operating in spade culture often prevented the full intensification of tillage. Furthermore, because larger farms also meant greater potential for commercial orientation, farmers may have responded to the labor equilibrium in a more capitalistic way, i.e., with wage labor. For these reasons, the large farmer's experience differed from the small and middling farmers'; but in all cases we can still identify the operation of the variables discussed above when dealing with farmers as a group.

To carry out the analysis of farm size and family structure, I have divided the farming community into three groups according to their acreage as reported in the Tithe Applotment Book for Killashandra:[20]

Group	No. Statute Acres	No. Farms
Small Farmers	1 to 12 Acres	123
Middling Farmers	13 to 25 Acres	158
Large Farmers	More Than 25 Acres	101

Of course, the definitions of small, middling, and large are a question of judgment. I chose these parameters because they fulfilled the qualitative requirement that the groups conform to contemporary standards.[21] Fortunately, the parameters create three groups of households of sufficient size to permit statistical analysis without violating the pre-famine usage of the qualifying adjectives.

Figures 4.16 through 4.18 display the results of family analysis for these three groups.[22] These figures show no clear, uniform relationship between farm size and family experience. One unexpected

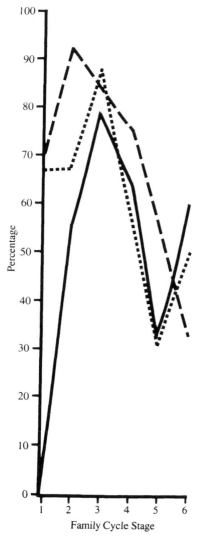

Small farmer, 1–12 acres (Irish) (N = 123)
Middling farmer, 13–25 acres (Irish) (N = 158)
Large farmer, 26–100 acres (Irish) (N = 101)

Figure 4.16 Percentage of Nuclearity in the Families of Small, Middling, and Large Farmers, by Family Cycle Stage. (Killashandra Study File.) Some cells in figures 4.16, 4.17, and 4.18 contain insufficient cases for meaningful commentary. Stage 1 for small farmers and stage 6 for small and middling farmers contain only three cases each.

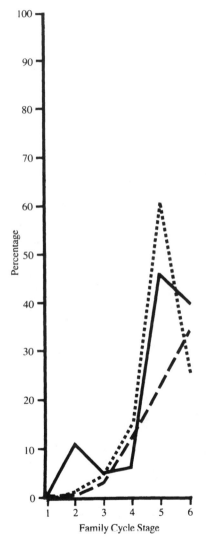

Figure 4.17 Percentage of Vertical Extension in the Families of Small, Middling, and Large Farmers, by Family Cycle Stage. (Killashandra Study File.)

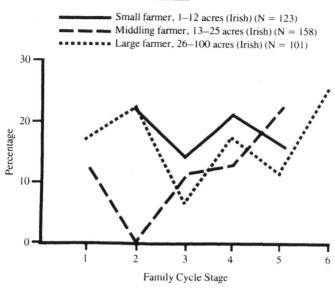

Figure 4.18   Percentage of Lateral Extension in the Families of Small, Middling, and Large Farmers, by Family Cycle Stage. (Killashandra Study File.)

finding is that middling farmers appear far more nucleated than both the small and large farmers (figure 4.16). Only in the third stage of the cycle are the middling farmers surpassed in nuclearity, and then only by a small margin. (In stage 6 there are only three middling farming families and comparison is therefore impossible.) The reason behind this inconsistent relationship between the three groups is the absence of a strict linear relationship between farm size and family structure. The relationship which does exist becomes more understandable if viewed in conjunction with the percentages of vertical and lateral extension.

Figures 4.17 and 4.18 together contain evidence that middling farmers did indeed occupy an intermediate position between the small and large farmers, but that evidence requires considerable explanation. As noted before, lateral extension among farmers indicates the impact of the labor equilibrium on family structure. Small farmers relied more heavily on familial extension for labor requirements than either middling or large farmers (figure 4.18). Of course the labor requirements of the larger farmers were greater, but they were likely to meet those needs through recourse to the labor market (see table 4.3).

It is not so easy to explain why, during most stages of the cycle, the large farmers were also more likely than middling farmers to be extended laterally. Perhaps their labor requirements were so large that both family extension and wage labor were possible or necessary. Perhaps their laterial extension was as much a sign of charity toward landless relatives as of economic rationality, and the large farmers were the only group with sufficient resources to consider such action. The fact that the large farmers fell below the middling farmers in lateral extension at the height of child bearing (when the household was crowded but not well-supplied with workers) might reflect this. My information precludes more definite answers. However, it is clear that small farmers were more likely to seek a familial rather than a commercial answer to their labor needs.

In the case of vertical family extension, the situation appears reversed, with large farmers showing a dramatic propensity for vertical extension during the fifth stage of the cycle (see table 4.17). The large and middling farmers appear to have had very similar experiences, with no vertical extension during the first and second stages and moderate extension during the third and fourth stages. Small farmers had moderate extension during the second stage and lower extension during the third and fourth stages. Although the

Table 4.3

Extra-Familial Labor on Farms, by Farm Size

FARM SIZE	AVERAGE NUMBER OF LABORERS AND FARM SERVANTS RESIDENT IN THE HOUSEHOLD	AVERAGE NUMBER OF DAY LABORERS
Small	.10	.37
Middling	.21	.43
Large	.51	.64

SOURCE: Killashandra Study File.

differences were not so great as to produce a clear relationship in these early stages of the family cycle, both middling and large farmers had fewer ascendant relatives during the early- and high-fertility stages and rapidly increasing extension during late fertility and after the end of fertility.[23] During the fifth stage the large farmers reached an amazing rate of 60.0 percent vertical extension. Of course, this reflects the inheritance and family-transmission process discussed above, and it is clear from these figures that the importance of the inheritance process was far greater among the large farmers.

This brief discussion of the family experience of different types of farmers confirms the importance of the relationship between the family and the farm in rural Cavan. It also confirms that this relationship in turn depended on the labor equilibrium and the inheritance process. Because of the different effects of these phenomena on family structure, there is no simple relationship between relative wealth and family extension. The wealthiest farmers were less likely to be nucleated than the middling farmers, but more likely than the poorest farmers. As we have seen, this was due to the variable importance of the labor equilibrium and the inheritance process to these different groups.

It is interesting that the laborers' family experience resembled the middling farmers' more than they did the small farmers'. Both laborers and middling farmers show a high percentage of nuclearity, low lateral extension, and relatively low overall extension. The small farmers were far less likely to be nucleated and far more likely to live in laterally extended households than either their laboring or wealthier farming neighbors. Given the poverty of many of these small farmers, it is clear that there was no simple relationship between poverty and family experience; rather a connection must be sought in the family's relationship to labor and production.

Small farmers faced a different set of problems then did large farmers during times of increasing economic activity. As we have seen, with the dramatic exception of 1818–25, the higher agricultural prices and the more advanced agricultural trade during the first half of the nineteenth century helped drive rents higher. While in many cases rent increases reflected increased profits, this was less likely to be true of small farmers. The small farmer was unable to participate in a market economy for a number of reasons. In addition to the obvious limitation imposed by the smaller area available for market crops (both in absolute and proportionate measures), the small farmer faced more severe marketing and capital problems than did his strong farming neighbors. For example, because of the limited quantities of produce which the small farmer had to deal with and the importance of his labor on the farm, he often entrusted his produce to a carter for delivery and sale at a market town, a procedure that was rife with abuse. One witness testified before a government commission studying the corn trade that it was common practice for carters to bypass the public scale and sell this grain at the private scales of dealers, where the farmer was shortchanged by dishonest weights and dishonest merchants who were in collusion with the carters.[24] Small farmers also struggled to meet rents without being forced to sell in a glutted market and were less likely to have a manure supply of their own or the cash or credit to purchase manure. As a result, they had a more difficult time increasing their productivity.

Small farmers who by and large were without wage labor and capital, were locked into the difficult position of having to compete for occupation of land with their better-endowed neighbors. Thus, the high incidence of lateral extension is a sign of increasing economic stress and self-exploitation. Paradoxically, the generally low incidence of lateral extension among agricultural laborers indicates the difficulties that confronted them. Without a productive unit of their own, they could not utilize the labor of additional adults.

The middling farmers, with between thirteen and twenty-five acres, were above the threshold of commercial participation. That they hired much more of their labor and practiced lateral extension less frequently demonstrates their ability to manage within a more fully monetized agricultural system than could their small farm neighbors.

Family experience, then, was directly affected by the relationship between the family and the productive unit. The dispersed settlement of the countryside and the general poverty of many of its inhabitants were not the major determinants of family structure.

Instead, the relationship between family and farm was the major determinant. Laborers, divorced from any control over the only major source of production, the land, had to adapt to a harsh economic climate; hence the high incidence of vertical extension early in marriage and the exceedingly high percentage of nuclearity which dominated all other stages of family life. For farmers, the forces behind family extension were tied to their control over the farm. Labor requirements and family transmission patterns affected farms of different sizes in different ways, creating varying degrees and types of family extension; but in all cases farm families responded as producers as well as workers.

Population

5

The rapid growth of population in Ireland during the late eighteenth and early nineteenth centuries has been the cause of considerable debate among historians. Much of the debate has centered around Kenneth Connell's pioneering work, *The Population of Ireland*, which established the high quality of Irish demographic historiography. Connell was one of the first European demographic historians to challenge the linkage of population growth in modern Europe to lower mortality rates, which in turn were credited to improving material conditions. Connell argued that Ireland's growth in population, especially the tremendous expansion between 1750 and 1845, was the result of increasing fertility rates (rather than declining mortality rates) created by lower marriage age.[1] Both developments, Connell believed, depended upon the potato and its role in subdividing land and supplying food for the poor. As he saw it, Irish population grew in a Malthusian way, with the impoverished masses pushing on the means of subsistence.

Connell has been criticized on a number of specific points. Michael Drake has questioned the existence of unusually early marriage in Ireland before the famine, pointing out that most of Connell's evidence consisted of contemporary witnesses who were seldom disinterested.[2] Louis Cullen has questioned the dominant role of the potato in population dynamics, suggesting that the potato was really the result rather than the cause of population growth[3] (a view consistent with the fact, noted in chapter 2 above, that the potato was hardly the dominant tillage crop). The lack of any reliable statistics regarding marriage age before 1841 census, and confusion over the actual timing and speed of the adoption of the potato, perpetuate the argument.

In addition, there is one major conceptual limitation which Connell's methodology imposed upon him and which few of his critics have escaped. Because Connell worked with aggregate figures (i.e., the published census-summary tables), he was unable to examine the influence of his variables across different occupational groups, or the effects of intermediary variables upon his arguments. For instance, he could not study marriage age across occupational groups, nor could he study the effect which farm size, literacy, or emigration had upon marriage age and fertility. Connell's arguments, therefore, and those of most other researchers in the field, either have had to ignore the nuances of the demographic process in Ireland or to offer theoretical arguments based on inconclusive evidence.[4]

This one-dimensional view is particularly unfortunate because Connell's basic argument rests upon a fairly solid economic foundation. His discussion of marriage age centers on the lack of real economic opportunities in Ireland, constantly increasing rent demands, and a culture of poverty, based on the potato, that left early marriage and the love and support of a family the only comforts for impoverished young Irish men and women. To fully understand the operation of the economic forces behind the decrease in marriage age and the consequent rise in fertility, we need to know more about the specific experience of the various social groups in the rural community. As has been shown, there were considerable differences between farming and laboring groups in both their economic and family experiences. If Connell's arguments regarding poverty and marriage age are correct, then differences should also be reflected in the marriage decisions of the two groups, and ultimately in their fertility rates and their contributions to the population increase of this period. The Killashandra evidence suggests the even

more surprising possibility that the curtailment of rising fertility and
the assertion of social controls over the increasingly dangerous imbalance between resources and population most likely began before
the famine and within the poorest sector of the agricultural community.

Connell identified 1780–1830 as the period of rapid population
growth, tying the origins of increased fertility to the movement of
Irish agriculture toward tillage during the last quarter of the century.[5] He linked the marked decrease in the rate of population
growth during the intercensal period of 1831–41 to pre-famine economic difficulties.[6] The aggregate figures for Killashandra parish
actually show a decrease in population during this time.[7]

	Killashandra	Cavan
1831	14,462	228,050
1841	12,562	243,158

The available nominative census information dates from the 1841
census. This census represents either the penultimate point of the
rapid growth of the previous sixty years or, as I shall argue, a
transition stage between the relatively high and relatively low general fertility periods which appear to straddle the famine. Because
the data reveal little about the early phase of the high fertility period, they cannot be taken as new evidence of the origins of this
growth. However, much can be learned about the first four decades
of the nineteenth century, the era of crisis, by studying the elder
cohorts of the parish.

The study of family structure (chapter 4) has shown that the
commercialization of Cavan's agriculture affected farming and laboring families each in quite different ways; and that even within
the farming group there were considerable differences among the
size categories. Unfortunately, Connell's arguments generally ignore these differences. Michael Drake has already pointed out how
this oversight could distort the data, especially regarding marriage
age.[8] At some points Connell did introduce the idea of differences
between the groups, such as when quoting the Poor Law inquiry
witness who reported that below "the class of middling farmers,
unmarried men above 25 years are very common";[9] but he hardly
comments about what the middling and strong farmers may or may

not have been doing to be cited as an exception. Elsewhere, when explaining the desire to marry young, he states bluntly that "no middle class helped to narrow the social wilderness between proprietor and cotter,"[10] and that lacking an intermediate social class, the peasant lost all hope of improving his material well-being.

We have already seen that there were substantial numbers of middling and strong farmers. Furthermore, the family experiences of small farmers differed from those of agricultural laborers, even though their material conditions were similar. If population grew because of the increase in fertility, which in turn was brought on by the changing agricultural economy, there is reason to expect that the differing positions of the groups within that economy would demand different responses to change.

FERTILITY

FAMILY AND HOUSEHOLD SIZE

Since census returns do not contain information regarding live births, it is impossible to obtain precise measurements of fertility.[11] We can, however, gain valuable evidence regarding fertility with which to follow general trends in population growth and compare the relationships between the various social groups and population growth or decline.

Household and family size[12] are, in many ways, two of the most useful variables for understanding population dynamics. In Killashandra parish in 1841, households and families were smaller among small farmers and laborers than among the upper economic groups of middling and large farmers (table 5.1). The enormous gap between laboring and farming families is especially important and raises some serious questions regarding Connell's general argument linking the lower social groups with population growth and his image of the peasantry as a homogeneous group.

The figures for the family size of the farming population mirror the curious relationship noted in the discussion of family experience (chapter 4): those for small and large farmers were nearly identical, while those for middling farmers were the highest of any group in the total population. As argued above, economic conditions of the farming groups, the variable role the family played in agricultural

Table 5.1

Mean Family and Household Size in Killashandra Parish, 1841

GROUP	N	FAMILY SIZE	HOUSE SIZE	FAMILY AS % OF HOUSEHOLD
Laborers	623	4.84	5.21	92.9
Farmers (all)	783	5.71	6.48	88.2
Small Farmers	123	6.19	6.56	94.4
Medium Farmers	158	6.57	7.04	93.3
Large Farmers	101	6.23	7.77	80.0

SOURCE: Killashandra Study File.

production, and the relative importance of the inheritance system contributed to this phenomenon. The smaller family of the one-to-twelve-acre farmers reflects the economic adversity of this group and its inability to utilize surplus labor. Large farmers had smaller families because they married later to accommodate the inheritance process. The substantially larger family unit of the middling farmers demonstrates both their ability to utilize their family labor fully and the lesser importance to them of the inheritance process. The anomaly disappears when we look at household rather than family size, in which case the relationship between wealth and household size is clearly positive, reflecting the overall labor needs of the various farming groups.

There are some figures available for comparison. Francis J. Carney has recently published similar data for a few districts in 1821 (table 5.2).[13] His figures for Cavan are based on a sample of 857 households across the county, and therefore do not bear direct comparison with the 1841 figures. Even so, as the 1841 figures for family and household size are lower than those Carney identified in 1821, it appears unlikely that household or family size increased in the third and fourth decades of the century. This does not necessarily mean that the population stopped growing; an echo effect allowed the total number of families to continue to increase. Still, the force behind the increase in marital fertility apparently was no longer effectively operating to any significant degree. For comparative purposes it is also worth noting that Cavan's experience was fairly typical. The one interesting difference between Cavan and the

Table 5.2

Mean Family and Household Size in Selected Irish Districts, 1821

COUNTY	N	FAMILY SIZE	HOUSEHOLD SIZE	% NON-FAMILY IN HOUSE
Cavan	857	5.13	5.69	9.84
Meath	528	4.86	5.45	10.83
Fermanagh	271	4.97	5.82	14.61
Kings	501	4.94	5.68	13.03
Galway	506	5.25	5.86	10.41

SOURCE: Carney, ''Aspects of Pre-famine Irish Household Size,'' p. 36.

other counties is the relatively small difference between family and household size; while Cavan had the second-largest family size of the five counties, it had the smallest non-family household component. It is also interesting that Cavan most nearly resembled Galway, not its Ulster neighbor Fermanagh. This seems to confirm that human factors, not geography, caused variations in family size and structure.

The guidelines to the relationship between social structure and population dynamics suggested by household and family size data are certainly rough, and may also be misleading. It is possible that emigration and labor patterns could reduce the family size of some social groups while increasing the household size of other groups. Laboring children left home earlier than farming children, and were more likely to take up residence in the household of the farming family for which they worked (chapter 4). This would have decreased the average size of laboring families and households and increased the size of farming households. Thus, family and household size are only an indirect measure of fertility. Those groups with family and household sizes larger than their neighbors must have been more ''favorably'' disposed for high fertility. Families that could absorb the children of other families bore less pressure to limit their own size.

Emigration also affected family size, but here the relationship among social groups is not so well defined (see table 5.3). The poorest (laborers) and wealthiest (large farmers) left the county with the highest frequency. The exodus of laborers is quite understand-

Table 5.3

Migration by Social Group, Killashandra Parish, 1841

GROUP	N	NO. MIGRANTS PER HOUSEHOLD	NO. MIGRANTS/ HOUSEHOLD SENDING MIGRANTS	% MIGRANTS TO NORTH AMERICA
Laborers	244	.42	1.78	62.3
Farmers (all)	276	.38	1.58	65.0
Small Farmers	46	.37	1.34	70.0
Medium Farmers	58	.37	1.51	68.2
Large Farmers	51	.51	1.76	52.6

SOURCE: Killashandra Study File.

Note: This table summarizes the responses of families who were asked to record members who were absent on the night of the census taking. This question was designed to "catch" individuals who might be temporarily transient; it was not designed to measure migration. Only those who misunderstood the question gave information on true migration. Hence, these figures probably understate the true extent of emigration.

able given their economic situation, but the frequency with which they headed to North America is surprising for the same reason. This may be explained in part by chain migration: laboring families were the most likely to have more than one emigrant per household, and of those households sending emigrants to America, 59.4 percent sent more than one. Chain migration, if it did often occur, would help to account for the laborers' ability to overcome the financial barrier which separated them from America. It would also underline the critical importance of the family to the poor and help explain why Cavanites were so conscious of those who had left and why the families considered them very much a part of the family unit.

The precise effect of emigration upon family and household size remains uncertain because these figures do not necessarily reflect the distribution of total migrants over the social groups involved. Still, the data seem to indicate that migration had little overall impact on the relative family size of farmers and laborers; but when acreage is taken into account, it is evident that emigration may have substantially decreased the average family size of the three farming groups vis-à-vis laborers—a difference of at least .138 per household.

The true relationship between family size and fertility can be

Table 5.4

Mean Family Size by Family Cycle, Killashandra Parish

STAGE OF FAMILY CYCLE	FARMING FAMILY SIZE	(N)	LABORING FAMILY SIZE	(N)	% DIFFERENCE
1	2.58	(90)	2.42	(72)	6.24
2	4.40	(116)	4.01	(126)	11.28
3	7.67	(280)	6.60	(212)	13.94
4	6.12	(182)	4.87	(122)	20.45
5	4.59	(52)	3.92	(24)	13.33
6	2.72	(36)	2.12	(25)	22.12
All	5.71		4.84		15.24

SOURCE: Killashandra Study File.

drawn more precisely through the use of the family cycle model. Because the six stages of the model were developed to be sensitive to fertility changes in a household, they are particularly useful for comparing groups in terms of their fertility experiences. If emigration, the more rapid departure of laboring children from their parents' household, or some other "hidden" variable were responsible for the large differences between the sizes of laboring and farming families, family sizes during fertile periods should have been nearly equal. In fact, during stages 2 and 3, which represent the early and middle stages of the family's fertility, the difference between farming and laboring households was considerable; and this was true at every stage of family development (table 5.4). These figures confirm that the difference in family size was attributable to differences in the number of children born to and surviving in the families of both groups.

It appears from this indirect evidence that the laboring sector was less responsible for population growth in the immediate pre-famine period than was the farming sector.

THE CHILD/WOMAN RATIO

Although the census data do not allow the calculation of an accurate general fertility rate, they can be used to generate one of the most frequently used indices of fertility, the child/woman ratio—the number of children zero to four years of age per 1,000 women of childbearing age (here defined as fifteen to forty-nine years of age). This statistic is in some ways more useful than the crude fertility rate, because it is age-specific and therefore more reliable in a population suspected of having undergone significant demographic change. Its drawback as a measure of actual fertility is its vulnerability to distortion created by high rates of infant mortality. In a society where infant mortality is high but constant over the entire population, the child/woman ratio can be used as an effective measure of relative fertility; unfortunately, nothing can be assumed about infant mortality in pre-famine Cavan. Indeed, given the general level of physical suffering among the poorest members of society, the only reasonable surmise would be that they experienced higher infant mortality.

Despite its limitations, the child/woman ratio is still an extremely valuable tool for the study of the critical question of population change. Although it cannot be accepted uncritically as indicating the rate of childbirth, it does permit a detailed analysis of child-survival. From this we can deduce which groups and factors were primarily responsible for changes in the rate of population growth. Population increase, rather than the fertility rate itself, decides the demographic experience of a community.

Table 5.5 gives the child/woman ratios for five-year cohorts of married farming and laboring women. These figures provide very

Table 5.5
Child/Woman Ratios, Killashandra Parish

AGE	FARMING WIVES	(N)	LABORING WIVES	(N)
15–19	.40	(5)	.40	(5)
20–24	.63	(46)	.82	(57)
25–29	1.54	(79)	1.25	(68)
30–34	1.58	(95)	1.30	(91)
35–39	1.27	(74)	1.16	(62)
40–44	.89	(88)	.77	(61)
45–49	.38	(66)	.19	(32)
Average	1.06		1.00	

SOURCE: Killashandra Study File.

important evidence on the nature of population growth in Cavan. For every five-year cohort but one, farming households contained more children under age five per married woman. The only point at which laboring women had more young children living with them was in the first cohort containing significant cases, age twenty to twenty-four. The reasons for this are uncertain; however, as this cohort is at the age of first marriage for most women, it may be a sign of bridal pregnancy, a possibility which would coincide with the general hypothesis regarding laborers advanced earlier: laborers, finding it increasingly unattractive economically to marry, would have attempted to postpone marriage, but as they had no motive for delaying marriage for a specific goal, such as farm inheritance, they had no reason to limit romantic contact with members of the opposite sex. Given Irish social custom and the power of the clergy, a pregnancy in most cases led to marriage—and the start of a new family cycle.

Another analysis (table 5.6) shows that during the first year of marriage, laboring women were slightly more likely to have a child under five living with them; during the next three years, children under five numbered about the same for farming and laboring women; and after the third year, farming women had far more small children at home. These figures are consistent with the hypothesis of different patterns of infant care. It is possible that farming women, in this dairy culture, were already bottle-feeding their infants, while the poorer laboring women, who had limited access to cows' milk, were almost certainly breast-feeding. If such differences existed, the postpartum amenorrhea of laboring women would have been relatively protracted. The first birth of course would have been unaffected, and assuming the typical first birth occurred within the first eighteen months of marriage, we would expect a similar child/woman ratio for the first three years or so; thereafter the extended infertile periods of laboring women would have lowered their relative rate of childbirth.

However likely an assumption of bottle-feeding in pre-famine Ireland may be, it has one major flaw: in traditional societies, the transition from breast to bottle characteristically resulted in dramatic increases in infant mortality, an increase which would more than offset any increase in natural fertility.[14] Virtually nothing is known

Table 5.6
Number of Children under Age Five
of Farming and Laboring Women,
by Years Married, Killashandra Parish

YEARS MARRIED	FARMERS	(N)	LABORERS	(N)
Less than 1	0.45	(20)	0.47	(16)
1	0.61	(23)	0.50	(20)
2	1.08	(13)	1.12	(34)
3	1.13	(16)	1.37	(19)
4	1.56	(25)	1.22	(23)
5	2.08	(13)	1.55	(22)
6	1.86	(21)	1.24	(17)
7	1.58	(14)	1.36	(11)
8	1.59	(27)	1.13	(16)
9	1.17	(18)	1.41	(17)
10	1.69	(16)	1.56	(18)
11	1.62	(26)	0.74	(19)
12	1.33	(15)	1.00	(13)
13	1.19	(21)	1.24	(17)
14	1.11	(18)	1.35	(23)
15	1.36	(22)	0.82	(11)
16	1.40	(10)	1.00	(13)
17	0.50	(6)	0.33	(3)

SOURCE: Killashandra Study File.

about child-feeding in Ireland, so I can offer no conclusions on that subject. Not much more is known about infant mortality; but there is one tantalizing piece of related, indirect evidence. Table 5.7 shows the sex ratio of children aged zero to five in farming and laboring families. While the figures for farming children indicate a normal ratio, with boys outnumbering girls in the early years, among laboring children, girls outnumbered boys during ages one through five.[15] Such a distorted sex ratio in the early years of childhood could have resulted either from poor reporting or from high infant mortality. As there is no reason to suspect underreporting of male children in an agricultural society (the opposite is sometimes found), and as there is every reason to believe that laboring mothers and their children were malnourished, the second explanation seems far more likely. As male fetuses are known to suffer a dispropor-

Table 5.7

Sex Ratio (M/F) of Children Aged 0–5, Killashandra Parish

AGE	FARMERS	(N)	LABORERS	(N)
Less than 1	1.32	(79)	1.06	(74)
1	1.10	(109)	.88	(98)
2	1.11	(133)	1.17	(100)
3	.98	(123)	.87	(101)
4	1.09	(138)	1.00	(94)
5	1.13	(128)	.75	(107)
All	1.11	(710)	.94	(574)

SOURCE: Killashandra Study File.

tionately high incidence of miscarriage and stillbirth, a population which is malnourished or unhealthy would produce an inordinate percentage of female births.[16]

A higher rate of infant mortality among laboring children is also consistent with our knowledge of their living conditions, but it weakens the credibility of the hypothesis regarding breast and artificial feeding. Therefore any conclusions as to the causes of the lower child/woman ratio in laboring families will have to await further work in the field. But the startling fact emerging from this data is that, for whatever reason, laboring families had fewer surviving children than farming families.

One other variable appears to have an association with fertility as measured by the child/woman ratio, but its association is also quite surprising. Demographers usually treat literacy as a sign of cultural modernization and therefore as a variable which is positively correlated with the advance of a low fertility system. My information on literacy and fertility suggests not only that this thesis is not universally valid, but that there may actually be a positive correlation between literacy and fertility in pre-famine Cavan.

Table 5.8 breaks down the child/woman ratio by occupational category (farmer/laborer) and by the level of literacy. The census form from which this information came asked individuals whether they could read and write, read only, or neither read nor write. As with all such questions, this imposed a certain arbitrariness, especially between the "read only" and the "read and write" cate-

Table 5.8

The Child/Woman Ratio and Literacy, Killashandra Parish

| AGE | ILLITERATE | | READ/NOT WRITE | | FULLY LITERATE | |
	Farming (N = 301)	Laboring (N = 203)	Farming (N = 176)	Laboring (N = 131)	Farming (N = 177)	Laboring (N = 41)
20–24		.73	.72	.92	.64	.78
25–29	.83	1.08	1.54	1.42	1.66	1.60
30–34	1.32	1.26	1.66	1.39	1.69	1.23
35–39	1.44	1.06	1.39	1.27	1.04	1.50
40–44	.76	.75	.94	.75	.88	1.00
45–49	.10	.17	.32	.20	.67	.33
Average	.87	.89	1.17	1.15	1.16	1.22

SOURCE: Killashandra Study File.

gories. Furthermore, as no test was required, some individuals were likely to have reported themselves as more accomplished than they actually were. Assuming that this temptation worked only in one direction, it is reasonably certain that those women who listed themselves as illiterate truly were so. It is also a fair assumption that some members of the "read only" and "read and write" groups may have had lower levels of literacy than they indicated. Even so, the information in the table still demonstrates that illiterate women had, at virtually every period in their lives, fewer resident children. The positive relationship between literacy and the child/woman ratio is so strong that it even overcomes the aggregate differences between laboring and farming families: illiterate farming women had a much lower child/woman ratio than literate laboring women.

Of course, literacy is closely tied to other variables which ultimately may have caused the differences in the child/woman ratios, the most likely of which is wealth. The persistence of the differences across occupational categories should partially allay such suspicions, but it is possible that illiterate wives from the small farming group were actually worse off than some of their laboring neighbors. Greater precision is not possible without more specific data regarding wealth, although, at least within the occupational groups, it is fairly certain that literacy and wealth co-vary. The one startling fact of which we can be quite certain is that illiterate women had fewer very young resident children than did literate women.

From these observations regarding the child/woman ratio, the age structure of the child populations, and the relationship between literacy and the child/woman ratio, we can begin to assemble a fairly concrete model of Cavan's population dynamics during the immediate pre-famine period. This information undeniably challenges the traditional interpretation of Irish population movements at that time, consistently pointing to lower fertility—or, at least, lower child-survival—among laboring and illiterate groups than among the more prosperous and secure farming classes. Because of the nature of the fertility data, there is no clear answer as to whether this represents a sudden change in Cavan society or the continuation of a historical pattern. But given the weight of contemporary testimony, the changes in the aggregate census figures for 1831–41, and the general logic of Cavan's economic development during the late eighteenth and early nineteenth centuries, the former seems far more likely. The numerous reasons for such a change include deteriorating physical and material conditions for Cavan's laborers; declining labor opportunity for Cavan's agricultural and industrial labor; the dearth of conacre ground and cots; and large-scale migration of laborers. Ultimately all these were symptoms of the rapid but incomplete commercialization of Cavan agriculture.

This proposed revision of current thinking about the social forces contributing to Irish population dynamics raises several questions concerning other aspects of the traditional demographic argument, most notably the relationship between marriage age and population dynamics. If Connell's general thesis tying fertility to marriage age and my revision reversing the role of economic deprivation are correct, we should find evidence that marriage age moved upward, especially among agricultural laborers and their wives, during the last decade before the famine.

MARRIAGE AGE

Table 5.9 presents the simplest measure of the age at marriage of farmers and laborers in Killashandra in 1841. This mean was calculated from the nominative census forms of the inhabitants of the parish, the year of marriage being recorded for each individual. It is particularly fortunate that the actual year of marriage was recorded,

Table 5.9
Mean Age at First Marriage by Group,
Killashandra Parish, 1841

GROUP	MALES	(N)	FEMALES	(N)
Farmers (all)	26.04	(635)	21.7	(573)
Small Farmers	27.07	(112)	23.78	(98)
Middling Farmers	25.6	(130)	21.557	(114)
Large Farmers	28.42	(89)	23.07	(81)
Laborers	24.5	(509)	22.26	(458)

SOURCE: Killashandra Study File.

as the population's unstable age structure (caused principally by dramatic changes in emigration) makes the singulate mean age of marriage unreliable. These figures indicate that the age of first marriage was not remarkably low in Cavan. They also illustrate two particularly important relationships.

As expected, the figures vary considerably among social groups. Even more important, this relationship is different for the two sexes: while farmers as a group were a mean 1.54 years older at marriage than agricultural laborers, their wives were .56 years younger than laboring wives. Michael Drake suggested this sort of relationship as a possibility in Ireland after uncovering a similar relationship in a Scandinavian study. According to Drake, farmers might have delayed marriage to insure receipt of their inheritances, but because economically they were desirable mates, once they decided to marry they could choose from among the most attractive young women. On the other hand, male laborers, although able to marry earlier, were not nearly as competitive in the marriage "market."[17] Drake suggested that this anomaly might undermine Connell's argument, which, because it was based on aggregate figures, may have overestimated the effect of economic deprivation as a depressant of marriage age and a stimulant of fertility.

While the figures seem to bear out Drake's cautions, it is worth stressing that the mean figures for all age groups tell nothing about either the historical development of marriage trends or the immediate experience of individuals marrying at the time of the census. Rather, they reveal a confused combination of the two. The mean figures for marriage age are subject to distortion by age differences in the subpopulations in 1841, as well as by the different social and economic experiences of these groups over the previous half-century or more (a very erratic half-century).

There are several other ways to approach the question of retrospective marriage age from the census data, none of which alone is entirely satisfactory, but which, when considered together, provide a model of both the historical trends in marriage age and the experience of individuals of marriageable age in the years just before the famine. Figure 5.1 incorporates two of the most useful relative measures of marriage age that I can generate from the nominative census data: the mean age of first marriage, analyzed by age cohorts (represented by line CD) and by the decade in which that marriage took place (represented by line DE). The difficulties of reconstructing the past experiences of individuals of different ages recorded in a single census necessitate this rather cumbersome method of measurement. The want of other Irish evidence is such that the effort is warranted. First, measurement by age cohort suffers from a serious flaw when used for the entire population, because the younger cohorts have not completed their exposure to risk; i.e., many twenty-five-year-olds who were still single at the time of the census would have soon married, increasing the "true" mean for that cohort. It is a good indicator, however, of the marriage experience of older cohorts. The graph confirms the general relationships already noted between occupational groups and sexes. For every cohort, laboring wives were older than farming wives. The data indicate that marriage age fell during the last decade of the eighteenth century and the first decade of the nineteenth. A note on farm size and marriage age is useful here. Laboring husbands remained single longer than both small and middling farmers. Only the large farmers consistently married much later than laborers and other farming groups. The experience of women was similar: wives of large farmers were the eldest within the farming group, but still younger than laboring wives. This would seem to negate any simple linear connection between marriage age and wealth.

Line DE, the measurement by decade, is responsive to past changes in marriage patterns and allows more precise observation of the most recent experience, the area in which the cohort information

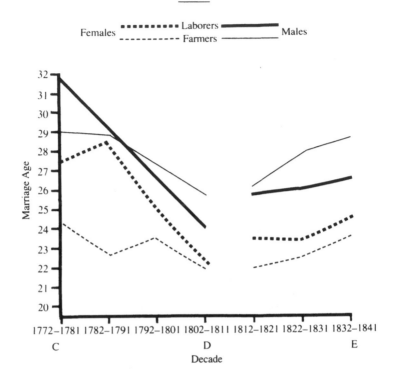

Figure 5.1 Two Measures of Marriage Age. (Killashandra Study File.) Farmers: N = 635 males, 573 females. Laborers: N = 509 males, 458 females. For explanation, see text.

is the least reliable. However, it too has one serious drawback: because those marrying at a relatively later age in a past decade ran a greater risk of mortality than those who married at a relatively early age in the same decade, the mean age of marriage in the earlier decades is artificially depressed. Furthermore, as this damping effect is directly proportional to the percentage of late marriages in past time, it has the most serious effect upon groups with large numbers of such marriages. Thus the mean age of marriage for the various groups tends to converge in the distant past.

Therefore, this measure is most useful in the decades immediately prior to the census, 1811–41, and only these decades appear on the graph. Especially during 1821–41, the damping effect was minimal, as the exposure to mortality of those marrying in their late twenties or early thirties in 1826 was not substantially greater than for those marrying in their early twenties. Still, the information for 1821–41 should not be regarded as a precise measurement, but as a good estimate of recent marriage experience among these groups. The relationship is quite clear and is consistent with the cohort measurements. Again, while laboring men married younger than farmers, their brides were older. This relationship remained constant over the three decades. However, the evidence indicates a slowly rising age of marriage for all groups in the two decades before the famine.

The evidence thus affords no reason for supposing that laborers as a group married considerably younger than farmers, but rather every indication that laborers' wives married later than farmers' wives throughout the pre-famine period.

The information regarding the direction of change over the first half of the nineteenth century is less precise, but still convincing. The form of measurement most sensitive in the recent past, the decade method, indicates that the age of marriage rose for all groups in the immediate pre-famine decade. The cohort method indicates that during the early years of the century marriage age declined. Exactly where lines CD and DE intersect is impossible to say; however, if the accurate portions of each are accepted, the result is certainly compatible with the economic argument that marriage age declined between 1800 and 1820 and increased between 1821 and 1841.

Figure 5.2 represents the best estimate I can advance. It is the result of fitting together the most accurate portions of the two measurements and interpolating from these figures to provide the most likely "fit" between the measurements. Notice the much steeper slope of the lines representing laboring men and women. Most important, the very sharp decline in mean age of marriage for laboring women of 5.1 years (from those marrying ca. 1796–1805 to those marrying 1822–31) could represent the type of radical demographic change which Connell believed responsible for Ireland's population explosion. Yet, as we have seen, laboring women had fewer surviving children, and laboring wives, for whatever reasons, married

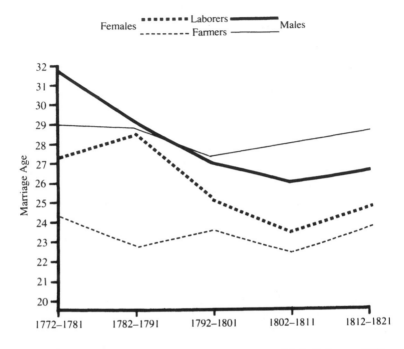

Figure 5.2 Estimate of Mean Marriage Age, by Birth Cohorts. (Killa-shandra Study File.) To provide continuity, I have reconstructed the scale of the decade of marriage portion of the graph to approximate birth cohorts. E.g., those farming women married 1822–31 had a mean age at marriage of 22.39, and thus the birth cohort 1800–1809 includes most of these same women.

later than did farming wives throughout the pre-famine period. There is no contradiction here. During the years before 1831 laboring women nearly gained equality of opportunity for marriage: an opportunity which began to recede before the famine and which became notoriously rare in post-famine Ireland. Connell suggested that this opportunity to marry was the critical demographic variable in Irish rural society, but his equation of poverty and early marriage was too simplistic. It is quite likely that despite maintaining marriage ages higher and fertility rates lower than farming wives did, laboring women were the primary contributors to the overall increase in fertility. Expressed in another way, laboring women represent the variable component of Cavan marriage age and fertility rates. While farming women constantly maintained a lower mean age of marriage and higher rates of fertility, laboring women experienced radical changes in both demographic variables which altered the fertility rate of the entire population.

One final variable remains to be considered. The general fertility rate and direction of population change are not exclusively determined by the marriage age and the fertility rate of the married population. As the demographic history of post-famine Ireland dramatically demonstrates, a very high marital fertility rate and a population decline can coexist as long as the proportion of individuals marrying remains low and emigration high.[18] The high levels of nuptiality demonstrated here indicate that this was not so in pre-famine Killashandra (see table 5.10).

In describing the post-famine period, Connell cited the 1951 census to demonstrate Ireland's low percentage of marriage. Among the 40–49 cohort, only 66 percent of males and 73.5 percent of females had ever married. The corresponding figures in table 5.10 are 86.6 to 88.9 for males and 87.8 to 90.5 for females. It should be remarked that these figures, even more than Connell's, may suffer from serious distortion. As emigration had reached high levels only in the fifteen years before the census, and as migrants were overwhelmingly single and young during this period, it is very likely that the percentage married in the younger cohorts (under age forty) is inflated. It is interesting that this profile still fits within the Western European late-marriage pattern as discussed by Coale and Anderson:[19] Only 28.8 percent of females aged twenty to twenty-four were married, and 10 percent remained unmarried at age fifty. However erratic Irish marriage patterns may have been, they fit within the main Western European experience.

In this regard, it should be noted that the figures for farmers and laborers overstate the actual marriage rate among those groups because of the relationship between occupational titles and marriage.[20] The figures merely demonstrate the consistency of this very

Table 5.10
Percentage Ever Married by Age Cohorts, Killashandra Parish, 1841

AGE	ENTIRE POPULATION				FARMERS				LABORERS			
	Male	(N)	Female	(N)	Male	(N)	Female	(N)	Male	(N)	Female	(N)
15–19	2.80	(709)	2.60	(726)	0	(223)	2.22	(225)	.95	(105)	5.77	(104)
20–24	14.21	(556)	28.76	(619)	9.55	(157)	32.16	(171)	48.24	(85)	70.00	(90)
25–29	46.48	(355)	64.97	(394)	48.08	(104)	79.64	(113)	75.29	(86)	87.64	(89)
30–34	69.97	(365)	84.97	(415)	76.79	(112)	95.80	(119)	90.82	(109)	96.64	(119)
35–39	82.97	(276)	86.97	(284)	91.00	(100)	96.59	(88)	93.43	(76)	97.18	(71)
40–44	86.65	(367)	87.80	(377)	94.07	(118)	99.06	(106)	94.69	(113)	98.72	(78)
45–49	88.88	(200)	90.54	(222)	95.35	(86)	98.63	(73)	92.69	(41)	97.37	(38)
50–54	92.65	(272)	89.01	(273)	95.19	(104)	98.39	(62)	96.36	(55)	100.00	(43)
55–59	94.96	(139)	95.50	(111)	98.80	(51)	100.00	(30)	100.00	(43)	100.00	(23)
60–69	92.96	(173)	89.50	(200)	98.84	(86)	100.00	(35)	94.87	(39)	100.00	(22)
65–69	98.59	(71)	92.16	(51)	96.43	(27)	100.00	(12)	100.00	(13)	100.00	(3)

SOURCE: Killashandra Study File.

184

high marriage rate across the social groups. Pre-famine Cavan had a very low celibacy rate, and consequently marriage age should directly influence the rate of population growth.

The evidence presented in this chapter does not constitute a "solution" to the demographic debate. However, several visible trends in the demographic variables of the late pre-famine period raise serious questions about traditional interpretations of population growth in Ireland. Furthermore, these trends are theoretically important to the general argument of the relationship between economic modernization and the so-called demographic transition.

All the variables measuring the contributions of various groups to population growth in the immediate pre-famine period indicate that the laboring population was suffering a severe crisis. Marriage age, household and family size, the child/woman ratio, and the age structure of households all differed significantly between farming and laboring families. My model suggests the explanation. As labor supply surpassed demand, farmers no longer had the incentive to provide housing for the laboring population. Hence, marriage became more difficult. The insecurity of by-the-day employment, linked with a growing population of laborers, resulted in widespread underemployment and a lower standard of living with all of the attendant miseries. None of these factors seriously affected the more prosperous farming class.

The long-term pattern is less clear. There is evidence of a general increase in marriage age, but as just observed, there is no reason to believe that the proportion of individuals marrying was decreasing. These two facts may fit the general model of a society departing from generally high fertility. If, as is argued here, the age of marriage was largely determined by certain preconditions, such as succession to control of a farm or the ability to find a cottage and labor (which in turn depended on the immediate economy), individuals were likely to delay marriage until they had either met these conditions or had lost all hope of meeting them. However, the proportion ever marrying was largely determined by the general expectations of the community regarding the "normal" marriage and family experience. Thus, as long as individuals attempted to fulfill those expectations, a high proportion were likely to marry, even if economic

conditions delayed the wedding day beyond the socially desirable
age of marriage. Emigration then was a safety valve, perhaps the
only escape for those who felt, or perceived, the greatest tension
between traditional expectations and changing economic reality.

These hypotheses may help to explain the increasingly contradic-
tory views of the famine held by demographers and social and
cultural historians. It now appears more than likely that both a later
age of marriage and a slower rate of population growth were pre-
famine, not post-famine, developments. But the famine, in addition
to dramatically altering the social structure of the country by annihi-
lating a large part of the laboring population, also radically altered
the community's expectations regarding marriage. Seen in this
light, the reaction of the Irish peasants was not a fatalistic acceptance of the famine as a decree by God (or Fate) that their past ways
were wrong. Rather, it was the realization that the marked deterioration of their material well-being during the early nineteenth century was determined by gradual, fundamental changes in the
economy and not a temporary streak of bad luck. This would also
explain why the famine caused fundamental changes only where
such economic changes had been taking place before the famine. In
those parts of the country which retained a Chayanovian organization, the pre-famine marriage and fertility patterns remained unchanged for another quarter of a century.[21]

Conclusion

The evidence presented in this study led me to the model of agricultural and demographic change proposed in the Introduction. Cavan's agricultural economy did not follow a Malthusian path from the eighteenth century to the famine. Instead, a complicated series of relationships between economic, social, and demographic variables regulated the rate of population growth. The major development responsible for the population increase was the growing involvement of Cavan's rural population in a commercially oriented system of agriculture.

Pre-famine farmers responded to increasing demands for rent by utilizing the limited means at their disposal to maximize their cash income and minimize their cash requirements. These efforts were facilitated by the availability of the potato, which was a traditional part of the tillage rotation, and by the growing demand for food in Britain's industrial cities. While the greater intensification of tillage (as compared to pasture) confirmed the importance of agricultural labor and encouraged the expansion of the landless laboring population, the increasing demand for labor was not translated into higher real wages for agricultural laborers. Because of the farmers' need to keep capital expenditure at a minimum, laborers were coerced into one of two undermonetized labor systems: either they exchanged their labor for subsistence land in the cot system, or they worked irregularly as day laborers and were forced to pay back their cash wages to the farming community through the conacre system. Both of these alternatives resulted in a dependent relationship which one might be tempted to call either reinfeudation or proletarianization, depending upon one's perspective. Both forms of labor were facilitated by the prolific nature of the potato, but neither was caused by it.

The demographic results of this surplus-producing stage most likely consisted of two distinct but closely related stages. The early effects of the increased market orientation of Cavan farmers and the consequent tillage intensification were an increased demand for labor and an increased supply of potatoes for local consumption. Demographically, this was manifested by a declining marriage age for laborers, a direct result of farmers' willingness to provide cots and conacre land in lieu of cash wages. Coupled with the high nutritional value of the potato and milk diet of the laboring population, these developments probably led to an increase in marital fertility and an increase in the proportion of the population marrying.

Most of my evidence relates to the second stage of the demographic response to the process of agricultural commercialization. In Cavan, sometime during the second or third decade of the nineteenth century the increasing labor supply began to press upon the upper limits of potential tillage labor demands. The short-term depressions of 1819–22 and 1825–26 helped to magnify the problem by throwing many textile workers into the agricultural labor market, but its underlying cause was the pressure of population upon the ecological limits of the area. Profitable tillage could be carried out only on the better dry fields, and by 1830 most of these were already in tillage (Irish cereal exports peaked in the years 1824–28). Consequently, while the laboring population continued to grow, farmers became more and more reluctant to provide additional land for laboring settlement. Cots became increasingly difficult to find and conacre rents rose beyond the land's productive capacity.

For laborers, the demographic results of this late pre-famine agricultural commercialization were an increased difficulty in forming families and a decline in marital fertility which was caused by the increasing age of marriage and possibly by higher infant mortality rates due to the rapidly deteriorating living conditions of the laborers.

For farming families, the late pre-famine period probably was not very different from the earlier years of the century; family structure, marriage age, and family size depended upon the labor (not consumption) requirements of the farm being managed. Families living on large farms tended to marry later because of the importance of the inheritance system, and to have nuclear living arrangements because their land requirements were more likely to be met by non-family members. The families living on the middle-sized farms tended to marry earlier than the large farmers and were the most likely to be nuclear families, because their economic limitations made it difficult to support nonproductive relatives and made temporary wage labor at the peak labor seasons the most efficient means of meeting their labor requirements. On the small farm, labor requirements seldom exceeded the family supply. For these farmers, resident kin may have functioned more like boarders, providing additional household resources earned elsewhere through wage labor.

According to this hypothesis, then, both the population expansion of the late eighteenth and early nineteenth centuries and the declining fertility rate of Cavan in the late pre-famine period reflected an equilibrium between population and environmental capacity which was maintained by economic forces. The variables which originally provoked change were landlords' demands for competitive rents and the increasing British demand for agricultural products. The eventual reassertion of population controls was forced by the environmental limits of the region and the diminishing return of labor investment. The reassertion of fertility limitations was partially delayed by the rising level of permanent emigration, so the transition to low or negative population growth was not completed before the famine. Still, it appears fairly certain that in Cavan the famine was an environmental accident and not the result of prior population increases.

The role of the famine in subsequent demographic change in Cavan falls outside the time frame of this study; but because the famine singled out the laboring population for virtual obliteration, it is likely that post-famine Cavan marriage and fertility patterns more nearly approximated those of the farming groups discussed here.[1] Furthermore, with population pressure greatly eased (Cavan lost approximately 28 percent of its population between 1841 and 1851), the county's agricultural organization could more easily be reoriented along less labor-intensive lines and turned to the dairy production which the soils and climate of the county favored. Together, these developments would lead to a much more homogeneous social structure dominated by the larger farming group and its demographic behavior.

The implications of these developments in Cavan for the reconstruction of demographic and agricultural change at the national level must be drawn with care. The experience of Cavan's rural community was substantially affected by the geographic location of the county. Because the developments in Cavan were closely linked to British economic development and European economic and political events, it is unlikely that events in areas undergoing market integration at an earlier or later period would experience these changes in precisely the same way. In areas with easier access to the eastern coastal cities, from Derry to Cork, the early stages of commercialization probably were well under way before the boom and bust cycle of the war years. This probably would have permitted a slower and therefore less harsh transition to capitalistic organization in these areas. Furthermore, the depressions of the 1820s and 1830s would have helped to speed the second stage of the transition before the famine and thus to make that event less traumatic; and indeed this all appears to have been the case.

Following a similar line of reasoning, those areas more isolated from ports with easy access to British markets may not have begun their development at all before the famine, and so would not have experienced the social differentiation which played a major role in population dynamics. These areas with an overwhelmingly Chayanovian agricultural orientation would be the most vulnerable to the famine and experience the highest mortality. Yet because of the social homogeneity of the population, mortality would have relatively little effect upon social and agricultural organization.[2]

The twentieth-century social problems of these more remote districts are echoes (perhaps more pathetic, but not more painful) of the process of depopulation and social "simplification" which took place elsewhere from 1850 to 1922. The "classic" type of peasant family and community which Arensberg and Kimball found early in our century may have been the last surviving element of an older and more complicated social world.[3] Likewise, the work of more recent observers might benefit from a sense of time. The family structure and demographic experience of "remote" areas are of considerable interest; however, it is dangerous to assume that they represent some sort of magical continuity with an unchanging "traditional" system.

Taking these qualifications into account, the most important Cavan findings vis-à-vis the national discussion are those concerning the nature of the relationship between population and agricultural changes, not the precise timing of those changes. The preeminence of economic development as a determinant of demographic change, and the role of the landless laborers as the group primarily responsible for the expansion of population *and* the eventual curtailment of that expansion, suggest that the population trends in Ireland were tied closely to labor demands and in turn to the agricultural needs of industrial Britain. Further research will be necessary to confirm this theory for other parts of the country. Not enough is yet known about the local experiences of areas with different relationships to the British market, and the study of Cavan has to be carried into the post-famine period in order to complete the history of agricultural modernization and document the complete transition to the developed stage of the market impulsion model.

The implications of this research at the broader theoretical level are similar. The most important generalization for testing is that peasant societies possess an equilibrium between population and productive capacity, and that structural economic changes are of considerable importance in this equilibrium. The three-stage economic model helps to explain both the shifting relationships involved in this dynamic and the conundrum of successive independent variables. As Marx noted, there is no single equation, but a specific one for each set of circumstances.

In its most extended form, my evidence supports those demographers and economists who stress the fundamental rationality of human communities (rationality does not imply compassion) and their ability to accommodate themselves to changing economic and environmental circumstances caused by industrialization. The evidence also suggests that the rural and urban poor seem to pass through similar difficulties as a result of the increased capitalization of the world economy. My conclusions parallel those reached by David Levine for proto-industrial England: "It is my belief that the critical factors in promoting rapid demographic growth were the proletarianization of the mass of producers, peasants and artisans and their integration into an extralocal commercial system."[4] It seems that the population dynamics of urban and developed England and rural and underdeveloped Ireland may have both responded to the same set of economic forces: the development of a regional industrial economy.

The extension of these arguments into the contemporary world may be a bit bold; but Charles Tilly has already suggested that the international economy may be the most important influence upon Third World demographics.[5] While only contemporary studies can define the contemporary problem, my evidence suggests that world demographers may need to reorient their conceptualization of the divisions between rural and urban economic and demographic change if they wish to come to any meaningful generalizations regarding these phenomena. Tilly has also observed that today's Third World development takes place "under conditions of more complete proletarianization and more thorough penetration of capital than occurred in the rural west."[6] I would conclude by suggesting that, as the nineteenth-century Irish peasantry were the most exposed to and least protected from the intervention of aggressive capitalism, their experience may provide the most useful model for predictions concerning parallel cases today. Such a suggestion, if valid, is cause for more than a little anxiety regarding the future relationship between industrial and "underdeveloped" regions.

APPENDIX

NOTES

BIBLIOGRAPHY

INDEX

Appendix:
The Killashandra
Study File

I compiled the Killashandra Study File from four major sources: (1) the manuscript census forms for the parish, 1841; (2) the Tithe Applotment Book of the parish, compiled in 1832; (3) Griffith's Valuation, 1853; and (4) the parish registers of the Catholic and Church of Ireland communities, 1820–80.

The base of the file consists of the information taken from the manuscript census forms which were completed on 6 June 1841. No sampling was attempted; each of the 12,529 individuals in the parish was coded as a separate case. The normal census data plus information on the year of marriage, literacy, and missing family members were recorded directly from the forms. Information on each individual's relationship to primary and secondary subnuclear units was also derived by the coder from the original forms.

Information on the extent and value of farm holdings from the Tithe Applotment Books and the Griffith's Valuation records was collected on the townland level. This information was linked manually to the census information before machine processing. I linked only those cases in which townland address, surname, and Christian name agreed and were unique.

The parish registers provided information permitting the religious identification of many of the parish inhabitants. The registers were too incomplete to permit family reconstitution. I assumed that if one individual in a family could be identified as a member of a particular religious group, all members of the family (not household) were of the same faith.

From the original thirty-two variables recorded for each individual, household, and family, summary and reference variables were constructed which were then imprinted with each case. They include family type, family cycle, age of youngest and eldest child/girl/boy in the family, number of lodgers, visitors, ascendant and descendant relatives, laborers, servants, etc. in the household. This difficult task was performed through utilization of the Comparative Cities Project programs and with the invaluable assistance of R. Burr Litchfield, one of the creators and directors of that project. Additional information on landholding and stocking of individual farms was collected from estate papers (for the Gosford and Farnham estates) and an estate census (for the Gosford estate, 1853) and added to the file. As of this date, the file contains 243 variables for each of the 12,529 individuals who lived in Killashandra parish in 1841. Much of the information collected pertains to post-famine times and awaits analysis. The figure and tables that follow are all based on the Killashandra Study File.

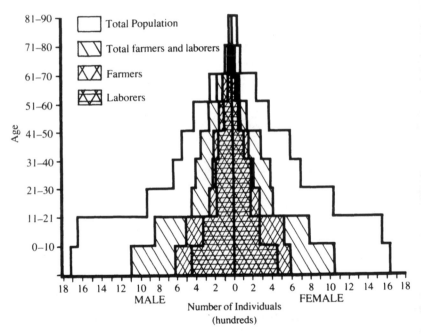

Figure A.1   Age/Sex Pyramid, Killashandra Parish, 1841. (Killashandra Study File.)

Table A.1
Female Age Structure, Killashandra Parish, 1841

AGE	ALL FEMALES		FARMING* FEMALES		LABORING* FEMALES	
	No.	%	No.	%	No.	%
0–10	1,620	25.9	595	30.6	450	34.4
11–20	1,560	24.9	529	27.2	275	21.0
21–30	1,013	16.2	284	14.6	179	13.7
31–40	699	11.2	207	10.6	190	14.5
41–50	599	9.6	179	9.2	116	8.9
51–60	384	6.1	92	4.7	66	5.0
61–70	251	4.0	47	2.4	25	1.9
71–80	97	1.5	12	.6	8	.6
81–90	43	.6	0	.0	1	.1
Mean Age	29.97		26.76		26.87	
Median Age	20.47		20.21		20.25	

* In tables A.1–A.6, the terms "farming" and "laboring" refer to the occupational identification of the head of the family unit.

Table A.2
Male Age Structure, Killashandra Parish, 1841

AGE	ALL MALES		FARMING* MALES		LABORING* MALES	
	No.	%	No.	%	No.	%
0–10	1,719	27.4	627	29.4	471	31.9
11–20	1,653	26.4	523	24.5	323	21.9
21–30	911	14.5	261	12.2	171	11.6
31–40	641	10.2	212	9.9	185	12.5
41–50	567	9.1	204	9.6	154	10.4
51–60	411	6.6	155	7.3	98	6.6
61–70	244	3.9	113	5.3	52	3.5
71–80	85	1.4	31	1.5	16	1.1
81–90	32	.5	10	.4	5	.3
Mean Age	29.17		29.86		28.92	
Median Age	20.35		20.34		20.33	

Table A.3

Household and Family Size of Selected Groups,
Killashandra Parish, 1841

		HOUSEHOLD SIZE		FAMILY SIZE	
GROUP	(N)	Mean	Median	Mean	Median
All	2,273	5.51	5.25	4.92	4.68
Farmers	773	6.48	6.37	5.71	5.67
Laborers	588	5.21	5.10	4.84	4.72
Weavers	151	5.44	5.11	5.29	4.98
Artisans	101	5.49	5.44	5.04	4.78

Table A.4

Household Size by Family Cycle Stage,
Killashandra Parish, 1841

FAMILY CYCLE STAGE	FARMING HOUSEHOLDS (N = 733)	LABORING HOUSEHOLDS (N = 588)
1	3.656	2.589
2	5.198	4.416
3	8.339	6.939
4	6.573	5.155
5	5.509	4.680
6	4.405	2.840

Table A.5
Children of Household Head per Family,
by Family Cycle Stage

FAMILY CYCLE STAGE	FARMING HOUSEHOLDS (N = 733)	LABORING HOUSEHOLDS (N = 588)
1	0	0 000
2	1.980	1.728
3	5.527	4.505
4	3.946	2.764
5	1.746	1.520
6	0	0

Table A.6
Household Structure of Killashandra in 1841 (b)

HOUSEHOLD TYPE	FARMING HOUSEHOLD	LABORING HOUSEHOLD
Head alone	16	17
Co-related kin present	5	18
Nuclear	3,618	2,457
Extended	106	135
Complex	319	147

Note: These figures are comparable with those suggested by Peter Laslett. His "upwards" and "downwards" categories are here combined. See Peter Laslett, "The History of the Family."

Notes

INTRODUCTION

1 George O'Brien, *The Economic History of Ireland from the Union to the Famine* (London: Longmans, Green, 1921).
2 E. R. R. Green, *The Lagan Valley* (London: Faber, 1949); C. Gill, *The Rise of the Irish Linen Industry* (Oxford: Clarendon Press, 1925); W. H. Crawford, *Domestic Industry in Ireland: The Experience of the Linen Industry* (Dublin: Gill & Macmillan, 1968); Peter Gibbon, *The Origins of Ulster Unionism* (Manchester: Manchester University Press, 1975).
3 Kenneth H. Connell, *The Population of Ireland, 1750–1845* (Oxford: Oxford University Press, 1950); Raymond D. Crotty, *Irish Agricultural Production: Its Volume and Structure* (Cork: Cork University Press, 1966).
4 For some of the major criticism, see Joseph Lee, "Irish Agriculture," *Agricultural History Review* 22, pt. 1 (1969): 64–76.
5 Joseph Lee, "Marriage and Population in Pre-famine Ireland," *Economic History Review*, ser. 2, 21:2 (1968): 295.
6 The most notable examples are: Louis M. Cullen, *Anglo-Irish Trade, 1660–1800* (Manchester: Manchester University Press, 1968); Crawford, *Domestic Industry in Ireland*; James S. Donnelly, *The Land and the People of Nineteenth-Century Cork: The Rural Economy and the Land Question* (Boston: Routledge & Kegan Paul, 1975). For a thorough and useful review of the literature, see Joseph Lee, ed., *Irish Historiography 1970–79* (Cork: Cork University Press, 1981).
7 Daniel Thorner, "Peasant Economy as a Category in Economic History," *Economic Weekly* 15 (special number, July 1963): 1243–52; reprinted in *Peasants and Peasant Societies*, ed. T. Shanin (London: Hammondsworth, 1971), pp. 11–19.
8 See D. B. Grigg, *Population Growth and Agrarian Change* (Cambridge: Cambridge University Press, 1980), pp. 9–48, for a useful summary of this literature. See also Ester Boserup, *The Conditions of Agricultural*

Growth: The Economics of Agrarian Change under Population Pressure (Chicago: Aldine, 1966), pp. 41–44.

9 Aleksander V. Chayanov, *The Theory of Peasant Economy*, ed. Daniel Thorner, Basile Kerblay, and R. E. F. Smith (Homewood, Ill.: R. D. Irwin, 1966), p. 40.

10 Richard Smith, "Some Reflections on the Evidence for the Origins of the 'European Marriage Pattern' in England," in *The Sociology of The Family*, ed. C. Harris (Keele: University of Keele, 1979), p. 93.

11 Jacek Kochanowicz, "The Peasant Family as an Economic Unit in the Polish Feudal Economy of the Eighteenth Century," in *Family Forms in Historic Europe*, ed. Richard Wall, Jean Robin, and Peter Laslett (Cambridge: Cambridge University Press, 1983), pp. 153–66.

12 Ronald Meek, *Marx and Engels on Malthus* (London: Lawrence & Wishart, 1953), p. 88; Karl Marx, *Capital*, ed. Friedrich Engels, trans. Samuel Moore and Edward Eveling (Moscow: Foreign Language Publishing House, 1961), 1:632.

13 Meek, *Marx and Engels on Malthus*, p. 99; Marx, *Capital*, p. 642.

14 See Clifford Geertz, *Agricultural Involution: The Processes of Ecological Change in Indonesia* (Berkeley: University of California Press, 1963), pp. xi–xiv, for an example of such short-circuiting of Marx's pattern of development.

15 Max Black, *Models and Metaphors* (Ithaca: Cornell University Press, 1962), p. 220.

16 This is part of Chayanov's system; i.e., his labor inputs were determined by the consumer/worker ratio, not the labor supply or the productive capacity of the land.

17 See Rudolf Bicanic, "Three Concepts of Agricultural Over-Population," in *International Explorations of Agricultural Economics*, ed. Roger N. Dixey (Ames: Iowa State University Press, 1964) for a discussion of the varying notions of labor capacity.

18 Frank Tipton, *Regional Variations in the Economic Development of Germany During the Nineteenth Century* (Middleton, Conn.: Wesleyan University Press, 1976), p. 12. Also see Richard Baldwin, ed., *Trade, Growth and the Balance of Payments* (Chicago: Rand McNally, 1965).

19 Tipton, *Regional Variations*, p. 12.

20 For one of the best examples, see Barbara Solow, *The Land Question and the Irish Economy, 1870–1903* (Cambridge: Harvard University Press, 1971), pp. 8–20.

21 Cormac O'Grada, "The Investment Bahaviour of Irish Landlords 1850–1875: Some Preliminary Findings," *Agricultural History Review* 23 (1975): 129–55.

22 John Messenger, *Inis Beag: Isle of Ireland* (New York: Holt, Rinehart & Winston, 1969), p. 125.

23 For a sensitive but depressing view of this process, see Hugh Brody, *Innishkilanne: Change and Decline in the West of Ireland* (London: Allen Lane, 1973). The characteristics he ascribes to the twentieth century were well in place in many areas a half-century earlier.

24 The potato, used as a fodder crop, did have an important role in commercial activity. See below, pp. 86–90.

25 I am currently researching this phase of development.

26 See Alan MacFarland, *Reconstructing Historical Communities* (Cambridge: Cambridge University Press, 1977); and Colin Bell and Howard Newby, *Community Studies: An Introduction to the Sociology of the Local Community* (New York: Praeger, 1972) for two useful discussions of the question.

27 The published census figure was 12,562. The surviving forms contain information on 12,529 persons. It is not clear whether some forms are missing or the published figure is in error.There were several variants of the parish name in use in 1841, including Killashandra, Killeshandra, and Killyshandra. I have chosen the older spelling.

28 John Orme, *Ireland* (London: Harlow, 1970), pp. 65–67.

29 Ibid., p. 78.

30 Quarto books of the 1840 Valuation (Public Record Office, Dublin [hereafter referred to as PRO]).

31 T. W. Freeman, *Pre-Famine Ireland: A Study in Historical Geography* (Manchester: Manchester University Press, 1957), p. 113.

32 *Census of 1841*, returns for Killashandra parish (PRO).

CHAPTER 1: AGRICULTURAL STRUCTURE: TENURE, RENTS, AND FARM SIZE

1 See below, p. 105, and Michael Beames, "Cottiers and Conacre in Pre-Famine Ireland," *Journal of Peasant Studies* 2:3 (1975): 352–54, for a description of this system.

2 See below, p. 87.

3 For the seventeenth-century origin of this system, see David Dickson, "Middlemen," in *Penal Era and Golden Age: Essays in Irish History, 1690–1800*, ed. Thomas Bartlett and D. W. Hayton (Belfast: Ulster Historical Foundation, 1979), pp. 162–85.

4 It is important to recognize the difference between subletting and subdivision. The former refers to the process of subleasing a large parcel of land to several undertenants, usually but not always in separate farms.

Subdivision refers to the practice universally criticized as one of the causes of population growth, by which a father divided his farm among his children. Of course both practices led to smaller farms, but their motives and results differed considerably. The subdivider broke up his property permanently and out of a desire to help his children survive; the subletter retained legal control of his property and divided it merely to increase his income.

5 Charles Coote, *Statistical Survey of the County of Cavan, with Observations on the Means of Improvement; Drawn up in the Year 1801 for the Consideration and under the Direction of the Dublin Society* (Dublin: Graisberry & Campbell, 1802), p. 58.

6 Rentals, Accounts, etc. of the Estate of Dowager Lady Garvagh in Corraneary, Co. Cavan, 1829–1865 (M5535, PRO).

7 Rental of the Estates in and near Bailieboro, Co. Cavan of Edward Groome, 1822 (M5559, PRO).

8 Papers relating to the estates in Co. Cavan, mainly in Corraneary, of W. F. Greville, 1809–1844 (M6178[64], PRO).

9 Royal School Estate Papers; H. Tilson, agent. Rentals and Correspondence, 1834–1864 (Ms17, 920, National Library of Ireland [hereafter referred to as NLI]).

10 *Evidence Taken before Her Majesty's Commissioners of Inquiry into the State of the Law and Practice in Respect to the Occupation of Land in Ireland*, ii (H.C. 1845, xx [hereafter cited as Devon Commission]), p. 99.

11 Ibid., p. 96.

12 Greville estate papers (M6178[64], PRO).

13 See William A. Maguire, *The Downshire Estates in Ireland 1801–1845: The Management of Irish Landed Estates in the Early Nineteenth Century* (Oxford: Clarendon Press, 1972), pp. 108–9; and Solow, *The Land Question and the Irish Economy*, pp. 7ff.

14 Solow, *The Land Question and the Irish Economy*, pp. 10ff.

15 Garvagh estate papers (M5535, PRO).

16 See Devon Commission, xx, pp. 1204–12; xxi, pp. 779ff.

17 Seamus O'Loingsigh, "The Burning of Ballinagh," *Breifne* 2:7 (1965): 362ff.

18 Randall M'Collum, *Sketches of the Highlands of Cavan* (Belfast: J. Reed, 1856), p. 260.

19 O'Loingsigh, "The Burning of Ballinagh," p. 363.

20 Devon Commission, xxi, p. 799.

21 Beresford denied the charges which were made against him at the Devon Commission hearings, but a letter from Beresford to Farnham expressing the need to take action against the Catholic tenantry would seem to

indicate that his evictions of the Catholic tenantry were undertaken as a deliberate sectarian attack. In any case, Beresford did remove the Catholic tenantry from one townland and replaced them with a purely Protestant group. See Devon Commission, xx, p. 112, and letter of 24 December, 1831, from Beresford to Farnham in the Farnham correspondence (Ms18,600, NLI).

22 Crotty, *Irish Agricultural Production*, p. 44.

23 Crofton Estate Papers: Rentals and Accounts of the Crofton Estates in Counties Cavan and Monaghan, 1769–1851 (Ms8150, NLI).

24 Coote, *Cavan*, p. 43.

25 Ibid., p. 117.

26 Ibid., p. 253.

27 Ibid., p. 148.

28 Ibid., p. 42.

29 Sneyd Papers: Survey of Estate, 1824 (D270/36, PRO Belfast).

30 Coote, *Cavan*, p. 273.

31 Greville estate papers (M6178[64], PRO).

32 The variable unit of measure recorded seriously limits the comparative value of these statistics between different counties and regions. See P. M. A. Bourke, "Notes on Some Agricultural Units of Measurement in Use in Pre-Famine Ireland," *Irish Historical Studies* 14:55 (March 1965): 36–45.

33 Rev. Terence P. Cunningham, "Notes on the 1821 Census of Lavey Parish," *Breifne* 1:3 (1960): 202.

34 The figures given in the Tithe Applotment Book are for holdings. I have combined multiple holdings whenever possible in preparing these figures. The average for the 423 holdings not combined to farm size was 15.7 acres. See Tithe Applotment Book of Killashandra, 1832 (PRO).

35 See Lutz Berkner and Franklin Mendels, "Inheritance Systems, Family Structure and Demographic Patterns in Western Europe, 1700–1900," in *Historical Studies of Changing Fertility*, ed. Charles Tilly (Princeton: Princeton University Press, 1978), esp. p. 217, for the method of calculation used here.

36 *First Report of the Commissioners for Inquiring into the Condition of the Poorer Classes in Ireland*, Supplement to Appendix F (H.C. 1836, xxxiii), pp. 293ff.

37 The average figure would be inflated by the few large farms in the area.

38 John Wilson, "Drumlommon in 1835," *Breifne* 2:7 (1965): 373.

39 Devon Commission, xx, p. 107.

40 Ibid., p. 97.

41 Ibid., p. 110.

42 Ibid., p. 919.
43 Hodson Papers: Rentals and accounts, 1810–1898 (Ms 16,399, NLI).
44 See Wilson, "Drumlommon," p. 373.
45 Greville estate papers (M6178[64], PRO).
46 If the object were to determine the true opportunity cost of occupy-
    ing land in Cavan, tithes, rates, and tenant right payments would have
    to be added to the base rent. Here the concern is only with the explicit
    relationship between landlord and tenant.
47 Greville estate papers (M6178[64], PRO).
48 Coote, *Cavan*, p. 253.
49 Greville estate papers (M6178[64], PRO).
50 Devon Commission, xx, p. 113.
51 [Lord Farnham], *Statement of the Management of the Farnham Es-
    tates* (Dublin: William Curry, 1830), p. 34.
52 *First Report of the Commissioners*, Appendix F, p. 74.
53 Letter to William Fluke Greville (1842), in Greville estate papers
    (M6178, PRO). Also see Devon Commission, xx, p. 113.
54 *First Report of the Commissioners*, Appendix F, p. 198.
55 Ibid., p. 70.
56 Hodson estate papers (Ms16,397–400, NLI).
57 It would be wise at this point to recall that on the Hodson estate in
    1847, undertenants still outnumbered direct tenants 126 to 106.
58 Letter to Sir Hugh Crofton, July 1822, in Crofton estate papers
    (Ms20,773, NLI).
59 Crofton estate papers (Ms20,773, NLI).
60 Garvagh estate papers (M5535, PRO).
61 Crofton estate papers (Ms20,773, NLI).
62 Coote, *Cavan*, p. 2.
63 Compiled from Garvagh (M5535) and Hodson (Ms 16,397–400) papers.
64 Rental of the Groome estate (M5559, PRO).
65 Crofton estate papers (Ms8150, NLI).
66 Ibid.
67 Shankey Papers: Rentals, etc., 1818–1826 (D1550/7, PRO Belfast).
68 Hodson estate papers (Ms16,397, NLI).
69 Garvagh estate papers (M5535, PRO).
70 Crofton estate papers (Ms2089, NLI).
71 Letter of 17 August 1843 in Royal School papers (Ms 17,920, NLI).
72 Garvagh estate papers (M5535, PRO).
73 Compiled from the Greville (M6178) and Royal School (Ms17,920)
    papers. 1841–45 figures are averages.
74 *First Report of the Commissioners*, Supplement to Appendix F, p. 298.

75 Devon Commission, xx, p. 100.
76 Greville estate papers (M6178[64], PRO).
77 Nicholson succeeded in having the agent fired and himself designated the new agent in August 1846. Several years later he was fired for incompetence and chicanery, and Lord Greville apologized to the former agent for having believed the slander which Nicholson had reported. See the Fitzpatrick/Greville correspondence in the Greville estate papers (M6178, PRO).
78 Greville estate papers (M6178, PRO).
79 See p. 45 above.
80 Hodson estate papers (Ms16,399, NLI); see p. 44 above.
81 See p. 14 above regarding this important question.
82 Letter from O'Brien to Crofton in Letters to Sir Hugh Crofton (Ms 20801, NLI).
83 Crofton rent roll of 1823 (Ms20800, NLI).
84 Greville estate papers (M6178[64], PRO).
85 I am indebted to David Buckley for this observation.
86 Tithe Applotment Book of Killashandra, 1832 (PRO).

CHAPTER 2: AGRICULTURAL STRUCTURE: MARKETS, CAPITAL, AND PRODUCTION

1 See Jan DeVries, *The Dutch Rural Economy in the Golden Age, 1500–1700* (New Haven: Yale University Press, 1974), p. 155.
2 See Greville estate papers (M6178, PRO).
3 Crotty, *Irish Agricultural Production,* pp. 51–57.
4 In terms of total population, the high point in Cavan was reached somewhere between 1831 and 1841; but given the bottom-heavy age structure of the population, the peak of adult population (especially young adults who would be seeking new farms) must have occurred immediately before the famine.
5 Devon Commission, xx, p. 97.
6 Ibid.
7 Greville estate papers (M6178[64], PRO).
8 Edward Wakefield, *An Account of Ireland, Statistical and Political,* 2 vols. (London: Longman, Hurst, Rees, Orme, & Brown, 1812), p. 427.
9 Devon Commission, xx, pp. 97, 111.
10 M'Collum, *Highlands of Cavan,* p. 19.
11 Greville estate papers (M6178[64], PRO).
12 Ibid. (M6178[65], PRO).
13 Ibid.

14 See William Carleton, *The Courtship of Phelim O'Toole* (Cork: Mercier Press, 1973) for an example of the operation of the dowry system among even the poorest.

15 Coote, *Cavan*, p. 48.

16 See margin notes to Hodson estate papers (MS 16,397–411, NLI).

17 Greville estate papers (M6178[64], PRO).

18 See Wakefield, *Ireland*, 2:219; *Freeman's Journal*, December 1811.

19 *The Commissioners of Valuation Table Showing the Average Price of Agricultural Produce in Forty Towns in Ireland in the Years 1849, 1850, 1851* (General Valuation Office, Dublin, 1852).

20 Coote, *Cavan*, p. 148.

21 Ibid., p. 18.

22 Ibid., p. 271.

23 There is another possible explanation for this tremendous increase in the volume of exports. It might possibly represent the expropriation of the former food supply of the farming population. I agree with J. Donnelly that the bulk of this grain came from increased acreage. See J. Donnelly, *The Land and the People of Nineteenth-Century Cork*, p. 32n.

24 Devon Commission, xx, p. 110.

25 Greville estate papers (M6178[64], PRO).

26 Coote, *Cavan*, p. 74.

27 Wakefield, *Ireland*, 1:323, 324.

28 Crotty, *Irish Agricultural Production*, p. 36.

29 For the best discussion of the market responsiveness of Irish farmers, see Cormac O'Grada, "Supply Responsiveness in Irish Agriculture During the Nineteenth Century," *Economic History Review*, ser. 2, 28:2 (1975): 312–17.

30 *First Report of the Commissioners*, Appendix F, p. 310.

31 Ibid.

32 *Second Report of the Commissioners Appointed to Consider and Recommend a General System of Railways for Ireland* (145) (H.C. 1837–38, xxxv), p. 9.

33 ibid., p. 36.

34 Ibid., p. 22.

35 Ibid., p. 24.

36 Greville estate papers (M6178[64], PRO).

37 Railway Commission, *Second Report*, p. 14.

38 Ibid., p. 92.

39 Figured at 6*s*. 4*d*. per hundredweight.

40 Railway Commission, *Second Report*, Appendix B.

41 See James S. Donnelly, "Cork Market: Its Role in the Nineteenth Century Irish Butter Trade," *Studia Hibernica* 11 (1971): 130–63.

42 Greville estate papers (M6178[64], PRO).

43 M'Collum, *Highlands of Cavan*, p. 5.

44 *Anglo-Celt*, 6 March 1846.

45 Ibid., 12 June 1846.

46 Ibid., 27 February 1846.

47 *First Report of the Commissioners*, Appendix F, H.C. xxxii, p. 310.

48 Ibid.

49 Redcliffe N. Salaman, in *The History and Social Influence of the Potato* (Cambridge: Cambridge University Press, 1949), p. 234, notes the incredible similarities between Peruvian and Irish potato culture and speculates that the requirements of the potato led the Irish to rediscover the wisdom of the Peruvians. Actually the similarities were not due to the potato but to the similar climates and topography. The Irish lazy bed and spade were probably as old as their Peruvian counterparts.

50 Coote, *Cavan*, p. 30.

51 *First Report of the Commissioners*, Appendix F, p. 310.

52 Greville estate papers (M6178[64], PRO).

53 Donnelly, *The Land and the People of Nineteenth-Century Cork*, p. 42.

54 Greville estate papers (M6178[64], PRO).

55 *Report of George Nicholls, Esq. to His Majesty's Principal Secretary of State for the Home Department, on Poor Laws, Ireland* (H.C. 1837, li), p. 4.

56 *First Report of the Commissioners*, Appendix E, pp. 293–302.

57 Ibid., pp. 293, 296.

58 Ibid., pp. 301, 295, 294.

59 *Report of George Nicholls*, p. 9.

60 Railway Commission, *Second Report*, pp. 15, 17.

61 Ibid., p. 22.

62 Ibid., p. 9.

63 Devon Commission, xix, p. 12.

64 Ibid., xx, p. 92.

65 Ibid., p. 108.

66 Crotty, *Irish Agricultural Production*, p. 31.

CHAPTER 3: AGRICULTURAL LABOR

1 Sneyd Papers: Survey of Estate, 1824 (D270/36, PRO Belfast).

2 Alexander Faris: Labor accounts in the Killashandra area, 1826–31 (Ms10,226, NLI).

3 *First Report of the Commissioners*, Appendix D, p. 67.

4 Coote, *Cavan*, p. 48.

5 Wakefield, *Ireland*, 1:362.

6 *Report of George Nicholls*, (H.C. 1837), pp. 4–5.
7 William Carleton, *The Party Fight and Funeral* (Cork: Mercier Press, 1973), p. 67.
8 *First Report of the Commissioners*, Appendix D, p. 67, and Appendix E, p. 108.
9 Ibid., Appendix D, p. 91.
10 Ibid., Supplement to Appendix F, pp. 293–302.
11 Ibid., p. 30.
12 Ibid.
13 Ibid.
14 Ibid.
15 Ibid., p. 31.
16 Ibid. However, it is worth noting that during the boom prices of the Napoleonic period, conacre land was set with oats, another sign of the responsiveness of these producers. See Wakefield, *Ireland*, 2:210.
17 *First Report of the Commissioners*, Supplement to Appendix A, p. 316.
18 Ibid., p. 308–11.
19 Ibid., Appendix D, p. 91.
20 Ibid., p. 301. There is reason to doubt his testimony, however; see p. 148ff. below.
21 Chayanov, *Theory of Peasant Economy*, p. xxiv.
22 Coote, *Cavan*, p. 300.
23 Wakefield, *Ireland*, 2:234.
24 Coote, *Cavan*, p. 46.
25 See C. Gill, *Rise of the Irish Linen Industry*, ch. 1.
26 A. Faris: Labor accounts (Ms10,226, NLI).
27 Compiled from Manuscript *Census of 1841*, returns from Killashandra (PRO).
28 *First Report of the Commissioners*, Supplement to Appendix D, p. 295.
29 Ibid., Appendix D, p. 67.
30 Ibid., Supplement to Appendix E, p. 309.
31 Ibid., p. 38.
32 Ibid., Supplement to Appendix D, p. 293.
33 Ibid., p. 35.
34 Ibid., Supplement to Appendix E, p. 293.
35 *Anglo-Celt*, 9 January 1845.
36 *First Report of the Commissioners*, Appendix E, p. 91.
37 Parish Register, Church of Ireland, in possession of Rector of Killashandra Parish, Rev. George Kingston.
38 *First Report of the Commissioners*, Appendix E, p. 91.
39 Ibid., p. 108.

40 Ibid., Appendix D, p. 112.
41 Ibid.
42 Ibid., Appendix E, p. 99.
43 Ibid., p. 299.
44 Ibid., p. 64.
45 Connell, *Population of Ireland*, p. 15.
46 *First Report of the Commissioners*, Appendix E, p. 126.
47 Devon Commission, xx, p. 97. Also see Donnelly, *The Land and the People of Nineteenth-Century Cork*, pp. 52–72, esp. pp. 59–60.
48 *First Report of the Commissioners*, Supplement to Appendix E, p. 295.
49 Ibid., p. 297.
50 Ibid., p. 298.
51 *Third Report of the Commissioners* (H.C. 1836, xxx), p. 2.
52 Ibid., p. 8.
53 See William F. Adams, *Ireland and Irish Emigration to the New World from 1815 to the Famine* (New Haven: Yale University Press, 1932), pp. 193–95.
54 *First Report of the Commissioners*, Appendix F, p. 139.
55 Ibid., Supplement to Appendix F, p. 293.
56 Ibid. As a Church of Ireland clergyman, he may have had a selective view of the community.
57 Killashandra Study File. (See Appendix, this volume.)
58 *First Report of the Commissioners*, Supplement to Appendix F, p. 12.
59 Devon Commission, xx, p. 91.
60 Ibid., p. 98.
61 See pp. 94ff.

CHAPTER 4: FAMILY STRUCTURE

1 See Peter Laslett, "The History of the Family," in his *Household and Family in Past Time* (Cambridge: Cambridge University Press, 1972), for a discussion of the historiography of the family.
2 The pioneering work of Chayanov in Russia first demonstrated the nature of rural village population dynamics. Recently the work of the Cambridge Group for the History of Population and Social Structure on English villages and Lutz Berkner on Austrian villages has explored the family patterns of rural villages in European history. The literature on areas of dispersed population concentrations is more limited; Michael Drake's *Population and Society in Norway, 1735–1865* (Cambridge: Cambridge University Press, 1969) is the most significant. See Richard Wall, Jean Robin, and Peter Laslett, eds., *Family Forms in Historic*

Europe (Cambridge: Cambridge University Press, 1983); and Lutz Berkner, "The Stem Family and the Developmental Cycle of the Peasant Household: An Eighteenth-Century Austrian Example," *American Historical Review* 77 (Spring 1972): 398–418.

3 Extension is defined here as any augmentation of the nuclear family unit by other related individuals. See Berkner, "The Stem Family." All figures presented here are from the Killashandra rural study file I compiled from the 1841 manuscript census for Killashandra parish, the Tithe Applotment Book of Killashandra parish, the Church of Ireland and the Catholic parish registers of Killashandra, and various other sources. See Appendix.

4 Connell, *Population of Ireland*, p. 161.

5 Berkner, "The Stem Family."

6 See Louis M. Cullen, "Irish History without the Potato," *Past and Present* 40 (July 1968): 72–83.

7 This family cycle schema was developed by R. Burr Litchfield and H. Chudacoff for the Comparative Cities Project at Brown University.

8 Laslett, *Household and Family*, pp. 28–32. Families with both lateral and vertical extension were too few to permit analysis. They have been grouped with the vertical families here. (All but one consisted of a vertically extended family with one newly married sibling present.)

9 Inheritance does not require freehold ownership, merely an inheritable right of occupation.

10 Chayanov, *The Theory of Peasant Economy*, p. 40.

11 Ibid., p. 7.

12 Ibid., p. 9.

13 A discussion of the differences between large and small farmers is included at the end of this section. A tripolar exploration of the family cycle was not attempted because of the incomplete nature of my information regarding farm size.

14 Killashandra Study File.

15 Richard Wall has noted that the English housing problem was solved by the sharing of dwellings. The Irish one-room cabin precluded this solution to the housing shortage. See R. Wall, "Mean Household Size in England from Printed Sources," in *Household and Family in Past Time*, ed. P. Laslett and R. Wall (Cambridge: Cambridge University Press, 1972), pp. 159–204.

16 Conrad M. Arensberg and S. T. Kimball's description, although old, remains the best: *Family and Community in Ireland* (Cambridge: Harvard University Press, 1940), pp. 126–28. Also see Robert E. Kennedy, *The Irish: Emigration, Marriage, and Fertility* (Berkeley: University of California Press, 1973), pp. 154–55.

17 Coote, *Cavan*, p. 41.

18 The occupational classification is probably responsible for the absence of laboring widows with children. Such an individual would most likely be reported as having "no occupation" or as a "mendicant" unless an adult child was designated as the head of household.

19 See Colin Clark and Margaret Haswell, *The Economics of Subsistence Agriculture* (New York: St. Martin's Press, 1967), pp. 111–38; Keith Griffin, *The Political Economy of Agrarian Change: An Essay on the Green Revolution* (London: McMillan, 1974), pp. 66–69; Sudhir Sen, *Reaping the Green Generation: Food and Jobs for All* (Maryknoll, N. Y.: Orbis, 1975), pp. 241–56; Don Kanel, "Creating Opportunity for Small Farmers: The Role of Land Tenure and Service Institutions," in *Problems of Rural Development*, ed. Raymond E. Dumett and Laurence J. Brainard (Leiden: E. J. Brill, 1975).

20 Tithe Applotment Book of Killashandra, 1832 (PRO). The Tithe Applotment Book alone is used here because the additional information which I have regarding farm size comes from the post-famine period.

21 See pp. 39ff. above for a discussion of farm size.

22 These figures are calculated through the heads of household, a procedure necessitated by the nature of the landholding information; therefore they do not correspond exactly to the similar figures for farmers and laborers given above, which were calculated according to subnuclear heads. The major shortcoming here appears in the early stages of the family cycle when married children of the head of household are often excluded from the analysis; hence the very low stem extension in stages 1 and 2.

23 The ratios of ascendant relatives to households for the different groups during the high fertility period are:

	Small	Medium	Large
F. cycle 2	.222	.083	.111
F. cycle 3	.070	.043	.048

SOURCE: Killashandra Study File.

24 *Report from Select Committee on the Sale of Corn; with the Minutes of Evidence, Appendix and Index* (H.C. 25 July 1834), p. 176.

CHAPTER 5: POPULATION

1 For the general arguments, see the conclusion to Connell, *Population of Ireland*. Recent studies of the developing world suggest that even in the contraceptive era, marriage age may be the key variable in population change. See Jane S. Durch, *Nuptiality Patterns in Developing Coun-*

tries: Implications for Fertility (Washington: Population Reference Bureau, 1981).

2 Michael Drake, "Marriage and Population Growth in Ireland, 1750–1845," *Economic History Review*, ser. 2, 16:2 (December 1963): 301–13; Joseph Lee, "Marriage and Population in Pre-famine Ireland," *Economic History Review*, ser. 2, 21:2 (August 1968): 283–95.

3 Cullen, "Irish History without the Potato," pp. 72–83.

4 For the notable exceptions to this rule, see Francis J. Carney, "Aspects of Pre-famine Irish Household Size: Composition and Differentials," in *Comparative Aspects of Scottish and Irish Economic and Social History 1600–1900*, ed. L. M. Cullen and T. C. Smout (Edinburgh: J. Donald, 1978).

5 Connell, *Population of Ireland*, p. 95.

6 Ibid., p. 3.

7 *Report of the Commissioners Appointed to Take the Census for the Year 1841* (H.C. 1843, xxiv).

8 Drake, "Marriage and Population Growth," pp. 301–13.

9 Connell, *Population of Ireland*, p. 58.

10 Ibid., p. 63.

11 There are some theoretical solutions. However, in the absence of reliable information on age-specific mortality, there is no sound basis for attempting regressions.

12 Family size is defined here as the number of individuals in the household head's nuclear family. Household size is defined as the total number of individuals residing in the household head's domicile.

13 My use of the term *household* differs from Carney's; the "household" figures quoted here are those which he calls "houseful" figures.

14 John Knodel, "Breast Feeding and Population Growth," *Science* 198: 4322 (December 1977): 1111–15.

15 The number of cases in each cohort is small, and therefore subject to distortion. Comparison between cohorts could be misleading. The significant figure here is the "All" category.

16 Donald J. Bogue, *Principles of Demography* (New York: John Wiley, 1969), p. 166. See also John Knodel and Hallie Kintner, "The Impact of Breast Feeding Patterns on the Biometric Analysis of Infant Mortality," *Demography* 14:4 (November 1977): 391–408.

17 Drake, "Marriage and Population Growth," p. 305.

18 See Kenneth H. Connell, "Peasant Marriage in Ireland: Its Structure and Development Since the Famine," in *Economic History Review*, ser. 2, 14:3 (April 1962): 502–23.

19 Ansley J. Coale, Barbara A. Anderson, and Erna Harm, *Human Fertil-*

ity in Russia Since the Nineteenth Century (Princeton: Princeton University Press, 1979), p. 138.

20 Single laboring males were likely to be returned as "farm servants" and single females as "spinners"; thus, they appear in these figures under the "Entire Population" classification.

21 S. H. Cousens, "The Regional Variations in Population Changes in Ireland, 1861–1881," *Economic History Review*, ser. 2, 17:2 (December 1964): 301–21.

CONCLUSION

1 Preliminary results of a post-famine project confirm this. See Kevin O'Neill, "Marriage Age and Social Structure in Nineteenth Century Ireland" (paper delivered to the Cambridge Group for the History of Population and Social Structure, February 1981).

2 These deductions, which are derived from knowledge of the events in Cavan, are supported by the empirical and theoretic work of S. H. Cousens. See especially "The Regional Variations in Population Changes in Ireland, 1861–1881"; and "Emigration and Demographic Change in Ireland, 1851–61," *Economic History Review,* ser. 2, 14:2 (December 1961): 275–88.

3 Arensberg and Kimball, *Family and Community in Ireland.*

4 David Levine, *Family Formation in the Age of Nascent Capitalism* (New York: Academic Press, 1977), p. 146.

5 Charles Tilly, ed., *Historical Studies of Changing Fertility* (Princeton: Princeton University Press, 1978), p. 31.

6 Ibid., p. 223.

Bibliography

MANUSCRIPT MATERIAL

PUBLIC RECORD OFFICE, DUBLIN

Papers relating to the estates in Co. Cavan, mainly in Corraneary, of W. F. Greville, 1809–1844. M6178.

Rental of the Estates in and near Bailieboro, Co. Cavan of Edward Groome, 1822. M5559.

Rentals, Accounts, Etc. of the Estate of Dowager Lady Garvagh in Corraneary, Co. Cavan, 1829–1865. M5535.

Rentals of property of James Hamilton in Portaliffe, Killashandra, 1831–1852, with associated documents. M5571.

Tithe Applotment Book of Killashandra, 1832.

Quarto Books of the 1840 Valuation, County of Cavan.

Census of 1841. Manuscript census forms for the Parish of Killashandra, County of Cavan.

Griffith, Richard. *Valuation of the Several Tenements in the Union of Cavan, 1857.*

NATIONAL LIBRARY OF IRELAND

Crofton Estate Papers: Rentals and accounts of the Crofton Estates in Counties Cavan and Monaghan, 1769–1851. Letters, Ms20773; papers and accounts, Ms20789–20801.

Faris, Alexander: Labor accounts in the Killashandra area, 1826–1831. Ms10,226.

Farnham Estate Papers: Rental of Cavan Estates, 1820. Ms3502.

Two volumes giving summaries of applications and representations made by tenants and other persons to the Lords Farnham and decisions made in respect of those, 1832–1860. Ms3117–18.

Rentals of the estate of Lord Farnham, in County Cavan, 1841–1848. Ms5012–13.

Farnham Estate Household Papers and other accounts, 1734–1862.
    Ms11,492.
Farnham Estate Correspondence and accounts, 1818–1899. Ms18,600–
    630.
Hodson Papers: Rentals and accounts, 1810–1898. Ms16,397–471.
Killashandra Parish Register: the Catholic Parish, 1840–1880. Microfilm.
    With the permission of Rev. Thomas M'Cauley.
Pratt Estate Papers: Surveys, accounts, legal papers, letters, etc. relating to
    the estates at Kingscourt and Cabra, Co. Cavan, 1639–1914.
    Ms13,314–27.
Rental of Rev. Joseph Pratt of Cabra Castle, 1819. Ms. 5086.
Rentals of the Pratt family estate of Cabra, 1837, 1844, 1847, 1855.
    Ms3284.
Valuation Book of the Cavan Estates of Colonel Joseph Pratt, 1842.
    Ms5087.
Royal School Estate Papers; H. Tilson, agent. Rentals and Correspondence,
    1834–1864. Ms17,920.

                              ELSEWHERE

Ellis Papers: Rentals of Estates 1836–1853. Public Record Office, Belfast.
    D520/14.
Killashandra Parish Registers: Church of Ireland Parish, 1735–1875. In the
    possession of Rev. George Kingston, Church of Ireland Rectory, Killa-
    shandra, Co. Cavan.
Shankey Papers: Rentals, etc., 1818–1826. Public Record Office, Belfast.
    D1550/7.
Sneyd Papers: Survey of Estate, 1824. Public Record Office, Belfast.
    D270/36.
Southwell Papers: Correspondence, 1825–37. Public Record Office, Bel-
    fast. D946/3.

GOVERNMENT PAPERS

*Return of the Population of the Several Counties in Ireland, as Enumerated
    in 1831.* H.C. 1833, xxxix.
*Reported from Select Committee on the Sale of Corn; with the Minutes of
    Evidence, Appendix and Index.* H.C. July 1834.
*First Report from His Majesty's Commissioners for Inquiring into the Con-
    dition of the Poorer Classes in Ireland with Appendix (A) and Supple-
    ment.* H.C. 1835, xxxii.

——Appendix (D) containing baronial examinations relative to earnings of labourers, cottier tenants, employment of women and children, expenditures; and supplement containing answers to questions 1 to 12 circulated by the commissioners. H.C. 1836, xxxi.

——Appendix (E) containing baronial examinations relative to food, cottages and cabins, clothing and furniture, pawnbroking and savings banks, drinking; and supplement containing answers to questions 13 to 22 circulated by the commissioners. H.C. 1836, xxxii.

——Appendix (F) containing baronial examinations relative to con-acre, quarter or score ground, small tenantry, consolidation of farms and dislodged tenantry, emigration, landlord and tenant, nature and state of agriculture, taxation, roads, observations on the nature and state of agriculture; and supplement. H.C. 1836, xxxiii.

——Supplement to Appendices D, E, F. H.C. 1836, xxxiv.

Third Report of the Commissioners for Inquiring into the Condition of the Poorer Classes in Ireland. H.C. 1836, xxx.

Second Report of the Commissioners for Inquiring into the Condition of the Poorer Classes in Ireland. H.C. 1837, xxxi.

Report to His Majesty's Principal Secretary of State for the Home Department on Poor Laws, Ireland. H.C. 1837, li.

Second Report of the Commissioners Appointed to Consider and Recommend a General System of Railways for Ireland. H.C. 1837–38, xxxv.

Report of the Commissioners Appointed to Take the Census for the Year 1841. H.C. 1843, xxiv.

Evidence Taken before Her Majesty's Commissioners of Inquiry into the State of the Law and Practice in Respect to the Occupation of Land in Ireland. H.C. 1845, xx.

The Commissioners of Valuation Table Showing the Average Price of Agricultural Produce in Forty Towns in Ireland in the Years 1849, 1850, 1851. General Valuation Office, Dublin, 1852.

NEWSPAPERS

Anglo-Celt. 1845–48.
The *Freeman's Journal.* 1800–1845.

SECONDARY SOURCES

CONTEMPORARY WORKS

Carleton, William. *The Courtship of Phelim O'Toole.* 1833; Cork: Mercier Press, 1973.

Carleton, William. *The Party Fight and Funeral*. 1833; Cork: Mercier Press, 1973.

Coote, Charles. *Statistical Survey of the County of Cavan, with Observations on the Means of Improvement; Drawn up in the Year 1801 for the Consideration and under the Direction of the Dublin Society*. Dublin: Graisberry & Campbell, 1802.

[Farnham, Lord]. *Statement of the Management of the Farnham Estates*. Dublin: William Curry, 1830.

Fullerton, Alexander. *Fifty Years an Itinerant Preacher: Being Reminiscences of Fifty Years in the Irish Methodist Ministry*. Belfast: Irish Methodist Publishing Company, 1912.

Inglis, H.D. *Ireland in 1834: A Journey throughout Ireland During the Spring, Summer and Autumn of 1834*. 4th ed. London: Whittaker, 1836.

Lewis, Samuel. *A Topographical Dictionary of Ireland: With an Appendix Describing the Electoral Boundaries of the Several Boroughs, as Defined by the Act of the 2nd. and 3rd. of William IV*. 2 vols. London: Lewis, 1837.

M'Collum, Randall. *Sketches of the Highlands of Cavan and of Shirley Castle, Taken During the Irish Famine by a Looker-on*. Belfast: J. Reed, 1856.

Thom's Irish Almanac and Official Directory. Dublin: Thom & Co., 1844.

Wakefield, Edward. *An Account of Ireland, Statistical and Political*. 2 vols. London: Longman, Hurst, Rees, Orme, & Brown, 1812.

Young, Arthur. *Arthur Young's Tour in Ireland, 1776–1779*. Edited by A. W. Hutton. 2 vols. London: G. Bell & Sons, 1892.

LATER WORKS

Adams, William F. *Ireland and Irish Emigration to the New World from 1815 to the Famine*. New Haven: Yale University Press, 1932.

Arensberg, Conrad M., and S. T. Kimball. *Family and Community in Ireland*. Cambridge: Harvard University Press, 1940.

Baldwin, Richard. ed. *Trade, Growth and Balance of Payments*. Chicago: Rand McNally, 1965.

Barrington, T. "A Review of Irish Agricultural Prices." *Journal of the Statistical and Social Inquiry Society of Ireland* 101:15 (1927):249–80.

Beames, Michael. "Cottiers and Conacre in Pre-famine Ireland." *Journal of Peasant Studies* 2:3 (1975):352–54.

Bell, Colin, and Howard Newby. *Community Studies: An Introduction to the Sociology of the Local Community*. New York: Praeger, 1972.

Berkner, Lutz. "The Stem Family and the Development Cycle of the Peasant Household: An Eighteenth-Century Austrian Example." *American Historical Review* 77 (Spring 1972):398–418.

Berkner, Lutz, and Franklin Mendels. "Inheritance Systems, Family Structure and Demographic Patterns in Western Europe, 1700–1900." In *Historical Studies of Changing Fertility*, edited by Charles Tilly. Princeton: Princeton University Press, 1978.

Bicanic, Rudolf. "Three Concepts of Agricultural Over-Population." In *International Explorations of Agricultural Economics*, edited by Roger N. Dixey. Ames: Iowa State University Press, 1964.

Black, Max. *Models and Metaphors: Studies in Language and Philosophy.* Ithaca: Cornell University Press, 1962.

Bogue, Donald J. *Principles of Demography.* New York: John Wiley & Sons, 1969.

Boserup, Ester. *The Conditions of Agricultural Growth: The Economics of Agrarian Change under Population Pressure.* Chicago: Aldine, 1966.

Bourke, P. M. Austin. "The Extent of the Potato Crop in Ireland at the Time of the Famine." *Journal of Statistical and Social Inquiry Society of Ireland* 20, pt. 3 (1959):1–35.

Bourke, P. M. Austin. "Notes on Some Agricultural Units of Measurement in Use in Pre-Famine Ireland." *Irish Historical Studies* 14:55 (March 1965):36–45.

Bourke, P. M. Austin. "The Use of the Potato Crop in Pre-Famine Ireland." *Journal of the Statistical and Social Inquiry Society of Ireland* 21, pt. 6 (1968):72–96.

Brody, Hugh. *Inishkilanne: Change and Decline in the West of Ireland.* London: Allen Lane, 1973.

Carney, Francis J. "Aspects of Pre-famine Irish Household Size: Composition and Differentials." In *Comparative Aspects of Scottish and Irish Economic and Social History 1600–1900*, edited by L. M. Cullen and T. C. Smout. Edinburgh: J. Donald, 1978.

Chambers, J. D., and G. E. Mingay. *The Agricultural Revolution, 1750–1880.* London: Batsford, 1966.

Chayanov, Aleksander Vasil'evich. *The Theory of Peasant Economy.* Edited by Daniel Thorner, Basile Kerblay, and R. E. F. Smith. Homewood, Ill.: R. D. Irwin, 1966.

Clark, Colin, and Margaret Haswell. *The Economics of Subsistence Agriculture.* 3rd ed. New York: St. Martin's Press, 1967.

Cole, Ansley, Barbara Anderson, and Erna Harm. *Human Fertility in Russia Since the Nineteenth Century.* Princeton: Princeton University Press, 1979.

Connell, Kenneth H. "Land and Population in Ireland, 1750–1845." *Economic History Review*, ser. 2, 2:3 (1950):278–89.

Connell, Kenneth H. "The Colonization of Waste Land in Ireland, 1750–1845." *Economic History Review*, ser. 2, 3:1 (1950):44–71.

Connell, Kenneth H. *The Population of Ireland, 1750–1845*. Oxford: Oxford University Press, 1950.

Connell, Kenneth H. "The History of the Potato." *Economic History Review*, ser. 2, 3:3 (1951):388–95.

Connell, Kenneth H. "Peasant Marriage in Ireland: Its Structure and Development Since the Famine." *Economic History Review*, ser. 2, 14:3 (April 1962):502–23.

Connell, Kenneth. "The Potato in Ireland." *Past and Present* 23 (November 1962):57–71.

Cousens, S. H. "Regional Death Rates in Ireland During the Great Famine from 1846 to 1851." *Population Studies* 14:1 (July 1960):55–74.

Cousens, S. H. "The Regional Pattern of Emigration During the Great Famine, 1846–51." *Transactions and Papers of the Institute of British Geographers* 28 (1960):119–34.

Cousens, S. H. "Emigration and Demographic Change in Ireland, 1851–61." *Economic History Review*, ser. 2, 14:2 (December 1961):275–88.

Cousens, S. H. "The Regional Variations in Population Changes in Ireland, 1861–1881." *Economic History Review*, ser. 2, 17:2 (December 1964):301–21.

Crawford, William H. *Domestic Industry in Ireland: The Experience of the Linen Industry*. Dublin: Gill & Macmillan, 1972.

Crotty, Raymond D. *Irish Agricultural Production: Its Volume and Structure*. Cork: Cork University Press, 1966.

Cullen, Louis M. *Anglo-Irish Trade, 1660–1800*. Manchester: Manchester University Press, 1968.

Cullen, Louis M. "Irish History without the Potato." *Past and Present* 40 (July 1968):72–83.

Cullen, Louis M. *An Economic History of Ireland Since 1660*. New York: Barnes & Noble, 1972.

Cunningham, Rev. Terence P. "Notes on the 1821 Census of Lavey Parish." *Breifne: Journal of Cumann Seanchais Bhreifne* 1:3 (1960):192–208.

DeVries, Jan. *The Dutch Rural Economy in the Golden Age, 1500–1700*. New Haven: Yale University Press, 1974.

Dickson, David. "Middlemen." In *Penal Era and Golden Age: Essays in Irish History, 1690–1800*, edited by Thomas Bartlett and D. W. Hayton. Belfast: Ulster Historical Foundation, 1979.

Donnelly, James S. "Cork Market: Its Role in the Nineteenth Century Irish Butter Trade." *Studia Hibernica* 11 (1971):130–63.

Donnelly, James S. *The Land and the People of Nineteenth-Century Cork: The Rural Economy and the Land Question.* Boston: Routledge & Kegan Paul, 1975.

Drake, Michael. "Marriage and Population Growth in Ireland, 1750–1845." *Economic History Review*, ser. 2, 16:2 (December 1963):301–13.

Drake, Michael. *Population and Society in Norway, 1735–1865.* Cambridge: Cambridge University Press, 1969.

Durch, Jane S. *Nuptiality Patterns in Developing Countries: Implications for Fertility.* Washington: Population Reference Bureau, 1981.

Freeman, T. W. *Pre-Famine Ireland: A Study in Historical Geography.* Manchester: Manchester University Press, 1957.

Geertz, Clifford. *Agricultural Involution: The Processes of Ecological Change in Indonesia.* Berkeley: University of California Press, 1963.

Gibbon, Peter. *The Origins of Ulster Unionism.* Manchester: Manchester University Press, 1975.

Gill, Conrad. *The Rise of the Irish Linen Industry.* Oxford: Clarendon Press, 1925.

Green, E. R. R. *The Lagan Valley, 1800–50: A Local History of the Industrial Revolution.* London: Faber, 1949.

Griffith, Keith. *The Political Economy of Agrarian Change.* London: McMillan, 1974.

Grigg, David B. *Population Growth and Agrarian Change: An Historical Perspective.* Cambridge: Cambridge University Press, 1980.

Johnson, J. H. "Agriculture in Co. Derry at the Beginning of the Nineteenth Century." *Studia Hibernica* 4 (1964):95–103.

Kennedy, Robert E. *The Irish: Emigration, Marriage, and Fertility.* Berkeley: University of California Press, 1973.

Knodel, John. "Breast Feeding and Population Growth." *Science* 198:4322 (December 1977):1111–15.

Knodel, John, and Hallie Kintner. "The Impact of Breast Feeding Patterns on the Biometric Analysis of Infant Mortality." *Demography* 14:4 (November 1977):391–408.

Kochanowicz, Jacek. "The Peasant Family as an Economic Unit in the Polish Feudal Economy of the Eighteenth Century. In *Family Forms in Historic Europe*, edited by Richard Wall, Jean Robin, and Peter Laslett. Cambridge: Cambridge University Press, 1983.

Laslett, Pater. "The History of the Family." In his *Household and Family in Past Time.* Cambridge: Cambridge University Press, 1972.

Lee, Joseph. "Marriage and Population in Pre-famine Ireland." *Economic History Review*, ser. 2, 21:2 (August 1968):283–95.

Lee, Joseph. "Irish Agriculture." *Agricultural History Review* 22, pt. 1 (1969):64–76.

Lee, Joseph, ed. *Irish Historiography 1970–79*. Cork: Cork University Press, 1981.

Levine, David. *Family Formation in the Age of Nascent Capitalism*. New York: Academic Press, 1977.

MacFarland, Alan. *Reconstructing Historical Communities*. Cambridge: Cambridge University Press, 1977.

Maguire, William A. *The Downshire Estates in Ireland 1801–1845: The Management of Irish Landed Estates in the Early Nineteenth Century*. Oxford: Clarendon Press, 1972.

Meek, Ronald. *Marx and Engels on Malthus*. London: Lawrence & Wishart, 1953.

Messenger, John. *Inis Beag: Isle of Ireland*. New York: Holt, Rinehart & Winston, 1969.

O'Brien, George. *The Economic History of Ireland from the Union to the Famine*. London: Longmans, Green, 1921.

O'Grada, Cormac. "The Investment Behaviour of Irish Landlords 1850–1875: Some Preliminary Findings." *Agricultural History Review* 23 (1975):129–55.

O'Grada, Cormac. "Supply Responsiveness in Irish Agriculture During the Nineteenth Century." *Economic History Review* ser. 2, 28:2 (1975): 312–17.

O'Loingsigh, Seamus. "The Burning of Ballinagh—May 1794." *Breifne* 2:7 (1965):359–65.

O'Neill, Kevin. "Marriage Age and Social Structure in Nineteenth Century Ireland." Paper delivered to the Cambridge Group for the History of Population and Social Structure, February 1981.

Orme, A. R. *Ireland*. London: Harlow, 1970.

Razzell, Peter E. "Population Growth and Economic Change in Eighteenth and Early Nineteenth-Century England and Ireland." In *Land, Labour and Population in the Industrial Revolution: Essays Presented to J. D. Chambers*, edited by E. L. Jones and G. E. Mingay. London: Edward Arnold, 1967.

Salaman, Redcliffe N. *The Influence of the Potato on the Course of Irish History*. Dublin: Browne & Nolan, 1943.

Salaman, Redcliffe N. *The History and Social Influence of the Potato, with a Chapter on Industrial Uses*. Cambridge: Cambridge University Press, 1949.

Sen, Sudhir. *A Richer Harvest: New Horizons for Developing Countries*. Maryknoll, N.Y.: Orbis, 1974.

Smith, Richard. "Some Reflections on the Evidence for the Origins of the 'European Marriage Pattern' in England." In *The Sociology of the Family*, edited by C. Harris. Keele: University of Keele, 1979.

Solow, Barbara. *The Land Question and the Irish Economy, 1870–1903*. Cambridge: Harvard University Press, 1971.

Thorner, Daniel. "Peasant Economy as a Category in Economic History." *Economic Weekly* 15 (special number, July 1963):1243–52.

Tilly, Charles, ed. *Historical Studies of Changing Fertility*. Princeton: Princeton University Press, 1978.

Tipton, Frank. *Regional Variations in the Economic Development of Germany During the Nineteenth Century*. Middletown, Conn.: Wesleyan University Press, 1976.

Wall, Richard. "England: Mean Household Size from Printed Sources." In *Household and Family in Past Time*, edited by P. Laslett and R. Wall. Cambridge: Cambridge University Press, 1972.

Walsh, Brendan. "A Perspective on Irish Population Patterns." *Eire-Ireland* 4:3 (Autumn 1969):3–21.

Wilson, John. "Drumlommon in 1835." *Breifne* 2:7 (1965):366–75.

Index

Abatements, 49
Adolescence, 130, 146, 149
Agency fees, 48
Age structure, 149, 197
Agricultultural development, 4, 66, 96–98. *See also* Market impulsion model
Alcohol, 118
Amenorrhea, postpartum, 173–74
Anglo-Celt, 84
Armagh, 79
Arrears, 60–61, 62, 71–72
Arvagh, 29, 30
Ascendant relatives, 161, 213*n23*
Austria, 126

Bailieborough: farm size, 44; oat market, 83, 84; agricultural statistics, 89–90; mentioned, 29, 35
Bailiff, 48
Ballinagh, 38
Belderg, Mayo, 26
Belfast, 26
Belturbet, 29, 82, 84, 107
Beresford, Rev. Marcus, 38, 204*n21*
Bleach greens, 41. *See also* Linen industry
Bottle-feeding, 173–74
Brady, Rev. Bernard, 108, 119, 120, 122
Breed selection, 93
Bridal pregnancy, 173
Bruse Hill, 30

Butter: prices, 74, 76; exports, 77, 83; production, 79, 84, 85

Capital: and development, 8, 67; in Market Impulsion Model, 15, 16–17, 19; shortage of, 22, 67; and tenant right, 67, 69; stock, 69; dowry, 70; drainage, 70; and grass production, 80. *See also* Credit
Castle, John, 51
Castleraghan, 40
Castleterra, 107
Catholic Emancipation, 38, 39
Cavan: economic history, 22–24; sources, 24–25; prices 74
Cavan town, 29, 82, 83, 84
Celibacy rate, 184–85
Chayanov, Aleksander V., 6, 131
Chayanovian state. *See* Market impulsion model
Childhood experience: labor, 87, 103, 105, 146–49; education, 146–49
Child survival, 172
Child/woman ratio: and fertility 171–77; and infant mortality, 172–75; and literacy, 175–76
Chudacoff/Litchfield family cycle, 127–29
Clare, 74–75
Clearances. *See* Evictions
Clonchee, 40
Clonmoghan, 40

227

nov's model, 6; Marx on, 7–8; in market impulsion model, 9, 12, 17, 18, 19, 23; and the labor ration, 18, 23; social controls, 23; and tillage, 85; debate, 164–67; and the child/woman ratio, 177
Porter, Hugh, 44
Potato: place in commercial tillage, 22; as pig fodder, 33, 92; and population density, 39, 164, 165; as part of general rotation, 86, 87, 89, 90
Poultry, 92
Pratt estate, 44–45, 60
Prices, 39, 73–77
Primative accumulation, 22
Production/consumption units, 21
Production/rent ratio, 16
Productivity, agricultural: Malthus on, 5; and Chayanov's model, 6; in market impulsion model, 9, 15, 16, 19; and self-exploitation, 23
Profit, 16
Proletarianization, 17, 188
Property rights, 34

Rail transport, 24, 25
Rationalization: of land, 14, 46, 50, 51
Renny, landlord, 119
Rent: in market impulsion model, 11, 16–17, 22; as a coercive factor, 14; system described, 14–15, 46–47; trends, 52–64; reductions, 54–55; rack rents, 59, 80; and arrears, 62; and production factors, 80; conacre, 104
Repeal movement, 39
Rice, 9
Roscommon, 29
Royal School estate, 35–36, 55, 58
Russia, 6

Seasonal migration, 107
Seasonal work, 114
Secret societies, 85
Sectarian evictions, 204n21. See also Evictions
Sectarian violence, 38

Self-exploitation, 23, 85, 162
Settlement pattern, 126, 211n2
Sex ratio, 174
Shankey estate, 55
Shercock, 83, 84
Singulate mean age of marriage, 178
Slieve Russell, 28
Sligo, 29
Small farmers, 63
Sneyd estate, 41
Social controls on fertility, 24
Social differentiation: as a problem for Chayanov's model, 6; in market impulsion model, 11, 17, 18, 19; and peasant society, 101; and conacre, 107; and population dynamics, 190
Spade, 22, 87
Stock, 69
Stocking ratio, 91–93
Strong farmers, 63
Subdivision, 39, 41, 43, 203n4
Subletting, 39, 44–45, 203n4
Subtenantry, 34, 35, 40, 59, 60, 62
Surplus producing stage. See Market impulsion model
Swanlinbar, 36

Tenant right, 67–69
Tenure: direct, 33, 34, 60, 63; secondary, 33, 34
Tillage: labor requirements, 22; balance with pasture, 81, 90, 93. See also Oats; Potato
Tithe, 42, 43
Tobacco, 117
Topography, 28
Transportation, 72, 81, 82–83
Tullaghunco, 40
Turnip, 85, 86
Typicality, 25

Underemployment. See Labor
Undertenants. See Subtenantry
Unemployment. See Labor

Vent for surplus model, 12, 16
Vertical extension. See Family structure

DESIGNED BY ARLENE PUTTERMAN
COMPOSED BY PIED TYPER, LINCOLN, NEBRASKA
MANUFACTURED BY CUSHING MALLOY, INC., ANN ARBOR, MICHIGAN
TEXT AND DISPLAY LINES ARE SET IN TIMES ROMAN

Library of Congress Cataloging in Publication Data

O'Neill, Kevin, 1949–
  Family and farm in pre-famine Ireland.

  Bibliography: p.
  Includes index.
  1. Farm tenancy—Ireland—Killashandra (Cavan)—
History—19th century. 2. Agriculture—Economic aspects
—Ireland—Killashandra (Cavan)—History—19th century.
3. Poor—Ireland—Killashandra (Cavan)—History—19th
century. 4. Family—Ireland—Killashandra (Cavan)—
History—19th century. 5. Killashandran(Cavan)—Population
—History—19th century. I. Title.
HD1511.I732K546   1984   338.1'094169'8   84–40154
ISBN 0–299–09840–0